INDIANS, INFANTS AND INFANTRY

INDIANS, INFANTS AND INFANTRY

Andrew and Elizabeth Burt on the Frontier

by

Merrill J. Mattes

University of Nebraska Press
Lincoln and London

First Bison Book printing: 1988

Library of Congress Cataloging-in-Publication Data
Mattes, Merrill J.
   Indians, infants and infantry: Andrew and Elizabeth on the
Frontier / by Merrill J. Mattes.
      p.   cm.
   "Bison book."
   Reprint. Originally published: 1960.
   Includes index.
   ISBN 0-8032-8157-9 (pbk.)
   1. Pioneers—West (U.S.)—Biography. 2. Burt, Andrew, 1839–1915.
3. Burt, Elizabeth (Reynolds), b. 1839. 4. Frontier and pioneer
life—West (U.S.) 5. West (U.S.)—History—1848–1950. 6. Indians
of North America—Wars) 1866–1895. 7. United States. Army—
Military life—History—19th century. I. Title.
F594.M34   1988
978'.03—dc19   CIP 88-14335

Reprinted by arrangement with Merrill J. Mattes

⊗

Preface

In 1957, General Reynolds J. Burt, U.S.A. (retired) asked me to review his mother's manuscript, *An Army Wife's Forty Years in the Service,* which he had placed with the Library of Congress. The "true adventures" of Andrew and Elizabeth Burt on the Indian frontier were too remarkable to be dismissed. They opened up new and challenging vistas of research and publication.

A man achieves fame in various ways. He may be a truly great leader. He may be adopted by the crowd as a romantic symbol or a political figurehead, or he may simply have a good publicity agent. Frequently overlooked by historians are men of lesser fame who are the actual doers and builders, the "captains of the guard" on the watch-towers of history. Andrew Sheridan Burt was one of these men. He was an American whose love of country was founded on the solid rock of faith in American ideals—the dignity and freedom of the individual, and his inalienable right to carve out his own destiny. Andrew Burt knew little about rights to security or rights to the pursuit of pleasure. If he were with us today, he would be more interested in the evidence of a man's upright character than he would be in the signs of his financial status.

Western literature is replete with stories of flamboyant fur traders, law men, desperadoes, cowboys and cavalry commanders. "Brave Andy Burt," as he was called by Lieutenant John G. Bourke, was a different kind of frontiersman. He was an officer in the supposedly unglamorous infantry branch of the Indian-fighting army. He was also a model husband and father, raising a family under the most harrowing frontier conditions.

To occupy forever diminishing library shelf space every book must have its unique justification. This book is (1) the first book-length story of a frontier army officer's wife since Fougera's *With Custer's Cavalry,* published in 1942, (2) the first biographical treatment of a line infantry officer of the Indian-fighting army, (3) the first revealed history of remote, little-known and dangerous Fort C. F. Smith, Montana Territory, and (4) the first full account of activities at and based upon famous Fort Laramie, Wyoming, in the climactic years 1874-1876.

My principal indebtedness is to General Reynolds J. Burt, who provided the voluminous materials in the Burt Collection. Various libraries and Government repositories in Washington, D. C., Omaha, Nebraska, and other midwest centers were also consulted. The services of David D. Lloyd, Executive Director, the Harry S. Truman Library, Washington, D. C., and J. R. Fuchs of the same institution, Independence, Missouri, who acted as "catalytic agents," are gratefully acknowledged. Louise Stegner, dean of Omaha historians, gave liberally from her inexhaustible fund of knowledge and enthusiasm. Finally, it is of paramount importance to make record of the fact that, without the patient encouragement of my wife, Clare, this book could not have been written.

As this book is published, Reynolds J. Burt lives on serenely in "Jade Wood," 306 Woodland Terrace, Alexandria, Virginia, in a world which has travelled many years away from August 2, 1874, when he was born at Fort Omaha. Within two months he was the youngest resident of Fort Laramie, Wyoming Territory, and he was launched on his own military career. He vividly recalls boyhood incidents at Forts Omaha, Bidwell, McDowell, Robinson and Washakie. He also remembers his second residence at Fort Laramie, age 13, in 1887-1888, and through his recollections he is assisting the National Park Service on a project to restore the interior of "the Burt House," the officer's quarters with mansard roof, next to the old adobe sutler's store.

Reynolds was a graduate of the United States Military Academy in 1896, and in that year he brought his bride, Lilian Stewart, with him when he joined his father's regiment, the 25th Infantry, at Fort Missoula. In 1900-1901 he was active in various jungle campaigns in the Philippines. In 1911-1912 as Disbursing Officer, Signal Corps, he signed the $2,500 check paid to the Wright Brothers for the first U. S. Army airplane. In 1918 he was appointed Brigadier General and commanded the 22nd Infantry Brigade. The colorful climax of his career was in 1932-1935 as Colonel, 15th Infantry, commanding the garrison of U. S. Army troops at Tientsin, China, in concert with the garrisons of other nations, to keep open the railroad route to Peking. In 1937 he retired. His favorite hobby since that time has been the composition of military marches which, like his "Infantry, Kings of the Highway," have achieved wide popularity.

Reynolds J. Burt is a vigorous "living link" between the time of Crook's campaign against Crazy Horse, and the time of atomic bombs and planned trips to the moon.

Merrill J. Mattes

Contents

Illustrations

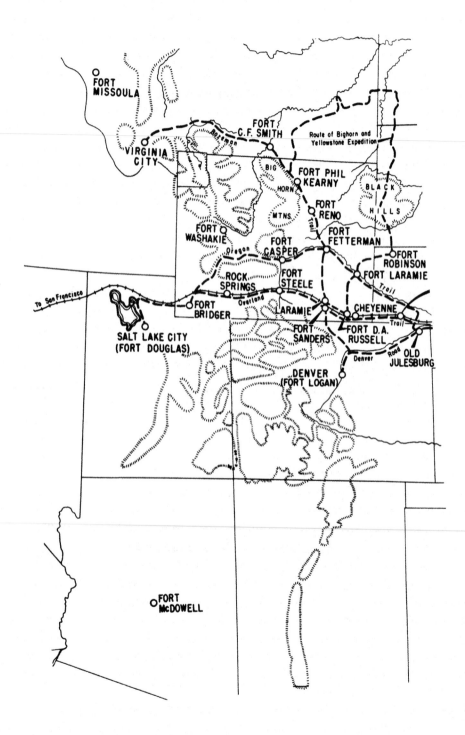

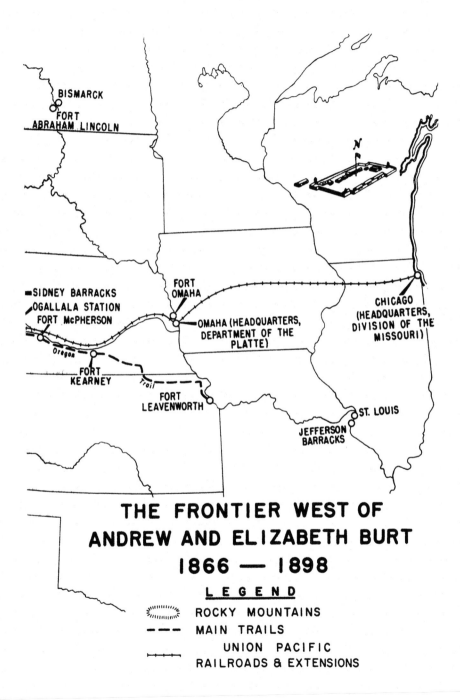

THE FRONTIER WEST OF
ANDREW AND ELIZABETH BURT
1866 — 1898

L E G E N D

ROCKY MOUNTAINS

MAIN TRAILS

UNION PACIFIC
RAILROADS & EXTENSIONS

1

Civil War Romance

This is the story of two Americans, Andrew and Elizabeth Burt, who were actors in the pageant of American history. They dedicated themselves in long and faithful patriotic service to a young nation under trial—torn asunder by civil war, pledged to protect its unsettled Western frontier, and thrust by colonial strife into the din and glare of global politics. They did not rise meteor-like above the horizon of their time, but they had moments illuminated by the lightning flashes of destiny, moments of dramatic grandeur.

For over half a century their lives were happily intertwined, often in defiance of custom and despite all dangers and hardships that fate could devise. Forty of these years they were hostages to fortune, while Andrew was an infantry officer in the United States

Army. His career was an epitome of American military history from Fort Sumter to the Philippines.

Andrew S. Burt was a far better soldier than George A. Custer, who was of comparable age. He was no fool and would have spurned a fame bought by a theatrical suicide. He was as able a soldier as Merritt, Mackenzie or Royall, but like Custer they also were cavalry commanders and in Indian warfare on the Great Plains the cavalry received the newspaper coverage. Burt admired the proclaimed manly virtues of Buffalo Bill Cody, Wild Bill Hickok and other lurid frontier characters, but was himself a sober, religious, family man, not a career celebrity.

The name of "Major Burt" appears frequently in published official reports and in such classics as Finerty's *Warpath and Bivouac* and Bourke's *On the Border With Crook*. It crops up on the pages of a surprising number of books on the West. Like mountain-man Jim Bridger of an earlier era, Burt seemed to be all over the frontier and personally involved in many historic events; but unlike Bridger, Burt did not cultivate a following with the use of elaborate yarns and picturesque attire. He has been an elusive, shadowy figure in the background of frontier literature. It is time for him to achieve belated recognition as an authentic and distinctive type of American frontiersman.

"Brave Andy Burt," as he was called by Finerty and others, had courage and self-reliance that was conspicuous among men to whom courage and self-reliance were routine necessities of survival. "Gallant Andy Burt" was the title of a regimental ballad sung in countless barracks sessions. In physical stature Andy Burt was a small man, but as friend or foe he made a forceful and memorable impression. He had "a heart four times too big for his body," as one admiring friend said in eulogy. He led his lowly foot soldiers on thousands of rugged miles until they all became as tough as boot leather, compelling the grudging admiration of their erstwhile cavalry tormentors. He was notoriously full of mischief, and his gray eyes could twinkle merrily, but they could also become stern and forbidding as the wrath of Jehovah in the presence of Southern sympathizers, wayward Indians or errant soldiers.

Citizen Andy Burt was among the first to enlist when Abraham Lincoln issued his call for volunteers after the attack upon Fort Sumter. Quicky promoted to the rank of Lieutenant, he was wounded by enemy fire at the Battle of Mill Springs and was in the first file of Union officers to be brevetted for gallantry.

Captain Burt's name is inscribed among those counted as the heroes of Chickamauga and Missionary Ridge. He was wounded and brevetted again for his skillful defense of the Union line at Jonesboro, before Atlanta.

In 1866 Major Burt with F Company, 1st Battalion, accompanied Colonel Carrington's 18th U. S. Regiment of Infantry up the old Oregon Trail to Julesburg, then followed the overland route west to become the first regular officer to resume command at historic Fort Bridger, Wyoming (then Dakota) Territory.

In 1867, following Colonel Carrington's disastrous efforts to pacify the Bozeman Trail, Major Burt was sent to remote Fort C. F. Smith, Montana Territory, there to assume command of "the last outpost" on the Indian frontier, to become a respected friend of the Crow Indians, and to bear the brunt of repeated attacks by hostile Sioux and Cheyenne. In 1868 he unhappily carried out orders to abandon Fort C. F. Smith in one of the rare "strategic withdrawals" of the United States Army.

In 1874-1876, while based at famous Fort Laramie, Wyoming Territory, he played a prime role in events culminating in the final showdown with hostile Sioux and Cheyenne, one of the climaxes of Western frontier history. He escorted Professor O. C. Marsh of Yale College on his historic trek to gather fossils in the Badlands in defiance of Sioux threats. He escorted Professor Jenney on his scientific exploration of the Black Hills which resulted in the official confirmation of the existence of gold, and witnessed the abortive conference at Red Cloud Agency which started the Sioux War. He fought with conspicuous gallantry under Crook at the Battle of the Rosebud, was a pillar of strength on the grueling "horsemeat" expedition, and accompanied Crook on his famous dash from Deadwood to Fort Laramie. He was the close friend of Sheridan, Crook, Stanton, Cody, Merritt, Bourke, Charles King and others whose names adorn the annals of Plains Indians warfare.

In later more tranquil years, as Major, Lieutenant Colonel and Colonel, on duty tours at the usual variety of military stations, he had much time for his own pursuits. The Indians merely required paternal surveillance, and there was only an occasional white man's riot to quell. He revealed an eager, curious, highly sociable temperament. He entertained celebrities, displayed his fossil and Indian collection to all comers, invented a better shelter tent, became the best rifle shot in the Army, organized baseball teams at every post, and composed a successful melodrama for stage-happy Buffalo Bill Cody. He took pride in his friendship with Chief Red Cloud and Chief

ANDREW SHERIDAN BURT, 1862.

Washakie, and assisted ethnologists in preserving the linguistics of the Crow, Sioux, Cheyenne and Shoshone, in which he had attained unusual proficiency.

Andy Burt and men of his mold were the backbone of the Union Army and the Indian-fighting army. During the peaceful decades he "kept his powder dry" and his men in first-class fighting trim. When there was fresh need of tested military leadership in the Spanish-American War, Colonel Burt was given key training assignments, acquitted himself with distinction, and was rewarded by President Theodore Roosevelt with the rank of Brigadier-General.

Andy Burt was an intense man, enjoying life to the last minute when he died quietly in his apartment in Washington, D. C., on the brink of American entry into World War I. Except for his brief fling at drama, his official reports, and a few reminiscences for newspaper consumption, he made no pretense of being a writer. He was not introspective and he kept no diary. The scattered references to him and his deeds, and his own meager literary efforts provide limited material for a biography. His wife made up the deficit.

Elizabeth Reynolds Burt was the family historian. Her Civil War romance with young Captain Burt blossomed into a marriage that lasted fifty-three years. During most of these years she kept diaries and wrote extensive letters to her mother and sister. It is regrettable that the diaries and the letters have disappeared without trace, lost or destroyed without her awareness of the historic value of such documents. But in 1912 she did a thoughtful thing, out of family sentiment. She sat down and proceeded to write the story of her life with Andrew Burt.[1] She had her diaries before her as she wrote, to aid her memory. The result properly comes under the heading of "recollections" or "reminiscences," but this is not the vague and wandering recall of an older person peering dimly through the mists of time. Her story, though simply told, is stamped with freshness and honesty. It is a gold mine of Western frontier lore. Over one-half of her story deals with events of 1866-1876, the period of maximum historic interest.

When Captain Burt returned with his company to the Army rest camp on Lookout Mountain in 1864, Elizabeth Burt turned heaven and earth to join him. She remained loyally by his side thereafter until his death in 1915, being separated only during his absences on dangerous field campaigns and her own rare trips back East. Thus, Elizabeth Burt was an eyewitness of historic times, places, personalities and events, and she has recorded these with fidelity.

The Author
Elizabeth J. Reynolds Burt
1862

ELIZABETH REYNOLDS BURT, 1862.

6

It is regrettable that she did not record some events with greater thoroughness. She included much admirable sentiment of a deeply devoted Christian woman, army wife and mother. She was brief or silent about some matters that clamor for attention. What was her estimate of Captain Anson Mills, her husband's successor at Fort Bridger, and a controversial figure in the Sioux War? Just what were the facts about General Bradley and the allegations of his "timidity" at the time of the Hayfield Fight? When the famous General Crook stayed with the Burts at Fort Laramie, how did he act, what did he say? When Elliott Coues, famed editor of the Lewis and Clark journals, visited Fort Missoula, what sage comments did he have?

Elizabeth Burt was not writing for historians; she was writing for herself and her children, telling what interested her, and leaving out what didn't interest her or didn't appear proper. Fortunately, most of what she did say is of signal historic value.

She reached Jefferson Barracks by walking across the frozen Mississippi River, rode in an "ambulance" to old Fort Kearney, saw the overland stage line at its booming climax, and witnessed the grading for the new Union Pacific Railroad while having her second baby in the Fort Sanders blockhouse. She was in a wagon train attacked by Indians, and she narrowly escaped kidnapping by Indians outside a stockade.

Mrs. Burt was the only resident of Fort Bridger to tell of events there during the transitional year, 1866. She was the first resident of remote and mysterious Fort C. F. Smith to leave a vital record of events long hidden in a cloud of speculation. She was the only writer who has provided a glimpse within the walls of the Officers' Quarters at Fort Laramie, if we except the fiction of General Charles King. She shed new light on Forts Omaha, Robinson, D. A. Russell, Washakie, Bidwell and Missoula. Aside from the array of military brass, she met the illustrious Captain Bonneville, entertained Chief Washakie, Mark Twain and Owen Wister, and described old John Robertson and other frontier notables.

But the greatest value of Elizabeth Burt's story is its voluminous contribution to the limited literature of frontier army wives. In this she joined the ranks of Elizabeth Custer, Margaret Carrington and a handful of others who described the frontier West from the petticoat angle.[2]

Almost every aspect of garrison and camp life came in for documentation by her pen: the eternal wife-baiting Army Regulations and the philosophy required to cope therewith; the frequent and

7

untimely changes of station; the vicissitudes of camping "on the march"; the protocol of rank and the scramble for quarters resembling the game of "musical chairs"; the chronic shortage of servants; the monotony of army rations and the ingenuity required to dream up a tasty meal; the low pay of an army captain and the economies required to make ends meet; the severe limitations of schooling for army youngsters; the prevailing attitude toward Mormons, enlisted men, colored troops and peaceful Indians; what to expect if captured by hostile Indians; the poignant refrain of the soldier's farewell song, *The Girl I Left Behind Me.*

Besides her journal of reminiscences and an accompanying album of contemporary scenes and portraits, Mrs. Burt left another testament which magically recalls historic scenes. This is a "landscape album" or "herbarium" of pressed flowers. Such mementos were commonplace enough in the last century, but where else are there specimens with such historic overtones as these?

> "Lookout Mountain, 1864."

> "Fort Bridger, 1866."

> "Gathered by Andrew and handed to me in the ambulance on the spot where Captain Brown fell at the Phil Kearny massacre, August, 1868."

> "Fort Sanders—Edith's Birthplace, 1872."

> "Yellowstone Expedition, 1873."

> "Fort Laramie, 1875."

> "Black Hills Expedition, 1875."

Andrew had a naturalist's passion for collecting fossils, birds' eggs, curios, minerals and plants. The flowers were often presented to Elizabeth upon Andrew's return from some battle or wilderness camp. Each faded blossom is pungent with the aroma of the parlor of an officer's quarters at some old Western military post.[3]

Elizabeth Johnston Reynolds was born on March 20, 1839, at Piqua, Marion County, Ohio, one of six children of William A. and Rachel Johnston Reynolds. Her paternal ancestry has been traced back to Christopher Reynolds, County Kent, England, in the 16th century. Great-great-grandfather John Reynolds removed to America in the early 18th century, acquiring large land holdings in Pennsylvania. Great-grandfather Joseph, 1747-1821, who gained prominence as an Indian fighter during the Revolution, took up his home in Maryland, and it was here that James Reynolds, Elizabeth's grandfather, married a daughter of the prosperous Lansdale clan.

Grandfather John Johnston, on the maternal side, had a colorful history. His family originated in Scotland but moved to Ireland when given large grants there by William III for valorous services at the Battle of the Boyne. John Johnston was born in County Donegal, Ireland, in 1775, migrating to America at age seventeen. At Philadelphia he became a clerk with the War Department, later going into the mercantile business at Carlisle, then the rendezvous for American troops marching against Indian raiders. He helped to supply Wayne's army and became a staunch friend of Daniel Boone. In 1802 he received an appointment as Indian agent or factor for the area around Fort Wayne. This same year he eloped with Rachel Robinson, a young Quakeress, and their wedding journey was a horseback ride of over 1,000 miles to his new station in the wilderness.

Elizabeth's mother, Rachel, was one of fifteen children of these pioneers. Two of Rachel's brothers were slain in the war with Mexico; a third died of malaria while with the Army of the Potomac.

In 1810 a patent was granted Colonel Johnston for a quarter section at Upper Piqua, Miami County, Ohio. At the outbreak of the War of 1812 a large blockhouse was built there to protect the community, and all the neutral tribes were removed to Piqua and placed under Johnston's supervision. After Hull's surrender of Detroit and the subsequent siege of Fort Niagara by Indian allies of the British, Piqua became the rallying point for the demoralized settlers. Colonel Johnston later became a central figure in Indian treaty councils held there.

Elizabeth's aunt, Julia Jefferson Patterson, had vivid memories of the frightened people in the stockade, visits there by General W. H. Harrison, General Cass and the noted Indian chiefs Tecumseh and Little Turtle. She also remembered how domestic fires were started by flintlocks sparked against punk, gun-powder being reserved only for hunting game and defense against hostile Indians. Home-made rugs were primarily red and blue, being fabricated of captured British and discarded American uniforms. One day while playing in the blockhouse she and Rachel were horrified to discover a collection of fresh Indian scalps which had been taken by white settlers. Their elders were even more fearful that this grisly cache might be discovered by Indian visitors.[4]

In Elizabeth Reynolds' girlhood, Piqua was reckoned to be one day's drive from Dayton, two days from Cincinnati. This quiet, shaded historic town on the Miami River was her home, and she would return to it as often as she could after her marriage to Andrew. But that would not be often, for Piqua was over 1,500 miles away from Wyoming and Montana Territories.

Elizabeth's younger sister, Katherine (Kate), was her faithful companion for ten years on the frontier. She eventually married Captain Winfield Scott Matson, whom she met at Fort C. F. Smith, where he was a fellow officer of Major Burt in the 27th U. S. Infantry.

Andrew and Elizabeth Burt had three children, all born under the shadow of Mars. Andrew Gano Burt was born in 1863 at Piqua, Ohio, while his father was deploying his troops before Lookout Mountain. Edith Sanders Burt was born in 1867 at new Fort Sanders, Wyoming Territory, just before Major Burt was ordered to Fort C. F. Smith, remote Montana outpost involved in "Red Cloud's War." Reynolds Johnston Burt was born in 1874 at Fort Omaha, just as his father's regiment was ordered by the Department of the Platte to march to Fort Laramie, at the beginning of the climactic war with the Sioux under Sitting Bull and Crazy Horse. Their infancy was identified with old forts, blockhouses, Indian raids and skirmishes. Their childhood playgrounds were parade grounds and stockade enclosures. They were frontier army children in the classic tradition.

General Burt's ancestor, Henry Burt, arrived in America from England in 1635. He was associated with William Pynchon in the founding of the Agawam colony on the Connecticut River, which later became Springfield, Massachusetts. A fifth generation Andrew Burt, 1771-1817, migrated from Massachusetts to Cincinnati, where in 1807 he married Sarah Gano, identified with the illustrious Goforth-Gano family of Revolutionary War fame. A brother, Major General John Gano, commanded the Ohio frontier during the War of 1812.

General Burt's father, Andrew Gano Burt, 1810-1875, became a successful banker in Cincinnati. In 1832 he married Anne Green Thompson, 1818-1892, native of London, England.[5]

The Burts, Johnstons and Reynolds were authentic pre-Revolutionary American pioneers, with a distinguished centuries-old record of leadership in peace and war. This included a fair share of Indian fighting, from Massachusetts Colony to the Ohio Valley. Andrew and Elizabeth Burt were well equipped by ancestral tradition for their forty years in the United States Army, thirty of which would be spent on the last wild Indian frontier.

General Andrew Sheridan Burt was born November 21, 1839, in Cincinnati. He attended Yale University until the end of the first term, junior year, and was then employed in his father's bank, A. G. Burt and Company, until the outbreak of the Civil War. On the first day of President Lincoln's call for volunteers in April, 1861, he enlisted as a private in the "Guthrie Grays," which became part of the 6th Ohio Volunteer Infantry. On April 20 he was made a Sergeant, and on May 14 he received a commission as First Lieutenant in the new 18th United States Infantry Regiment, for which he proceeded to recruit a company.[6]

The 18th, under the command of Colonel Henry B. Carrington, was trained at Camp Thomas, about four miles north of Columbus. General Carlos Buell, commanding the Army of the Ohio, assigned the regiment to the 3rd Brigade, 1st Division, under Colonel Robert L. McCook and Brigadier-General George B. Thomas, respectively. Young Lieutenant Burt was detailed as aide-de-camp on the brigade staff, and during the early months of his career was closely associated with the all-German 9th Ohio Infantry. Most of the volunteers, like him, "entered the military service from a variety of unwarlike professions."[7] But they gained experience in a hurry when Thomas collided with Crittenden at Logan's Crossroads, otherwise known as Mill Springs, Kentucky, on January 17, 1862.

This was the first significant Union victory after the debacle of Bull Run. Confederate General Zollicoffer was fatally shot from his horse and his forces were driven off in confusion. Union casualties, however, included General McCook and Lieutenant Burt, both severely wounded. The latter was transported back to Cincinnati to recuperate. On March 14, 1862, at "Camp near Nashville" General McCook addressed the Honorable Edwin Stanton, Secretary of War, commending his aide for bravery and coolness: "Burt was severely wounded whilst carrying a request to General Thomas to send me forward some cannon. He carried the order and did not leave the battlefield, or even stop to have the ball extracted from his side, until the battle was over and we had pursued the enemy to his works."[8] For this gallantry he was awarded the rank of Brevet-Captain, and several weeks of not unpleasant recuperation.

One of the most diligent and personable among the volunteer nurses was young Elizabeth Johnston Reynolds, and a wartime romance bloomed. At Mill Springs, Burt had "captured" a copy of Shakespeare's *Henry VI* from the Confederate camp, and the ardent young couple improved their time by quoting to each other from its immortal lines.

In April the Captain, fully recovered, was appointed aide-de-camp on the staff of General Halleck, and again assigned to serve

11

GENERAL GARFIELD AND STAFF, 1863.
Captain Andrew Burt standing, at left.

with Colonel McCook. He rapidly became Assistant Adjutant General of the Brigade, and was near at hand when McCook was murdered by bush-whackers in Tennessee, on August 16, 1862. In his dying moments McCook addressed his faithful adjutant in these terms: "Andy, the problem of life will soon be solved for me. You and I part now, but the loss of ten thousand such lives would be nothing if their sacrifice would save such a Government as ours." A wave of indignation and sorrow swept the city of Cincinnati when the tragic news was received, and flags on public buildings were flown at half-mast.[9]

Captain Burt accompanied the remains home, and was then placed temporarily on duty there with troops hastily organized to meet the threat of General Kirby Smith's knife-life thrust through Kentucky. When it appeared that he would have to hasten immediately to the battlelines, he took advantage of this opportunity to convince Elizabeth Reynolds that she should marry him at once. The hastily improvised wedding took place that very evening— on September 13, 1862. Then the Confederate invader suddenly retreated, making it unnecessary for Andrew to leave his bride right away for the field of combat.[10] Thus an army marriage which would endure for over half a century had an auspicious beginning.

In January, 1863, Andrew reported to General James A. Garfield, later to become an assassinated President of the United States, but now Chief of Staff to General Rosecrans, commanding the new Department of the Cumberland. He was designated "Acting Assistant Inspector General," but saw much action through the Hoover's Gap and Tullahoma campaigns, being cited among those on the field of battle who "discharged their duties with zeal and ability."[11]

On May 30, 1863, he was promoted to full Captain in the regular army, whereupon at his own request he relinquished his staff appointment and now assumed personal command of his own Company F, 1st Battalion, 18th U. S. Infantry. While Elizabeth was nursing her first child, born in July, Andrew was heavily involved in the great battles of the Chattanooga campaign, August-November, 1863. He played a conspicuous role under General Thomas in defending a gap necessary for the passage of the main army at Chicamauga. For this he was mentioned for gallant service by Major General Alexander McCook, commanding the 14th Corps, and the name of "Captain Andrew S. Burt" is engraved on one of the memorial stones erected by the Government at Chicamauga National Military Park. On November 25 he led his company in the daring and victorious assault upon Missionary Ridge which ended the Confederate hold on the area.

September 1, 1864, Burt was brevetted Major for splendid service in leading his company in the Atlanta campaign, showing conspicuous bravery at the battles of New Hope Church, Kenesaw Mountain, Peach Tree Creek, and Jonesboro. The depleted regiment remained in the vicinity of Atlanta until September 28, when it left for Chattanooga, where it arrived on the 30th, and then marched to Lookout Mountain and encamped on its southern slope for the winter.[12]

Elizabeth Burt left little Andrew Gano with her mother at Piqua and hurried to a joyful reunion with her husband at Louisville. The blissful couple then defied Confederate guerrillas and Union Army regulations, made a precarious dash by military railroad train to Chattanooga, and took up their abode in a tiny log cabin at the encampment on Lookout Mountain. She remembers:

> This was my first army home, and consisted of two rooms of logs, chinked with mud. The floors and all wood work, except window frames, were of unplaned boards. A half window sash in each room afforded light. A leather latch string was the fastening of the door. When it hung out, we were ready for visitors; drawing it in secured us from intrusion.
>
> Behind these rooms was a tiny kitchen, where a soldier was installed as cook, doing his best to please the Captain and the Madam. There was little from which to supply variety for the table and I began with ambitious ideas of making new dishes; but found cooking by a fire in the open air with a camp kettle and Dutch oven so very different from using a stove that I was soon obliged to acknowledge the soldier's superior skill as a camp cook. In time we became resigned to eat what he could give us from the meager variety of food; beef, sometimes, and potatoes when they could be purchased from the Commissary, as well as beans, rice, hard tack, flour, coffee, dried apples, salt pork and sugar. Flapjacks, mixed with water, flour and baking powder, when it was to be purchased, was a breakfast luxury, served with sugar syrup. Quite good biscuits were baked in a Dutch oven when it was possible to obtain baking powder.
>
> The Brigadier General in command was General John H. King, a delightful gentleman as well as a noted soldier.[13] I shall tell more of him later, when we were so fortunate as to belong to his regiment, the 9th Infantry, for many years on the Western frontier.
>
> After the railroad had been torn up by General Hood's forces, all communication from the North was cut off; neither letters nor papers were received by us. One day, a

far-away, dull rumbling was heard that was pronounced to be the firing of cannon, which indeed proved to be the case. It was the report of cannon at the hotly contested battle of Franklin, where Hood's army was repulsed by General Schofield's forces. We waited impatiently to know the result. The battles before Nashville soon followed, when General Thomas drove back the Confederates, deciding their fate west of the Alleghany mountains. Communication was soon resumed with the North, enabling us to receive letters from home, which comforted me with the news that all was well with baby and the family.

As Christmas approached, our minds were relieved from fear of danger in the West, allowing my thoughts to dwell upon the possibility of celebrating the day in some slight way. A dinner was all that seemed feasible and that was almost an impossibility, for what was a Christmas dinner without turkey?

In an interview with the cook we concocted a plan to surprise the Captain. My mother had put fruit for a plum pudding in my trunk with the recipe by which to make it and the cloth in which to boil it. The cook make an eager search in the surrounding country for viands but returned with the report that there was not a turkey nor chicken to be begged or purchased, but a wee pig had been promised. A few eggs were brought as treasures and enough sweet potatoes for the dinner, with some apples to make sauce to accompany the pig. A little milk, too, had been promised. The prospect seemed so bright that I suggested to my husband that I would like to invite four officers to dine with us. He scorned the idea of my being able to prepare a dinner for four guests. What could I give them for a Christmas dinner? At length, however, he yielded to my entreaties when I asked him to leave all arrangements to me except providing me the evergreens and holly. The latter were easily supplied, making our rooms very attractive in their decorations. Holly and red berries decorated the table.

A good beef soup was an appetizing course. Then came our wee pig with an apple in his mouth, apple sauce and sweet potatoes with rice, and beans baked beautifully, and hot baking powder biscuits. Home made candy supplied the bonbons, and when the big round plum pudding was brought in with a sprig of holly on the top, a burst of surprise and delight rewarded my efforts. Coffee followed as usual, but in very primitive cups. Our guests pronounced my first Christmas dinner a complete success. . . .

A great misfortune befell us New Year's night when an officer came to offer the greetings of the season. We smelt

15

smoke and at once opened the door into the adjoining room. Alas! The logs in our open fireplace were sending streams of fire up the wall. The officer ran to give the alarm, whilst I hurried to the closet in the burning room that consisted of a blanket tacked across one corner with nails behind it on which to hang clothing. Seizing as many garments as it was possible for me to carry, I escaped through the smoke and gave them to a soldier to remove to a place of safety. Numbers of soldiers were now on the scene, carrying out our trunks and whatever else they could save; but the flames spread like magic, making it impossible to re-enter. It is amazing how rapidly pitch pine logs burn when once started, as I learned to my sorrow. Our wardrobes were sadly depleted. No hat was left me and Chattanooga could not supply one. A large hole was burnt in my only coat. The fire was over in a very short time and before my husband could hear of it in the adjoining regiment where he had gone to wish "Happy New Year" to the ladies. One of the officers kindly loaned me a soft black felt hat to wear until one could be sent me from Cincinnati. The loss of my riding habit disturbed me greatly. Rather than give up the delightful rides, I substituted my long waterproof cape for a skirt. To ride then in a divided skirt and astride as is the custom of the present day, was unheard of.

Fortunately, the trunks contained the greater part of our wardrobes, enabling me to accept an invitation to attend a ball, given by citizens of Chattanooga to the officers. General Sherman was far away on his triumphant "march to the sea," and the minds of our forces were at rest, as the end of the war was in view. As far as possible the officers and their wives attended the entertainment. The former were all in uniform, not decorated with gold embroideries and glistening insignia, but bearing the marks of hard campaigning. Where so many ladies came from I did not know, but there was a goodly number of dancers. . . . To meet socially so many renowned heroes was a marked event, to say nothing of waltzing with so many officers of distinction. To meet General George H. Thomas was sufficient gratification for one occasion.[14] His commanding presence towered above those gathered about him. His noble countenance filled me with awe when I was presented to him. He, however, placed me at ease and filled my heart with pride when he said in a kindly way, "I am glad to meet the wife of Captain Burt, one of my good war captains who has served with me in the field since the Battle of Mill Springs. He did good work that day by his gallant ride under fire of the enemy."

All hearts were gladdened from day to day by the telegraphic reports of Sherman's progress and Grant's success about Richmond. The regret expressed by the officers and men of the Regular Brigade in the beginning, at not being able to take part in that renowned march, now increased into a wail, that they could not participate in the glories of the end and be in the grand review for President Lincoln. However, their consciences told them that they had done their full share in ending the bloody strife.

When I left my mother's home near Piqua I had named three months as the limit of my visit to the army. When the end approached, we took our last ride to Lookout Point overlooking Chattanooga and the beautiful valley of the Tennessee River, where had camped the great Union and Confederate armies of Rosecrans and Grant, and Bragg. . . . I tore myself away from my husband and my first home in the army, where we slept under army blankets and read by candlelight, where weeks passed without mail. Still there was a charm about it and my love for army life began then, though under conditions very primitive. The band played every day at guard mounting, giving untiring pleasure. Through the many years spent in different posts, watching this daily formation never lost its interest.

Upon leaving camp to start North I narrowly escaped a serious accident. The ambulance was one with side seats that could be made into a bed for the sick. My husband and our friend, Captain Lyster of General King's staff, were on horseback talking to me at the back. A slight wet snow caused the feet of the mules to slip on the mountain side, and they started to run. One wheel struck the stump of a tree, thus turning the ambulance on its side. Fortunately the four mules became detached. I was thrown on my trunk instead of it on me. Tremblingly my husband drew me from the ambulance. . . . Beyond the terrible jolting and nervous shock, nothing more serious appeared than a big bump on my forehead. . . . Word of the accident was carried to General King's headquarters, and very soon another ambulance arrived, bringing a surgeon with remedies in case of need.

Our journey was resumed and we found the General awaiting our arrival. After looking me over, he said: "You are the luckiest or unluckiest of women. First you startle us with a fire that burnt your worldly goods and threatened to destroy the camp; then comes the alarming news of the mules running away, upsetting the ambulance and endangering your life. At once I ordered the doctor to your assistance, fearing to see you brought back a fit inmate for the hospital, and here you are, apparently as well as ever."

"Yes, General, I have escaped with only bumps on my forehead and nose that make me feel that my face had better be hidden from view."

"Surely, you are not going to continue down the mountain?"

"Yes, indeed, with the doctor's services to prevent my face from becoming black and blue. I must keep on my way. All arrangements are made, and I must get home to baby. Most thankful am I to escape so easily." With a hurried goodbye we resumed our journey to Chattanooga.

With the shining armor of her strong religious faith, and the knowledge of Andrew's undying devotion, Elizabeth would be an ideal army wife, ready to meet any danger, any privation, any turn of the strange wheel of a soldier's fortune.

During its field service the 18th Infantry suffered staggering losses—39 officers and 929 men killed, wounded or captured.[15] Captain Burt (now entitled by brevet to be called "Major Burt") was among the officers sent to Cincinnati to recruit the regiment back to full strength. This would become the first regular infantry to march out into the wild Indian frontier, to replace volunteer companies at many scattered posts.

2

Jefferson Barracks
to Fort Kearney, 1866

The 2nd Battalion of the 18th U. S. Infantry left Lookout Mountain in August, 1865, for Louisville, there joining Regimental Headquarters under Colonel Carrington. On November 3 they entrained for Fort Leavenworth, and on the 26th of November left Leavenworth for Fort Kearney. "This march was very severe on account of the continuous cold and snow storm," reads the official report.[1] Mrs. Carrington is more specific: "The mercury was twelve degrees below zero and two feet of snow was first to be shoveled aside before a tent could be pitched."[2] The 2nd Battalion reached its destination December 11, and three companies were sent to Fort Cottonwood, Nebraska. During early 1866 Headquarters of the regiment remained at Fort Kearney.

After recruiting detail, Major Burt resumed command of his Old Company F, 1st Battalion, at Columbus Barracks. In November other companies of the 1st Battalion left Camp Thomas on Lookout Mountain for Fort Leavenworth, subsequently marching under severe conditions to various posts in Kansas and Colorado.³ In December Burt's company was ordered to accompany the 3d Battalion and several hundred recruits by train from Columbus to Jefferson Barracks below St. Louis, where they would remain for several months because of the severity of the winter. Elizabeth Burt vividly recalls the poignant departure:

. . . Hardships of long marches were undoubtedly ahead, but before this order came he and I had discussed the matter and agreed that wherever orders took him, baby and I would go too, if at all possible. When we announced this decision to our families a great outcry was raised together with urgent protests against this rash resolution. The idea of our taking our two-year-old baby out on the frontier, in the midst of the winter, was preposterous. Pictures of the trials of soldier life were given us from all quarters—principally of wild Indians, tent life, in the snow and again in burning sands, all painted in vivid colors.

Cousin Jane Jones, who had known many army people at Newport Barracks, Kentucky, tried to frighten me by saying: "You may live in the Rocky Mountains, where you will have no servant and must make Andrew's trousers and coats." Though the first part of this prediction was realized, and many trials fell to my lot in those early days, I never was called on to fill the role of tailor, as there was always one in the company sufficiently skillful to do the necessary work of that kind.

Waiting at Piqua for the troop train from Columbus that cold December morning, baby Andrew and I were the centre of an excited group of relatives and friends, who were sending us forth with caresses and blessings to begin our life in the Far West. They formed a tearful company.

When the train arrived my husband's welcoming smile and the bronzed faces of a few soldiers, made familiar to me on Lookout Mountain, cheered my homesick heart. Among them was big Sergeant St. John and he, holding the baby, stood with us on the rear car platform where we waved goodbyes. This was my parting from dear old Piqua for many years.

Here, travelling with the 18th U. S. Infantry, began my real army life. My husband never changed permanent

AT FORT LEAVENWORTH, 1866.

Top row: Captain Terry, Colonel Reeve, Mrs. George Sykes, Captain Rodenbaugh.
Bottom row: Major General George Sykes, Miss Kate Reynolds, Major Cushing,
Mrs. Elizabeth Burt, Lieutenant Newliss.

station thereafter that I and the children did not go along.
The long, weary separation of the late war filled with days
of anxiety and horrid suspense, when it was wired that a
battle had been fought, had determined me henceforth never
to be left behind. Of course I had to remain in garrison
when he and his company were ordered on an Indian campaign. True, that was often the case, for it seems to me there
were few summers during which he was not in the field with
his company. These partings were always great trials to me.
Our family farewells were always made in quarters behind
closed doors. Then he to his duty and I in a back room to
my tears and prayers. I would choose a back room to shut
out the tune the band played, marching the company out
of the post, "The Girl I Left Behind Me." To this day when
I hear that air tears come to my eyes.

When the troop train reached the Mississippi River, it
was frozen, and as there was no bridge, I was obliged to walk
over on the ice with the company, while a soldier carried

baby. After a short stay at a hotel I joined my husband at Jefferson Barracks and, ignorant of the customs of the service, began life in my first army post. As my husband's orders to me had been to bring little baggage, our home life started in a decidedly primitive way.

Colonel James Van Voast[4] and his adjutant, Lieutenant Henry Freeman, both retired brigadier generals now, extended to us the hospitality of their mess, thus providing our daily food. I soon learned that in an army mess, one officer orders the meals and controls the cook and assistant, if there is one, and at the end of the month divides the expenses among the members of the mess. Its hospitality is generally extended to those coming to the post and leaving it. What a relief it was to my mind to know that I need not worry about things to eat, for the present at least.

The "mess" is an institution unfamiliar to people in civil life, but in the army it is a most convenient arrangement at stations where there are no hotels, and where every officer's wife is called on so often to be hostess to new arrivals, who are frequently perfect strangers to her. However, when the necessity arises, no matter how few her bedrooms or scanty the larder, she rises to the occasion and fills the role to the best of her ability.

As my husband was not sure how soon orders might be received sending him further west, we did not consider it wise to invest in unnecessary household furnishings and only supplied ourselves from St. Louis with enough to make us comfortable in two rooms which were a family set. In the building there were four of the sets with a common family entrance. The kitchens were all below.[5]

The wife of a soldier of the regiment applied to us for a situation until she could join her husband, who was at old Fort Kearney, Nebraska. . . . Poor Bridget had just come from Ireland with her son Edward, a boy about twelve years old, expecting to join the sergeant at Jefferson Barracks. She was greatly disappointed to learn that he had gone so much further away. Following after her soldier husband, in a strange country, in the midst of winter, where all was so different from old Ireland, was not at all what she had expected. Fortunately for us, she and Edward were able to help us in many ways, especially as nurses, and stayed with us until she at last found her husband in the spring. Then what? A bright, active first sergeant, the picture of health and strength, always in immaculate uniform, made a startling contrast to this frail-looking wife with her withered face, black cap and Irish dress. How good, or otherwise, he was to her I never knew, as we then separated to meet no more.

Soon after our arrival at Jefferson Barracks we received a call from the post commander, General Benjamin Bonneville, a most interesting character. . . . When we met him, though retired, he had been put on duty at Jefferson Barracks. He was host at the first dinner party I attended in the army, filling the position delightfully, with the assistance of his charming nieces, Mrs. Crittenden and Miss Bacon.[6] The dismal picture that had been drawn for me before I started West, of eating from tin plates, was dispelled when we gathered round that beautiful table with its faultless napery, silver, glass, delicate china and flowers.

This was indeed the bright side of our new life. Immediately after this came an invitation to a ball to be given by the citizens of St. Louis. To attend this I sent home for a suitable gown and, the occasion offering, asked my mother to also send our box of silver, which we had never expected to use in the army, judging from the discouraging accounts given us before leaving Ohio. The gown and silver came safely, but before the ball took place an order was received [March, 1866] sending the company with its captain to Fort Leavenworth. We rejoiced that we had not invested in a great quantity of furniture which would not have to be packed. As it was, we were soon in readiness for the journey.

This was the beginning for me of many, many moves in the army. For years thereafter we looked for orders every spring to change station, and generally received the usually dreaded document in April. It seemed to me [now] that I was going out of the world, and my mother felt the same way; consequently she allowed my youngest sister Kate to join us before we left Jefferson Barracks.

In very uncomfortable cars, little resembling the Pullmans of today, we made that tedious trip, arriving at the town of Weston to find the Missouri River frozen over. Three wearisome days we spent in a forlorn hotel, waiting for the thaw to come. On the third day we watched hour by hour, the ice gradually break, and gladly welcomed at last the great cracking and rush which followed, of the running ice. Just before dark the ferry-boat succeeded in passing us over the river, when the command marched into Fort Leavenworth. An ambulance was sent to take the ladies to the post.

In 1827 Colonel Henry Leavenworth had been ordered to ascend the Missouri from Jefferson Barracks to the mouth of the

Little Platte, and there select a site for the permanent cantonment. The new post, which replaced Fort Atkinson above present Omaha, was the scene of many crucial treaties with the Osage, Pawnee, Missouri and other Plains tribes, and a base for west-bound emigrants and freighting outfits. In 1865 the Military Departments of Kansas and Missouri were merged under the name of the latter, with Fort Leavenworth as Departmental Headquarters. General Samuel B. Curtis was soon replaced by General Grenville M. Dodge as Commander, and in the summer and winter of 1865 Dodge launched expeditions against the Sioux, Cheyenne and Arapahoe which culminated in the Powder River Campaign. Dodge was in residence at Fort Leavenworth when the Burts arrived there, while General John Pope commanded the post. Shortly thereafter Dodge resigned from the Army to take on the job as Chief Engineer for the Union Pacific Railroad; at this same time a new Department of the Platte was created out of Nebraska and Wyoming Territories, with Headquarters in Omaha.[7] It was in this Indian-infested section of the West that Andrew and Elizabeth would spend their next quarter century.

Fort Leavenworth today is a huge sprawling establishment shaded by giant elms and lined with brick buildings, many of late 19th century vintage. Few buildings which Elizabeth Burt knew survive.[8] In 1866 a parade ground about 500 feet square was surrounded by two-story frame barracks, with porticoes, and fourteen sets of officers' quarters, variously constructed of logs, frame, brick and stone. The Surgeon-General of that period reported that "outbuildings are attached to all the officers' quarters, and there is a cistern in the rear of each set. None of them have water-closets or bathrooms."[9] Indeed, it would be twenty-five years before Elizabeth Burt would become situated at an army post that could boast such refinements! But Fort Leavenworth, she writes, did have its redeeming features:

A cordial invitation had been received by us before leaving Jefferson Barracks, to be the guests of General Washington Elliott, Lieutenant-Colonel, 1st Cavalry, and his wife, upon our arrival.[10] He was an old friend of our family and received us most graciously, at the entrance to the post, taking us to his quarters, where we were presented to his wife, who proved a most hospitable hostess, and who upon further acquaintance, gave me a most valuable suggestion for my guidance—never to borrow anything unless absolutely necessary. A good rule to follow, as has been proven. . . .

24

A vacant set of quarters was ready for us to occupy, which we did as soon as our household goods could be put in place by men from the company. In our house there was a basement dining room and kitchen with two rooms above them and two in the attic. Bathrooms were an unknown luxury in the army. Now-a-days every house, of course, has them, but my husband was a major who had served twenty years in the army before we possessed that luxury. At this time the water was hauled from the river and emptied into barrels at the kitchen door. Microbes were unheard of in those days, and we drank the water, and what milk we could purchase, with no thought of disaster.

The hall and stairway were in common with our next door neighbor, who was a volunteer paymaster, having his wife and daughter with him. This mode of building quarters prevailed generally in those early days, bringing families in closer contact than was sometimes pleasant.

Fortune favored us when a colored girl, Maggie, applied for a place as servant. She had lately been a slave, often working in the fields, though some experience as a maid and cook. We hailed her with joy, though we still had Bridget and Edward. . . .

Fort Leavenworth proved to be a very pleasant place in which to spend the remainder of our winter. Many officers were there, both regular and volunteer, the latter waiting to be mustered out, the former expecting orders to go west in the spring.

General Grenville Dodge was Department Commander, General George Sykes, Post Commander, General Potter, Quartermaster, General Morgan, Commissary. Colonel Reeve commanded the 13th Infantry.[11] In addition, there were in the garrison, parts of the 18th Infantry and of the 2nd Cavalry; also some artillery. General Sykes proved to be a delightful post commander, entering with his wife into all social gatherings that promoted pleasure and good feeling among the officers and their families, though he had the reputation of being very strict with those on duty. . . .

The winter was cold and snowy. We had many dances and social gatherings, all at our houses, as there was no "Pope Hall" as now, or any large room for a rendezvous. Colonel Reeve added greatly to our pleasure by his cordiality and kindness and often called the figures for the young people in the square dances, in the merriest manner. "Forward," "A la main, left," "ladies to the right," sound faintly in my ears now. The two-step was then unknown, but we waltzed with delight and danced the "galop."

General Dodge lived in the largest house facing the parade, which has been occupied by the Commanding Officer, I have been told, until lately. Colonel and Mrs. Lloyd Wheaton lived there when I visited Captain and Mrs. Trout, our son-in-law and daughter, in 1897. Our old home at the corner towards Pope Hall was made into a very comfortable set for a lieutenant.[12]

Life was then much more simple than of late years. No one had cut glass nor Oriental rugs. No one was rich or strived to live any better than his neighbors. Each knew what he could afford and lived within his means, which is certainly the secret of happiness in the army if not in civil life.

On April 20, 1866, while Regimental Headquarters and the 2nd Battalion, 18th U. S. Infantry, impatiently awaited at Fort Kearney, eight companies of the 3d Battalion, plus Major Burt's Company F of the 1st Battalion and a swarm of recruits, all commanded by Major Van Voast, left Fort Leavenworth on the epic march which is vividly described by Mrs. Burt:

. . . My husband's company was to take station at Fort Bridger, Utah. The idea of going to the land of Mormons was very strange and bewildering, and when we hunted it up on the map it looked very far away. I would be the only lady there, although a number of ladies and a few children were to begin the journey with us. The prospect seemed so doleful to me and so appalling to my mother that we asked the advice of officers and their wives who had lived on the frontier, as to the advisability of my sister going with us. Without exception they said, "Take her with you." After much persuasion, added to this advice, my mother gave her consent. My heart was lightened and my sister jubilant.

Our new home was to have an altitude of 7,000 feet in the Rocky Mountains. No need to prepare summer wardrobes for that climate.

Transportation was limited to one wagon to a company. It must carry tents, camping outfits, trunks, household goods and everything except commissaries, for three officers. "What about the ladies?" you ask. The Army Regulations provide nothing for wives and children, not even mentioning their existence. Happily there were no lieutenants [on duty at this time] in the company, for which we rejoiced, as we now had entire possession of that one wagon. Naturally the captain of the company would have preferred having lieutenants to help him . . . but where

26

could their trunks and other belongings have found space in that wagon? Suppose one had come with a wife?

It required judgment to select what was most necessary to take in that wagon, as there was no railroad to bring boxes from home, nor could packages come to us through the mail as in the present day. Expressage was too expensive a luxury for an army officer; so there was no possibility of our receiving any additions to our wardrobes or household effects before [army] freight could come from the East in the coming year.

The purchase of a cow proved a wise investment, giving our baby boy his good fresh milk three times a day during that long journey. A rooster and twelve hens also served us well. While at Fort Leavenworth we availed ourselves of the market of the city and supplied ourselves with a small quantity of luxuries to add to the table in the early stages of the journey. From the Commissary we could only buy what the Government issued to the enlisted men. There was great rejoicing when Major Cushing of the Commissary Department brought the news that an order had been issued naming canned goods among the supplies to be sent throughout the army. None could reach us at our far away home in Utah until the next year, as the supplies for Fort Bridger had already been ordered for the present year, and were to go with our command.

The day of departure from dear old Leavenworth was filled with the loveliness of spring that comes in April. Robins, bluebirds, violets, budding trees and fresh velvety grass made a scene of beauty.

Our wagon was packed to the bows—two large wicker chairs were tied on the outside, while to the back was fastened the coop containing our big buff Bramah rooster and his family. Early in the morning this load was started on its way. Then came a good breakfast at the bachelor's mess. Off started my husband marching with his company, leaving us surrounded by our friends, while we settled ourselves in the ambulance—my sister, baby Andrew, Maggie the cook, Mason the driver, and Betty the pet Skye-terrier, with me.

The parting from those who had made our stay at Leavenworth so pleasant was, with much regret, mingled with pleasure at their apparent sincere sorrow at losing us, as they waved a fond farewell to the wanderers, starting into an unknown land.

Though my husband had spent the years of the war in tent, he had never had his family with him and all was new

Courtesy, Burt Collection

ANDREW GANO BURT.

to us. However, it was but a few days before we became accustomed to the strange life. There were two wall and two "A" tents for the company commander and his family, the "A" tents serving as kitchen and sleeping room for Maggie. We soon learned to move, sleep and eat by order. The two wall tents were pitched with the openings facing each other, with the fly of one covering the space between, which formed our dining room in pleasant weather. A square of heavy Manila matting covered the ground in each wall tent, in one of which was a folding cot, and in the other was placed a rubber blanket and then the mattress. Tin basins and buckets supplied our toilets. There were a folding table and chairs for the dining room, and linen pockets on the tent sides were convenient for catch-alls. At first the uneven ground made a poor foundation for our bed, but the fatigue party that pitched the tents was careful to even the ground with spades to a certain extent and remove the stones, enabling our young, healthy bodies to sleep, in spite of ruts and hillocks.

Reveille sounded at four o'clock. Maggie had breakfast ready at five. Baby Andrew was rolled in a blanket and placed in the ambulance to continue his sleep. While we breakfasted, the fatigue party packed the wagon, and my sister and I were ready to start when the "General" sounded at five-thirty.

For a few days the chickens were kept in the coop, which was always the last thing placed on the back of the wagon. They soon became familiar with their new life and were let loose as soon as we reached camp, roaming about, laying their eggs sometimes in the tents or coop, here and there, sometimes three, sometimes seven. At times they strayed into strange tents, the occupants of which were kind enough to return the fresh egg to us. One motherly hen came slowly into my tent one day, looking around while I lay quietly on the bed. Between me and the tent wall she nestled closely and soon sent out a "cut-cut-ca-dar-cut," proclaiming her duty done. At their bed time they went into the coop and were fastened in, ready for the start the next morning.

Susy proved a great addition, giving several quarts of milk a day, for the table, providing cream for breakfast and milk to drink in abundance. She had been shod before starting on the trip and soon learned to follow with the command, after being led for a few days. Good old Susy, what a blessing she proved! When baby wakened, he had his cup of milk with cracker or baking-powder biscuit or sometimes hardtack.

29

We never stopped long enough to make bread except on Sunday when the command always remained in camp. Maggie could not make bread then as yeast cakes were unknown, but the Sabbath was devoted to washing and cleaning up generally, while everyone rested as far as possible and the mules benefited by a day of rest and grazing. The country was beautiful in its fresh garb of green. Grass, budding trees and wild flowers formed a picture to enchant the eye. The novelty of the life made us happy in the bracing air that brought good appetites and healthful sleep, regardless of the hard earth beneath the mattress. Youth, health and courage made us overlook the discomforts that in city life would have been considered unbearable.

When the "General" sounded in the morning, Major Van Voast and his staff officers led the command on horseback, followed by the captains and lieutenants, marching with their companies. Then came the ambulances carrying the wives and children of the officers, taking place in line according to the rank of the officer. There were four in front of us, keeping the same order each day, except when my husband was officer of the guard and remained in the rear of the command, and I was glad to keep back that day too, for a change. He had bought an ambulance and two mules for our use before leaving Leavenworth. Between the ambulances and the rear guard came the long line of six-mule teams carrying supplies needed for the trip as well as for the coming year and all the posts at which companies were to be stationed.

The command marched about three miles in fifty minutes and halted ten. The wagon master rode in advance and brought to the commanding officer a report about camp, that depended upon the supply of water and wood. The latter was scanty as trees in general were found only along streams. . . . The march was usually about eighteen miles. The Quartermaster carried a small amount of wood for fuel that was very carefully divided, when it was not possible to obtain any from the neighboring country. . . . Sometimes the ladies walked from one halting place to the next for exercise, always keeping ahead of the command at a short distance.

When the day's journey was ended, the adjutant had selected the sites of tents for companies and officers, always having them near each other. One lady objected to the proximity and told the pioneer party to change the locality appointed for her tents; but orders were orders and in that spot her tent must be pitched. This happened in the early part of the trip. We ladies soon learned the full significance of an order and that to submit gracefully was the only, as well as the happier, way.

Our wagon was soon on the appointed spot where the fatigue party quickly pitched the tents and placed the contents inside. Maggie arranged everything in order. The men filled the water pails and brought the fuel. Soon the smoke was puffing from the little pipe of the sheet-iron cooking stove and Maggie served us a cup of tea with a simple lunch, often consisting of a glass of milk and hardtack. . . . If there was a long day's march before us, we had a luncheon in the ambulance, where my husband joined us at a ten minutes' halt. After we were settled in camp, came a nap followed by necessary mending and writing letters, or in the diary, to be sent at intervals to my mother.[18] We made some little change in our wardrobe for five o'clock dinner, but it was very little. . . .

As our allowance of transportation was so limited, the extra supplies we had brought from Leavenworth were soon exhausted. We were more fortunate than the bachelors as we had milk and eggs in addition to the commissaries but soon found that good appetites made the plainest food palatable. Maggie made us many a simple pudding, varied by batter cakes with sugar syrup for dessert, as there was never time for them at breakfast.

After dinner visits were exchanged with the other ladies, who were all strangers to us when our journey began. An occasional game of whist in the evening or perhaps cribbage or bezique helped pass the time, until nine o'clock, when taps reminded us that we, as well as the soldiers, needed to retire early.

With the rear guard were the prisoners, and a hospital ambulance accompanied by the doctor, ready to care for the sick or those who became footsore and fell by the wayside. For the first few days there were many of these unhappy looking men, limping along, but it was not long before everyone was walking with a firm stride.

For a few days after starting we passed occasional ranches where we bought a little butter and had visits from the inmates of the homes and others about the country, who gathered with great curiosity to see so many soldiers. . . . General Carrington with one battalion of the regiment had passed over the same road a few months before this, in the midst of intense cold. . . .

On the seventeenth day after leaving Fort Leavenworth the command reached old Fort Kearney, Nebraska, completing a march of approximately 315 miles.[14] Through the field glasses we had seen the flag floating in the breeze from the flagstaff long before we heard the welcoming strains of the band that, to welcome us, had been brought from the fort by the officers who composed the 2nd Battalion, now with Colonel Carrington and Headquarters. . . . They were all war comrades of Major Burt, but many of them strangers to me. My husband, due to his brevet rank attained during the war, was officially ranked and called Major from this time on.[15] Brevet Lieutenant-Colonels Kinney and Haymond, Lieutenants Bisbee and Brown I had known on Lookout Mountain.[16] I had never met any of the ladies. The meeting was a joyful one and we were all glad to reach a post once more.

Alas! What a painful contrast to beautiful Fort Leavenworth! The old, dilapidated houses afforded scanty quarters for the officers and their families. Not a tree nor blade of grass was to be seen. However, we were received with the greatest hospitality, always, as I found, to be the custom in the army. Though Lieutenant Bisbee had but two rooms and a kitchen, he and his wife entertained us at as handsome a dinner as was possible to prepare in that destitute part of the world. Here I first met Mrs. Carrington, the wife of the Colonel, and Mrs. Horton, the wife of the Surgeon.[17]

We now felt the full force of the wind that blew almost daily over these plains, peppering our food with fine sand that would sift into everything, despite the greatest precaution. The country was a treeless plain with no beauty of landscape. However, the pleasure of meeting old friends and becoming acquainted with new officers and their families made the days pass pleasantly. The Adjutant, Mr. Phisterer, sent the band every evening to play in our camp, and one evening we had an impromptu dance at the Colonel's.

Elizabeth Burt spent a week at Fort Kearney, Nebraska Territory, the "jumping off place" for travelers on the Oregon Trail, the California Road, the overland stage line and the Denver Road. These historic routes had their initial beginnings at various points along the Missouri River but they all funneled into the old fort, which then represented the last citadel of civilization and the first stronghold of the Federal Government on the Great Plains.

In 1847 Lieutenant Daniel P. Woodbury, Corps of Topographical Engineers, had recommended the location of this post "at the southernmost part of the Platte River, where the Oregon Trail from Independence and St. Joe first touched that stream. In 1848 construction

SKETCH OF FORT KEARNEY, c. 1866 — Artist unknown.

of the original fort was completed by the Regiment of Mounted Riflemen; it was named in honor of General Stephen Watts Kearny, hero of the Mexican War.[18] It achieved its greatest fame during the California gold rush of 1849 and the early 1850's when over 200,000 people paused here to rest from their feverish journey. Here horses were shod, provisions could be obtained, and officers of the garrison were called upon to administer justice among quarreling nerve-taut emigrants. During the 1860's Fort Kearney was an important way station on the Overland Mail, freight and stage lines, and the famed Pony Express.

Elizabeth Burt did not know it at the time, but the overland stage she saw in all its glory was actually in the process of dying, having just suffered grievously from vengeful Indians during the uprisings of 1864-1865, and now doomed by the oncoming railroad. Like the plant said to give its best bloom just before it expires from a fatal infection, the old Fort Kearney stage station in 1866 was a beehive of activity. The heavy Concord coaches, driven by six-horse teams, and spilling over with passengers and mail, rolled in daily from Atchison, Omaha, Nebraska City, Denver, Salt Lake City and California. At this point the stages of the Western Stage Company, operating out of Omaha, connected with the Holladay lines from Missouri; there was great rivalry between these lines, and passengers seeking a transfer at this point were often compelled to wait for days. Stage coach days at Fort Kearney were finished after October 5, 1866, when the Union Pacific Railroad was completed to the 100th Parallel, on the opposite side of the river and fifty miles west of the fort.[19]

As officially described, the post was laid out in a regular square, with storehouses on the north; officers' quarters and one barrack on the south; the commanding officer's quarters and office buildings on the west, all surrounding a parade ground of four acres, flagstaff in center. A few cottonwood trees lined the sidewalks of the parade. To some stage passengers it was a grand sight, after travelling 150 miles without seeing a settlement of more than two or three houses, to gaze upon the old post, uninviting as it was, and see the few scattered buildings, a nice growth of shade trees, the cavalrymen mounted upon their steeds, the cannon planted within the hollow square, and the glorious stars and stripes proudly waving in the breeze above the garrison.[20] On the other hand, Elizabeth Burt's dismal impression was shared by Eugene F. Ware of the 7th Iowa Cavalry: "The post was a little old rusty frontier cantonment. The buildings were principally made out of native lumber hauled from the East. The fuel was cottonwood cordwood cut down on the island of the Platte. The parade ground was not very large, and had around it a few straggling trees that had evidently been set out in large numbers when the post had been made; a few had survived, and they showed the effect of the barrenness and aridity of the climate. They looked tough."[21]

The general effect was not improved by the proximity of Kearney City or Dobytown, two miles west of the Fort. It was a place of perhaps half a dozen sod structures, occupied by the worst kind of dives. The soldiers quartered at the post patronized these places, and teamsters looked forward to a pause there to fortify themselves with a dubious brew called "tanglefoot." Wagon bosses would try to arrange their journey so that they would never be obliged to camp in this vicinity.[22]

Inspector-General Babcock, who arrived at the place on May 17 to confer with Colonel Carrington, explained that "the transitory state of affairs at Fort Kearney prevented the neat appearance that would otherwise characterize the post," and, in view of the pending railroad, recommended that it be dispensed with forthwith.[23] The Fort Kearney situation at this period is further illuminated by a report of August 21, 1866, of General W. T. Sherman:

On Saturday, August 17, General Dodge gave us a special train and accompanied us to the end of the Pacific Railroad, the whole finished distance, 190 miles. The road lies in the flat prairie bottom of the Platte, and we found the construction trains laying rails within about five miles of Fort Kearny, where our ambulances awaited us. The railroad lies on the north side and Fort Kearny on the south side, and about four and a half miles will lie between the fort and its depot. . . . We had to cross the Platte, as mean a river as exists on earth, with its moving, shifting sands, and I feel a little lost as to what to say or do about Fort Kearny. It is no longer of any military use. . . . At Kearny the buildings are fast rotting down, and two of the largest were in such danger of tumbling that General Wessels had to pull them down. I will probably use it to shelter some horses this winter, and next year let it go to the prairie dogs. . . .[24]

3

To the Crest of the Continent

When Colonel Carrington arrived at Fort Kearney, his 2nd Battalion, 18th U. S. Regiment of Infantry, consisted of but 260 men. This force was swollen to nearly 2,000 men by May 15, 1866, with the gradual arrival of contingents of Major Van Voast's column, composed of the entire 3rd Battalion, Company F of the 1st Battalion, and recruits for the 1st and 2nd Battalions. The skeleton companies of the 2nd were now comfortably filled out to a force of about 700 men, and would march under Carrington via Fort Laramie to the Land of the Crows, to establish a line of posts along the Bozeman Trail, the new land route to the Montana gold fields. All other contingents would be scattered at posts along the old Oregon Trail or Platte route to Fort Laramie and beyond, and the overland stage route to Denver and Salt Lake City, replacing impatient volunteer units. They would all march together until they reached Fort Sedgwick near Julesburg, where the first unit was to be detached. This would be the largest body of soldiers ever to march across the Central Great Plains.[1]

Two volunteer cavalry regiments, the 7th Iowa and 6th West Virginia, en route from Fort Laramie to Fort Leavenworth to be mustered out of service, were induced by the Regimental Quartermaster to dismount and leave their horses at Fort Kearney for use of the Carrington expedition. Two hundred fortunate infantrymen were mounted, with only occasional mishaps, and a troop of cavalry thus improvised. The long Springfield rifle proved to be a dubious asset for the amateur horsemen, so they were packed in wagons on the optimistic assumption that the Indians would give no trouble.

The wagon train, drawn by 226 mule teams, was heavily laden with supplies and equipment for setting up a new civilization in the Crow wilderness—flour, bacon, salt, beans, canned fruits, all manner of provisions, medical gear (including several kegs of whiskey to anaesthetize or stimulate as occasion required), rocking chairs and sewing chairs, churns and washing machines, a steam saw mill, grinding stones, complete tools for the construction of log or adobe stockades, plows and garden tools, anvils, extra wagon parts, and a full complement of ordnance, including several shiny brass mountain howitzers. Mrs. Burt's cow and chickens added a domestic touch to the martial caravan. Another officer's wife boasted a small flock of turkeys and a brace of swine. The only things missing were Mrs. Carrington's best chair, bedstead, mattress and private stock of delicacies, all prematurely consumed in a fire which burned down their quarters shortly before the hour of departure.[2]

May 19 dawned "bright and promising, notwithstanding such a cloud of dust as only the plains can supply." Bugle calls set the regiment on the march, led by Colonel Carrington riding on the black Kentucky charger that had carried him through many Civil War campaigns. He was accompanied by Captains Phisterer and Brown, Major Horton and the illustrious "Major" James Bridger, chief guide of the expedition, and his assistant, H. Williams.[3] Then came one of the newly mounted companies, followed by the marching infantry and the serpentine wagon train. The remaining "cavalry" brought up the rear, while the ambulances carrying officers' families rode freely alongside the column.

The coppery sun glared down. The mass of men and animals created a small choking dust cloud of its own. No man knew what dangers lay ahead, but morale was excellent as the companies swung smartly away from Fort Kearney and Dobytown. The strains of martial music by the regimental band, thirty strong, kept steps and spirits high as the 18th Regiment of Infantry marched westward to bolster Federal sovereignty in the long neglected Great Plains and the Rockies.

It was General Sherman's suggestion, while visiting Carrington's quarters at Fort Kearney, that the ladies of the expedition keep a daily journal of events. It was already Mrs. Burt's habit to keep such a record:

> The country was here level along the Platte River with bluffs on one side showing plainly that in ages past they had been submerged. Their water-washed sides contained crevasses that afforded good hiding places for Indians, who undoubtedly were watching our movements, but kept out of sight. By the aid of good field glasses, what were sometimes thought to be Indians, were shown to be fantastic shapes in the water-washed bluffs. Antelope began to be numerous, giving animation and interest to the landscape, as their graceful forms seemed almost to fly over the country, offering great sport to the hunters after camp was made.

> We had now reached the land of sage brush that grew here in small bunches not more than a foot high. Farther west we found it sometimes much larger, looking like gnarled primeval trees. We have camped among sage brush higher than our heads and found it good firewood. That through which we were now traveling was a tender bluish-green herb. Colonel Lewis, who had served on the plains before the war, laughed heartily when a provident housewife suggested gathering a supply for seasoning when we first saw the sage brush. Little did she or any of us have any idea that our homes were to be among this herb for many years.

> We now travelled on the south bank of the Platte River, a wide, rushing torrent, dangerous in this month of June, when the melting snow was pouring into all streams. Sometimes the width of the river was a half mile and contained occasional small islands covered with swamp willows.

> We passed the land of ranches and found nothing but stage stations to relieve the monotony. They afforded nothing to interest us except the chance of receiving news from the passengers as they passed east and west each day, and occasionally left a precious newspaper. The stations of one story were built of adobe, which is sun dried brick,

made of yellowish soil. Each brick is about four times as large as our red brick. Every station had a room devoted to a store where supplies were kept for men—tobacco, whiskey, flour, bacon, hardtack, baking powder and things considered necessary for men, but nothing to replenish a woman's wardrobe. Some of them were able to supply breakfast or dinner or supper of a very primitive kind to the coach passengers.

Around the station was a stockade of adobe enclosing also the stables for the horses and whatever was necessary for the men employed, to take care of the teams and stock; but no cow had ever reached that part of the country. The horses were provided by the Overland Stage Company, and were necessarily selected as the best for the purpose and of course must receive especial care.

The wind constantly stirring up the dust surrounding the stations made life for a house keeper far from desirable. Occasionally we found a wife and children at the stations; more often men were alone. The occupants of the station, in addition to a daily paper, had the comfort of having the telegraph line with them. What joy there is in this I have experienced more than once.

The approach of the coaches was announced by a loud blast from a horn. The horses would then be ready for a speedy change, when on again went the stage, giving the occupants of the coach only time to stretch their limbs, unless it was the hour for meals that must be hastily swallowed. Even this brief rest was hailed with delight by passengers who had travelled, perhaps a week or sometimes longer, in a cramped position. The stages when crowded carried fifteen passengers besides large quantities of mail and express matter. It cost more for meals than is now charged for both railroad fare and meals.

At this period in the sixties it took six days and nights for the coach to make the distance from the Missouri River to Denver; the fare was $175, while now it is about $15 by the railroad. There were 153 stations on the line from the Missouri to the Pacific Coast. The time required was seventeen days and the cost without meals was $225. Salt Lake City was the only city between Denver and California. Our place of destination was far west of the present site of Denver. When my attention was called to the schedule of travelling expenses and the trials of a stage coach journey, I knew full well it would never be possible for me to return east until my husband came under orders and provided a less fatiguing and expensive mode of transportation.[4] . . .

On our route of march [Mrs. Burt continues] we found many prairie dog towns extended along the roadside, the houses consisting of mounds of sand and gravel with an opening at the top, used as doorways to their subterranean houses. The little gray fellows looked much like squirrels with short tails. They would sit on their hind legs and bark at us in the most saucy manner and seek refuge in their holes at our least attempt to approach them. Small grey owls were often seen sitting on the same mounds with them and were said to share their houses. Reports said that rattlesnakes sometimes joined them in their abode. However, we never saw any of the latter in the vicinity of a dog town.[5]

The beautiful pink and yellow blossoms of the prickly pear were profusely scattered over the sandy country among other lovely flowers new to us. We have found the prickly pear growing in all parts of the far west, but dreaded always by the pedestrian who has ever been so unfortunate as to step on its almost invisible but very sharp spines. They are most difficult to remove from the feet or hands of one who touches them. The Indians and frontiersmen used it as a cure for rattlesnake bite. The life of man or mule has often been saved by the application of one of these thick leaves, being split in two parts and then thrown on a camp fire until it became hot and soft, when it was applied to the affected part. Now Mr. Burbank, the horticulturist, announces that the western country may become rich in the manufacture of sugar made from this same prickly pear. Truly then the desert may be made to blossom as a rose.

On this march Mrs. Carrington also kept a journal, which achieved later fame as a book, *Ab-Sa-Ra-Ka, Land of Massacre*. Her travels coincided with those of Mrs. Burt from Fort Kearney to the South Platte crossing, and her observations, in polished literary form, make an interesting parallel:

The march was along the Platte River, whose quick-sands and fickle currents have been the bane of travelers since Lewis and Clarke abused it and Colonel Bonneville crossed it. Alkaline and muddy—sometimes disappearing under the sandy bed, so that a footman can cross from shore to shore without seeing water, and again flowing even with its banks; sometimes surfeiting the south channel, under the pressure of a strong north wind, and again, within the same sun, rolling back so as to foil the calculations of some traveler who crossed in the morning, expecting an equally safe crossing at night—it has no disputant to oppose its claim to be the most unaccountably contrary and ridiculous river the world ever saw.

But in our course along the Platte in 1866, we had, such as it was, all the water we wished. One day was much like another day, with the same march at the earliest dawn, the same adventure with rattlesnakes, the same pursuit of wild flowers, the same inopportune thunderstorms, the same routine of guard mounting at sunset, the same evening music from the band, and the same sound slumber. Recurring Sabbaths gave us our only intervals of rest; and the fact that at Fort Reno we overtook trains which started before us, but marched daily, is a substantial testimony, concurrent with all intelligent experience, that the observance of the Lord's day is indispensable alike to man and beast. On such occasions Lieutenants Adair, Kirtland and D'Isay, occasionally joined by Mr. Phisterer, tenor, helped to make something like true melody from the sweet Sabbath Bell sent us by the Sabbath school of Rev. Mr. Dimmick, of Omaha, before our departure from Kearney.[6]

General Sherman himself followed this same "dead level" route two months later:

I see little danger of Indians. The telegraph is unmolested; the stage passes daily; and I find the road filled with travellers, back and forth, with ranches every ten miles; yet there is a general apprehension of danger, though no one seems to have a definite idea of whence it is to come. I have met a few straggling parties of Indians who seemed pure beggars, and poor devils, more to be pitied than dreaded.

It is impossible to conceive of a more dreary waste than this whole road is—without tree or bush, grass thin, and the Platte running over its wide, shallow bottom with its rapid current; no game or birds; nothing but the long, dusty road, with its occasional ox team, and the everlasting line of telegraph poles. Oh, for the pine forests of the south, or anything to hide the endless view.[7]

Young William H. Jackson, helping to escort a bull-train to Salt Lake City that same summer, also heard echoes of impending Indian troubles:

. . . Along our route we have not seen the first single redskin with the exception of a half dozen some 3 days out

42

from Nebraska City. We have heard stories all along of anticipated trouble and of rumors of their intention to strip out this whole valley. Our route for the last few days has abounded with vestiges of their presence last fall. Deserted and ruined ranches are more numerous than inhabited ones. The country looks desolate enough anyway. The low mud huts called ranches were about once in six or eight miles so far, and their only redeeming feature is their wells. Some of them have most excellent water that is a real treat upon a hot and dusty day. In some the water is very strong of alkali. We always camp as near the river as possible and use that water. It is as muddy as the Missouri but is said to be not unhealthy. . . .[8]

The ranches referred to by Jackson, Sherman and Mesdames Burt and Carrington were in some instances the original Pony Express stations of 1860, now principally stage stations, sometimes fortified, which offered food and lodging to stage passengers and other travelers. The prices of these accommodations were uniformly high; their quality precarious. Women were free to sleep if they could in an uncurtained room full of snoring customers and stray dogs. At times one might have the good fortune to secure a meal of choice broiled buffalo steak; more often, stale bread, soggy bacon and bitter coffee were the fare. Also available were supplies and provisions, one account listing "nutmegs, peppermint, navy tobacco, clay pipes, salaratus, bologna, and ready-made clothing . . . canned fruits . . . black snake whips, tin cups, camp kettles and frying-pans." Withal, the ranches of the Platte were a boon to travelers until they were put out of business by the railroad. Mrs. Carrington had a fond regard for these establishments:

. . . it was after Kearney was passed, that the glory of legitimate ranching began. McLean and the genial Sydenham, our Fort Kearney Postmaster; Gallagher; Pat Mallaley; Dan Smith; Gilman, a man of business, straightforward and worthy, and Coles, were a few who ministered to our comfort on the way to McPherson. Then came Fitchies, Burkes, Morrows, Bakers, Browns, Beauvais, and Valentines, all accommodating and excellent.[9]

The Regimental Returns, with some misspellings, similarly identify the stations and camps on this march:

. . . May 19th the [Regimental] headquarters with Company F, 1st Battalion and the 2nd and 3d Battalions left

Fort Kearny enroute to Julesburgh, C. T. March 14 and encamped on Platte River 2 miles west of McDam's Ranche. May 20 marched 20 miles and encamped on Platte River near Plum Creek, N. T. May 21, marched 13 miles encamped on Platte River near Pat Malloy's ranche. May 22 marched 16 miles. Encamped on Platte river near Smith's Ranch. May 23 marched 22 miles and encamped on Platte River near Cole's Ranch. May 24th passed Fort McPherson camped on south Platte river near Jack Morrises ranch having marched 15 miles; May 25th marched 23 miles. Camped on South Platte river near O'Fallons Bluffs. May 26 marched 25 miles to Alkali Station camping on South Platte River. May 27 halted to rest. May 28 march 19 miles. Encamped on South Platte near Beavai's Station. May 29 marched 12 miles and camped on South Platte river 6 miles west of Beauvai's. May 30 march to Julesburgh 19 miles, camped on South Platte near Fort Sedgwick. Total distance . . . 198 miles.[10]

Cottonwood or McDonald's Station, 95 miles west of Fort Kearney, just below the forks of the Platte, was an important depot of the stage line, being midway between Fort Kearney and Julesburg, and near canyons full of cedar trees, a priceless item on the Plains. In 1863 the Army had set up Fort McKean near here to protect the stage and telegraph line. In 1864 this was renamed Fort Cottonwood. Early in 1866 General Dodge renamed it Fort McPherson after a fallen Civil War general.[11] The Carrington expedition paused here, five days out of Fort Kearney, only long enough to seek additional ammunition and pick up an idle saw mill. Mrs. Carrington mentions only "shabby log-cabins" but Mrs. Burt was most pleasantly impressed:

> A pleasant diversion was provided for us upon our arrival at Fort McPherson, a small post occupied by one troop of the 2nd Cavalry. The two officers called and invited us to a minstrel show given by the soldiers. It proved quite enjoyable and made an agreeable variety in our trip, giving us a pleasant impression of a clean little post on the banks of the Platte, where the officers and men exerted themselves to extend all possible hospitality. Very sleepy were we next morning when we started at five, as the "General" sounded as usual.[12]

In August General Sherman found here "General Mizner with two companies of the 2nd Cavalry, and two companies of the 5th United States Volunteers, who have been out all season escorting surveying parties for the Union Pacific Railroad." He found the famous cedars "being fast exhausted by persons engaged in collecting them for railroad ties" and states that "The railroad is progressing with such rapidity that I believe it will be done up and above this post by Christmas."[13] The "iron horse" was pawing and snorting hard on the heels of the Carrington expedition.

Mrs. Burt remembers:

> About May 29 we were most pleasantly surprised on the march when Colonel Otis from Fort Leavenworth appeared with an escort of cavalry, conducting a party of Indian Commissioners to Fort Laramie to be present at the signing of the peace treaty.[14]
>
> Soon after, we arrived at the mushroom town of Julesburg, 220 miles from Old Kearney, and the forlorn post of Fort Sedgwick four miles away. At this dreary spot we were to leave Captain Neil, his wife and young lady daughter, a lieutenant and a doctor with one company [E, 3d Battalion]—a poor prospect for them, especially for a young lady. Mrs. Neil was greatly discouraged at the surroundings. The quarters were very dilapidated and nothing was in sight but the river bottom and sandy plains; wood was $105 a cord and potatoes $8 a bushel, with other things in proportion. To raise vegetables in that sandy soil was declared impossible. However, Mrs. Neil was a capable manager who would find the bright side of life under all circumstances; and the result proved they were more fortunate than those who went on with Headquarters.

Original Julesburg was a ranch and Pony Express station on the south bank of the South Platte, opposite the mouth of Lodgepole Creek and by a ford called Upper California Crossing. It was named for Jules Beni, whose crude log establishment was regarded as a rendezvous for the toughest characters on the frontier. This was also a division point for stages going to Denver and Cheyenne, and Fort Rankin, later renamed Fort Sedgwick, was built a few miles west to protect it. In late 1864 Sioux and Cheyenne chased the citizens into Fort Rankin and burned out the village. What Mrs. Burt saw was a second rejuvenated Julesburg. Early in 1867 a third and even rowdier Julesburg would spring up on the north side of the South Platte, to accommodate the on-rushing construction crews of the Pacific Railroad. Julesburg, Colorado, today, with pavement and traffic lights, is a highly modern law-abiding fourth version. According to tradition Jules himself was killed in a Hollywood type gun fight with the notorious Joseph Slade, who then cut off his ears and used one of them for a watch-charm.[15]

Fort Sedgwick as of 1866 was a miserable place, with sod quarters General Sherman described as "hovels in which a negro would hardly go. Surely, had the Southern planters put their negroes in such hovels a sample would, ere this, be carried to Boston and exhibited as illustrative of the cruelty and inhumanity of the man-masters." Nevertheless, it was to these quarters that Captain and Mrs. Neil and their young daughter were assigned, along with one company, to protect Julesburg. At the same time Companies B and D, 3d Battalion, were sent up the South Platte to man Fort Wardwell near present Fort Morgan, Colorado; with them went Captain Kellogg and his wife and son.[16]

Before these separations occurred, reports Mrs. Carrington, there was a social entertainment never to be forgotten, the last reunion of the officers of the 18th Infantry:

> The young officers, full of regrets, but as full of life and devotion to the general comfort as ever, arranged a farewell concert of "Iron-clad Minstrels" under the supervision of Majors Van Voast and Burt. Hospital tents were unloaded and chairs from baggage wagons, or the fort, were brought into requisition, and a grand concert was the result.
>
> It is an old army fashion to enliven the monotony of frontier life by extemporized opera, charades, readings, and the miniature drama; and the illustrations on this occasion were excellent. The string band gave us a splendid orchestra, and the violins and violoncello, the clarinets and the flute, the French horns and the trumpet, the trombone and the tuba, alternately supplied the solo, or replenished the chorus, as the bones and banjo called for their interference. Faces only were unfamiliar; and the fifteen or twenty sergeants and soldiers, who, with fine voices, perfect harmony, and the usual bon-mots of Ethiopian minstrelsy, entertained the lovers of, now and then, a little sport, did as full justice to their music as they had effectually transformed themselves from Caucasian to African by the pervasive laws of burnt cork.[17]

The corresponding entry in Mrs. Burt's journal reads:

> During the wait at Sedgwick, one pleasant evening at least was spent at a vaudeville entertainment which blossomed forth under the management of Lieut. Colonel Van

Voast and Major Burt. This was the beginning of my husband's use of his theatrical talent, that afterward helped at so many posts, when officers and their ladies combined to brighten the evenings with amateur theatricals.

It took the depleted regiment three days to cross the South Platte River. With waters unpredictably rising and falling, and "booby-trapped" with quicksand, the cantankerous river interposed every obstacle to thwart the ingenuity of the soldiers; but by flat-boat ferry, by false-bottoming and half-loading the wagons, and double-teaming the mules, the regiment and all equipment was finally brought over to the north bank. The only casualties were a few mules who "got their ears under water to drown from innate stubbornness."[18] Mrs. Burt vividly recalls the incident:

> In addition to the desolation here surrounding us, we were also confronted with the necessary crossing of the dangerous South Fork of the Platte which we found a muddy swirling torrent.

> The remains of an ambulance and wagon protruding from the middle of the stream were a discouraging reminder that some unfortunate party had already met with disaster in attempting the ford. After three days spent in making preparations to ferry the river, the water fortunately fell about a foot, enabling the command to cross but with great labor and difficulty. Many of the soldiers were wet to the neck. Four of the largest and strongest walked at the sides of our ambulance to steady it in the water, if danger threatened.

> My husband on horseback kept at the side of the mules, directing, while a man rode one of the leaders, and Mason, our particular driver, handled the reins. We followed a wagon that unfortunately for the command drove into a quicksand, but which happily for us, gave warning of danger in time to avoid it. My sister and I drew our feet up on the seat and in this way with baby in my arms, we crossed in safety.

> False bottoms were put in the wagons to protect the contents from the water. All this necessitated unloading and reloading that meant hard work for officers and enlisted men. When the command was finally safely over, June 2, we found that the crossing had been accomplished with the loss of only two stubborn mules.

Beyond Sedgwick the regiment marched seventeen miles to Lodge Pole Creek, camping near present Brule, Nebraska. On the second day out they stopped at Louis' Ranch, east of present Sidney, Nebraska, described as "quite a fort," with outhouses and stables advanced like bastions, "so that enfilading fire can be had in all directions."[19] From here Colonel Carrington and the bulk of his forces would cross northward over tableland to the valley of the North Platte, reaching it near Court-house Rock at present Bridgeport, and then following the old Oregon Trail to Fort Laramie.[20] Major Burt's company, and other units would go due west via Lodge Pole Creek to the mountains. Mrs. Carrington paints the picture of this parting:

> The South Platte was left at Sedgwick. The first day's march is seventeen miles to Lodge Pole Creek, and the second is eighteen miles to Louis' ranche. Here we spent another social evening with those of the third battalion under Major Lewis, a true man and perfect soldier, whose destination was Camp Douglass, by way of Lodge Pole Creek canon, and so on to the pleasant land of Deseret and Salt Lake City. Here also we parted with Mrs. McClintock and Mrs. Burt and their husbands, and Mrs. Burt's sister, Miss Reynolds, thus still more reducing our coterie of ladies, and still farther separating us from the associations of the march and old times at home.[21]

From Fort Sedgwick to Fort Bridger the Lewis-Burt command followed a route which virtually coincides with the present Union Pacific Railroad. Indeed, within one year of their passage the railroad construction crews would follow in their footsteps, building to Cheyenne and grading far out on to the Laramie Plains. But as yet there was no Cheyenne, no towns of any description, no sign of surveyors or track crews. Even the stage and telegraph line had disappeared, branching up the North and South Platte routes, to be regained only after the crossing of Laramie River. Here was virgin land, unspoiled by steel plow or shining rails. Here was clear blue sky meeting grassland at infinite horizons, devoid of the sounds of carpenter's saw and hammer, the whistle of locomotive or the shrill noises of a white man's village. Elizabeth Burt's story is possibly the last record of a passage across Southern Wyoming before the wilderness-shattering arrival of the Union Pacific:

> For two days longer we marched with Headquarters, then on the evening of June 5 on Lodge Pole Creek, we all met at a farewell reception given by Colonel and Mrs. Carrington before their tent. We listened to the delightful music of the band for the last time, and then said "Good

Bye" with great regret, to those friends to whom we had been so closely drawn during the month just past.

The officers from whom we separated were Colonel Carrington; Lieut. Colonel Van Voast; Dr. Alexander; Captains Kinney, Haymond, Phisterer, Proctor; Lieutenants Bisbee, Adair, D'Orsey, Litchfield and Brown, with Dr. Horton, assistant surgeon. The ladies were Mrs. Carrington, Mrs. Bisbee and Mrs. Horton. The officers of our battalion were Major Lewis, commanding; Captain John McClintock, Quartermaster; Lieutenant Gill, Adjutant; Captains H. R. Mizner, Niel, Burt, Benham; Lieutenants Wilcox, Thompson, Bell, and Dr. Waters, surgeon.[22]

We started next morning in the early dawn, but our departing friends broke camp earlier than we. The head of their long column of soldiers, horsemen, ambulances and wagons was even then disappearing over the nearby bluffs, hurrying on its march towards Fort Laramie. . . . Our column could have marched with Headquarters as far as Fort Laramie and then continued southwest to Fort Bridger, but Colonel Lewis, our Commanding Officer, decided to follow a trail along Lodge Pole Creek which shortened the distance.[23]

We now lost sight of the telegraph poles and had only a faint trail to follow but our wagon master knew the country well. The only indication of a human being ever being in that locality was a solitary grave heaped with stones to protect it from the coyotes—a sad, sad sight in that lonely land. Then came the remains of wagons that filled our minds with the picture of an attack by Indians. How many victims had fallen was impossible to learn, as nothing was left to tell the sad tale but some bones, parts of wheels and other wagon fragments.

One day we were surprised to see coming towards us, what proved upon nearer approach to be an ox train sent by the sutler, Judge Carter, from Fort Bridger to St. Joseph for his yearly supply of stores. It had been twenty-four days in coming thus far. Travelling at the same rate, we might expect to reach Fort Bridger about the middle of July. We were ascending the foothills of the Rocky Mountains, though the ascent was so gradual it was difficult to realize that we were gaining any altitude. As days passed we had a glimpse of the snowy peaks that at first seemed no more than fleecy clouds. The winds from the icy summits made the mornings and evenings cold, while the middle of the day was delightful. The wraps and buffalo robes were then thrown into the boot of the ambulance—to be brought out in the evening.

We were now in the Indian country. Colonel Lewis gave orders that everyone should keep close to the camp and take no risk. Rumors were brought by Judge Carter's train that Red Cloud, the Sioux Chief, and his tribe were strongly opposed to the white people making a road across his country and building a post. They were now gathering from all parts of their country to meet the Commissioners appointed to make a treaty with them.

We met [an Indian] party hurrying north towards Fort Laramie. One of the chiefs made an astounding proposition to buy our dear baby boy. It took time for us to realize his offer was made in earnest. "Ten ponies?"—"No, indeed." "Twenty?" Then we began to feel he really meant this as a bona fide proposition. The monstrous idea! "Thirty ponies?" "No—no—no," and our dear boy was tightly clasped in my arms and carried into the tent. After this, when an Indian appeared, a terrible fear seized me that our boy might be stolen and we held a closer watch over him than ever.

A disagreeable, and to us a new experience, was a violent hail storm that threatened to tear our tents to shreds and, worse than this, to stampede the mules. I had heard of hailstones as large as hens' eggs and thought it an exaggeration but many of this size were among the quantity that covered the ground. Their jagged edges made them a formidable weapon missile from which many soldiers and mules suffered. Fortunately the storm soon ended and the woeful picture of being stranded in that wild country with our mules wandering far and wide, vanished.

Along the Platte we could sometimes get clear water by digging in the sand a few feet from the river. There was no fear of microbes. That danger was unheard of at that time, but the muddy water was not appetizing. [On the other hand] Lodge Pole Creek supplied cold, clear water from the mountains.

Antelope were plentiful and formed a pleasing feature of the landscape. Several young ones were brought to us for pets. The pretty little creatures with large black eyes, long slender legs, and tawny skins spotted with white, soon became tame enough to drink Susie's milk from a bottle, but we did not succeed in raising any and gave orders to the men to bring no more to us.

Instead of antelope the soldiers came in triumph with three "eaglets" that interested us greatly. They were very fierce and showed no signs of becoming tame. Great gluttons they proved to be, with a limitless capacity for raw antelope meat. Colonel Lewis was our authority upon all

50

uncertain points, connected with the country, as he had been stationed there before the war. Upon examining our "eaglets," he pronounced them no more than plebeian hawks, whereupon they were soon consigned to hands less considerate than ours.

One day my husband asked my sister and myself to join him and baby in a walk to see something pretty. We were taken to a wagon where there were pups and pups. Little white pointers with lemon-colored spots, just old enough to open their eyes. One was picked out for us and carried away in triumph by our baby boy. It was named "Beauty" and was a great pet with us and became a well trained hunting dog and faithful companion for her master on his hunting trips, which proved a source of happiness to him for years.

We were now still ascending the foothills with no signs of mountains until one day in June, we were convinced that the unchanging fleecy forms in the west were not clouds but snow-clad peaks far, far away. Yes, we were really in touch with the Rocky Mountains, now made so accessible by the power of steam, but then an almost unknown region.

At the end of seven weeks over country destitute of trees we revelled in the sight of evergreens, trees, and velvety grass. Here were the remains of Camp Walbach, a small military post that had been entirely destroyed by Indians years before, vividly reminding us of the deadly foe, not far away.[24] Still our command was too large to suffer from a surprise so long as we did not wander from its protection.

Colonel Lewis had been our Commanding Officer ever since we parted from Headquarters. His reputation was that of a fine officer and an experienced plainsman who was capable of guarding us from harm. We admired him and felt safe under his watchful eye, knowing he had his scouts on the alert and his officers always ready for duty. Socially he was agreeable, and often joined us in a game of whist, bezique or cribbage after dinner. None of us ever played for a stake.

The day's journey from Camp Walbach over the Wyoming Black Hills, was memorable for its grand scenery.[25] After travelling for so many weeks over level sandy ground covered with sage brush, grease wood, prickly pear and bunch grass, to drive over these hills among pine trees created a feeling of being in a magnificent park.

The command halted at the brow of the range while we gazed with ecstacy at the glorious view before us. The

51

green Laramie valley extended for miles with the Laramie River like a silver band in its midst, glistening in the sun. Beyond extended range after range of snow-capped mountain peaks as far as the eye could see.

Gladly we would have lingered there, but the bugles sounded for the men to fall in, which meant that we must get into our ambulance and join the line in its march to the river. To camp on a mountain ridge without water was impracticable and the command must reach the river before supper-time. It did not look far away but it was several hours before we halted for the night.

The fishermen soon were happy over their success with hook and line and furnished us with a delicious supper and breakfast. Here also we ladies revelled among beds of violets and fragrant white and pink primroses.

The camp was near the site of the future Fort Sanders, which had been selected by high military authorities, and was to be built by Brevet Lt. Col. Mizner. He was to go on with us as far as Fort Halleck and bring back from that place whatever building materials were worth transporting to the new post.

The next day we forded the Laramie River and were soon again on the old road, over which the stage travelled daily between Denver and Salt Lake City.[26] Again we were in sight of friendly telegraph poles, where from the stations messages might be sent home if necessary; however, a telegram was too costly a luxury for army officers to indulge in, unless obliged to do so.

When, out of a cloud of dust, four horses came at full speed, drawing a coach, there was great rejoicing at the prospect of papers at least, but we were doomed to disappointment, as the mail for the command had been ordered to be left at Fort Halleck, where we were supposed to arrive in three days. A few newspapers given by the stage passengers were passed from officer to officer, and then to the men to be eagerly devoured by each in turn. How hungry one becomes for news after being three weeks deprived of the accustomed newspaper, can be appreciated only by those who have been so situated!

We were now travelling over a hilly and rocky mountain road, where the quaking asp trees were beginning to burst into leaf while snow still lay in the crevasses about us. Sometimes the road rose as high as seven thousand feet and then descended into low valleys. At intervals it was cut out of the steep mountain side allowing room for one wagon only. Visions of ambulance and mules rolling down precipices filled the minds of my sister and myself with terror. One wagon did overturn, but did not roll far fortunately, and both driver and mules escaped without injury. The load consisted of commissaries and was uninjured.

We were in the land of wood where stockades and stations were built of logs instead of adobe. At the end of the third day we reached Fort Halleck, high up on Elk Mountain.[27] It was occupied by a troop of 6th Cavalry with the Captain and his wife, one lieutenant and a surgeon. All winter they had been in this lonely spot. The men had the pleasure of hunting deer, elk, bear, almost any large game, besides pheasants and grouse, to their hearts' content, but the little wife was snowbound in her log cabin, to gaze upon mountains white with snow for many months, with the only delight of seeing a mail arrive each day when storms did not prevent. However, she uttered no word of complaint but naturally rejoiced at the arrival of a company and officers to relieve their troop.

Captain and Brevet Lt. Colonel Mizner, a lieutenant and surgeon, were left here with a company to move the government property to the site for the post they were to build on the Laramie River. We were becoming impatient to arrive at our own place of destination. June twenty-second we reached the North Fork of the Platte River at the crossing.[28] Oh, this dreadful river! Were we never to escape its dangers at this time of year when the melting snows had filled its bed to the highest point? The banks are much higher and steeper here than those of the South Fork at Julesburg, where we crossed with such difficulty. Now the rushing torrent was too swift and deep to be crossed, except by a ferryboat worked by cables and pulleys.

For so large a command to be carried over, there was great danger to be apprehended. After waiting a few days hoping for a fall in the river, the perilous trip began. Part of the work was accomplished without accident. Mrs. McClintock, my sister and I sat with our two babies on the shore watching the progress with great interest. The Headquarters ambulance was over with safety; then came Mrs. McClintock's turn in her ambulance with her baby and nurse. All was safe thus far. Then came our ambulance with my husband's assurance that all would be well; he crossed with us in safety and then returned to bring his company over.

It was not long before a crash came. In a second we saw the boat overturned in the stream; the white wagon top was carried down; mules quickly disappeared and alas, also the three men who were with the wagon. All vanished like a flash. The wagon proved to be one belonging to Company F, and with it was Sergeant St. John, one of my husband's most reliable non-commissioned officers, and two good men of the company. The sergeant's wife and two children were sitting near us on the bank. The suspense was agonizing while we waited a long time before it was known who were the unfortunate victims.

How we grieved for the poor wife and desolate children who had lost husband-father in this unexpected way! Every possible kindness was shown them but it was hard for them to be comforted.

My own husband was on the other side with the company. How would he ever get over was now the question, and what were my sister, baby and I to do without him and the company? Part of the command, however, was on our side and the officers took care of us for three days while the boat was brought up stream and made ready again to bring over the rest of the command. When the last load had crossed in safety we breathed freely and gave thanks that no further disaster occurred. Gladly we began our onward journey with nothing but horror in our hearts for the dreadful North Platte. While we were waiting for the boat to be repaired, a startling episode occurred.

A large number of Indians appeared among us, with professions of friendship, but we knew the majority sympathized with their Chief Red Cloud in his protest against their hunting grounds being invaded by the white men. Could they be blamed for objecting to their lands being taken from them? They were now going north to join the rest of the tribe at the Peace Conference, taking teepees, squaws, papooses and large numbers of ponies.

Dressed in bright blankets and buckskin shirts and leggins, with necklaces and trimmings of elk teeth and beads, with their hair decorated in feathers, and ornamented moccasins on their feet, their appearance was very picturesque. Evidently they were in their gala attire for our benefit for they never travel in their "best clothes." Their trunks, called parfleches, were made of dried skins folded in an oblong shape and tied with thongs of buckskin, making a convenient trunk to be packed on ponies. Evidently the contents had been brought forth for this occasion.

At night when their camp fires lighted the bluffs, where their teepees were pitched, the scene was extremely picturesque. Their weird songs added interest to the novel sight.

However, there was great rejoicing when they stole quietly away in the early dawn, particularly so as the greater number of our soldiers with their guns, were on the other side of the river.

Glad we were to start once more, especially as we had no dangerous river before us. The dreaded Bitter Root country was yet in store for us and proved to be the most disagreeable part of the journey. It was a semi-desert region through which flowed Bitter Root creek, whose waters were undrinkable. Each man filled his canteen at the last spring of good water and our three-gallon keg was also filled and placed in the ambulance in addition to our two canteens. Sand, sage brush, alkali water and wind made a formidable combination against which we had to struggle for five days.

The Quartermaster had brought as much fresh water as possible with him; but we all rejoiced when we reached a good spring again. For a long time we had been in South Dakota, that is now Wyoming.[29] In a few days after leaving Bitter Root, we reached Green River which was crossed on a ferryboat worked as in the last case with pulleys; but the water was falling rapidly and the crossing was made in safety, in spite of our fears of a repetition of the late disaster.

The most memorable sight of this part of our journey was Church Buttes that consisted of a great mass of water-washed, brown columns of such fantastic shapes that we could readily imagine them the remains of a grand cathedral. On the ground surrounding it, numbers of moss agates were collected and kept to be cut and polished for rings, pins and other trinkets. In this early day these agates were a novelty eagerly sought by curio lovers in the East.

At last the happy day was near at hand, when we would reach our first home in the Rocky Mountains.

4

Fort Bridger, Autumn, 1866

Old Fort Bridger is one of the notable historic shrines of western America. For nearly half a century, from 1842 to 1890, it had an illustrious and checkered career as a trading post for trappers, Indians and emigrants, a Mormon outpost, a key United States military post, an Indian Agency, and a station on the famed Pony Express, the overland telegraph and the central overland stage lines. Andrew and Elizabeth Burt lived there for one year beginning July, 1866. When they arrived, joyful at beholding the charming oasis of Black's Fork Valley, Fort Bridger was still vibrant with the overtones of great historic events.

En route U. S. Highway 30 from Rock Springs, Wyoming, to Salt Lake City, after traversing a landscape which is barren and

burnt-out, relieved only by sage flats, the traveller today is grateful
for the green groves and meadows of Black's Fork, which one poetic
historian describes as "beautiful out of all reason, like a charming
but improbable stage setting, for which the snow-topped Uinta
Mountains provide a magnificent backdrop."[1] Knowing the affinity
of the mountain trappers for such scenic hide-outs it seems probable
that the locale was well known to them as early as the 1820's, when
they first invaded the Central Rockies. It is not far from here to
Henry's Fork of the Green where the first annual rendezvous of the
trappers occurred in 1824. Old John Robertson, whom the Burts
and others came to know as "Uncle Jack Robinson," is believed by
some historians to have lived there as early as 1834.[2] At any rate,
when the fur trade went into a decline after the last rendezvous of
1840, Jim Bridger and Louis Vasquez cast around for some other
source of income, and their eyes fell on this valley, squarely on the
prospective route of emigrants lured by the siren call of Oregon.

Most travellers agree that the scenery was superb but that the
early Fort Bridger was not a thing of beauty. In 1845 Joel Palmer
found it to be "built of poles and daubed with mud; it is a shabby
concern." The following year Edwin Bryant describes "two or three
miserable log cabins, rudely constructed." In the gold rush year of
1849 the Government explorer, Stansbury, found that "it is built in
the usual form of pickets, with the lodging apartments and offices
opening into a hollow square, protected from attack from without
by a strong gate of timber."[3]

In June, 1847, Bridger was en route from his establishment east-
ward to the American Fur Company post at Fort Laramie when he
had his fateful encounter with Brigham Young and his Mormon
pioneers. Despite Bridger's unflattering description of the Great Salt
Lake Basin, the Mormon leader decided to proceed there and establish
his colony. Bridger and the Mormons did not get on well. Possibly
his lack of enthusiasm for their project to settle Great Salt Lake was
a factor. Certainly they coveted his fort and his beautiful valley,
guarding the mountain gateways. In 1853 resentments came to a
head, Bridger was ousted and Brigham Young sent a posse of 150
"avenging angels" to take over his property. In 1856 the Mormons
built a more substantial fortification. This was described by Captain
Gove as a "wall 100 feet square inside, 5 feet at base and runs up to
15 feet, tapering to about 15 inches at top; attached to this is
another wall about 80x100 feet and 7½ feet height. These walls are
built of small round stone laid in mortar."[4]

Utah Territory had been part of the United States since 1848,
following the peace treaty with Mexico, but Brigham Young took his

national allegiance very lightly, creating his own private state of Deseret. Squabbles with the administration in Washington over territorial appointments, aggravated by long-standing grievances on both sides that harked back to earlier civil commotion in Missouri and Illinois, culminated in President Buchanan's order to send the United States Army to Utah to enforce the national will. This led to the "Utah War" and the conversion of Fort Bridger to a military post.

In the autumn of 1857 a sizeable expeditionary force under Colonel Albert S. Johnston, guided by Bridger, moved westward from Fort Laramie. The Mormons attacked and burned several supply trains encamped near Green River. Advancing against Fort Bridger under blizzard conditions, the troops arrived there in November to find the place a burning ruin. The Mormons retreated to strong entrenchments in Echo Canyon. Johnston elected to remain at Black's Fork for the winter. Sheltered only by canvas, his men sorely missed the supplies lost to the raiders. In the spring emissaries patched things up, the duly constituted Governor of Utah was accepted by Brigham Young, and the hungry army moved unopposed into Salt Lake Valley to establish Camp Floyd, later succeeded by Camp Douglas.[5]

Jim Bridger did not linger after the army took over. It was getting too crowded in that part of the world, and in 1859 he found congenial employment with Army Engineers who wanted to explore the Yellowstone wilderness. He and Elizabeth Burt were both in the great military march of May, 1866, from Fort Kearney to Fort Sedgwick, but he was far forward as expedition guide while she rode near the column rear. If they ever met face to face on this occasion she does not reveal it; and he could not possibly have been at Fort Bridger during her stay there. From Sedgwick he went on with Colonel Carrington to Fort Laramie, and thence up to the new Bozeman Trail forts. When the Burts went north from Fort Fetterman in November, 1867, Bridger had just left Fort Phil Kearny for Fort Laramie where he spent the winter, while the Burts were at Fort C. F. Smith. He was officially discharged from government service in the summer of 1868.[6]

Fort Bridger was formally designated an army depot by Colonel Johnston on June 7, 1858, when he departed for Salt Lake. Major William Hoffman, 6th U. S. Infantry, was left in command, and proceeded to rebuild to suit army requirements. The old stone fort was converted into store-houses and log quarters were erected for the troops. On August 16, 1858, Hoffman was relieved by Colonel E. R. S. Canby. The next three commanders at Fort Bridger, Major R. C. Gatlin, Captain Alfred Cuming and Captain Franklin Gardner, all serving briefly during 1860-1861, had the common distinction of resigning or deserting to the Confederate cause at the outbreak of the Civil War. It was during Captain Gardner's regime that the Pony Express stable, still standing, was erected. Captain Jessie A. Gove, 10th U. S. Infantry, assumed command on May 29, 1861, and withstood a determined effort by the Mormons to recapture the fort by legal strategems.

In August of that same year, when troops were required in the East on account of the Civil War, Colonel Cooke abandoned Camp Floyd and withdrew to Fort Bridger, where the bulk of the stores were sold at auction. Then both garrisons marched to Fort Leavenworth, leaving only a sergeant's guard. In December, 1862, Captain Lewis, 3d California Volunteers, assumed command. Thereafter until July, 1866, it was garrisoned by California and Nevada volunteers who performed the hard service of guarding the mails, escorting travellers and fighting Indians. The last volunteer commander was Major Noyes Baldwin, 1st Nevada Volunteer Cavalry, veteran of General Patrick Connor's Powder River campaign of 1865.[7]

Conditions at Fort Bridger just prior to Major Burt's arrival were given by Inspector-General Babcock, who visited there on June 17, 1866: "I passed this post and found it in a shameful condition— grounds not policed, buildings out of order, flooring burned up, bridges burned, shade trees broken down. Major N. Baldwin, in command. When his attention was called to the post, he said he had not men to do this work. He had between three and four hundred men, with no duty but to care for the post. As the regular garrison for the post would reach there in a few days, I gave no orders."[8]

On July 13 Major Burt arrived and took over the garrison with Companies F and H, 1st Battalion, 18th U. S. Infantry.[9] Elizabeth Burt was delighted:

Upon arriving at the bluff from which we looked down upon the valley and Ft. Bridger in which our new home was to be, our hearts were filled with joy. A mild day, bright with sunshine, prepared us to appreciate the beautiful scene. The bluish green sage brush was replaced by emerald grass extending for miles with several sparkling streams running through it. Mountain after mountain with snow-capped peaks stretched beyond, while the small post nestled in its green setting in the midst of the valley. The grass seemed more like the turf of the States than any we had seen in our journey of three months. Glad was our farewell to sage

60

brush, bunch grass, prickly pear and grease wood in the midst of which our tents had been pitched for so many weeks. The streams were bordered by wild rose bushes, pink with buds and flowers. How we rejoiced at our good fortune at being stationed in this lovely spot! No large trees were to be seen, but swamp willows were mingled with roses and other shrubs on the banks of the streams.

We drove to the quarters of the commanding officer, lately vacated by a volunteer and his family, who were still at the post. An invitation to dine with Judge and Mrs. Carter awaited us. This was gladly accepted and highly appreciated. An excellent dinner in a most comfortable dining room showed how attractive life might be in a one-story log house, even in far away Utah, the home of the Mormons.

The Judge was the post trader and a most agreeable gentleman, while his wife and family charmed us by their kind welcome and gracious manners, creating the feeling that we had found congenial companions who would prove good friends. There were children from sixteen down to two years of age, and their house servants were Shoshone Indians who had been trained for this service.

Our fellow travellers camped with us two days and then continued their journey to Camp Douglas, a post very near Salt Lake City. We regretted parting with each one, beginning with Colonel Lewis, who had proven to be a considerate Commanding Officer, whom we respected and admired. We never met him again, except when we made a short visit to Salt Lake in October. A few years after this, he lost his life in a fight with Cheyenne Indians on the Smoky Hill route, that was south of us. Mrs. McClintock was the only lady to go with the command. We wished greatly that her husband's orders had kept him at Fort Bridger, but they sent him to Camp Douglas as Quartermaster. We parted with her, the Major and their dear baby with great regret.

Either Lewis or McClintock could have been the author of an anonymous little volume, now extremely scarce, published in 1868 as *Life Among the Mormons, and a March to Their Zion*. Here Fort Bridger is revealed in further detail:

One day's march from Church Butte, and we were at Fort Bridger, which is the oldest military station passed on the march, save Fort Kearney. . . . It is situated 120 miles east of Salt Lake City, and the immediate site of the fort is a locality occupied by Brigham Young and his followers

GROUP AT FORT BRIDGER, c. 1870.
Ada, Edgar and Judge Carter seated, at right.

when seeking their new Zion in Salt Lake Valley in 1847. A tall stone wall—a parallelogram in shape—built by the Mormons for protection against the Indians, still stands below the parade grounds. Black's Fork . . . rises in the Uintah Mountains, and before reaching the fort divides into five branches, one of which passes directly through the post, affording an abundant supply of clear, cool, and the most delicious water. . . . About a mile below the post these branches unite again and form one stream . . . the spot appears a very desirable one for an officer's station, were it not for its isolated position.

. . . The quarters are constructed of hewn logs, and those of the officers neatly plastered and provided with such conveniences as to afford a comfortable home. . . .

In the vicinity game is abundant. . . . To an officer fond of hunting and fishing, the sport here afforded must in a great measure recompense for the want of society and little inconveniences incident to life at such a remote station and, indeed, taking all things into consideration, I felt like congratulating those who were to remain, for I considered it preferable to any post we had passed on the route. . . .

I have seldom met with a more hospitable gentleman than Judge Carter, and there is always a plate at his table for a visitor or a passing friend. . . .

Living on the reservation is another character, almost as generally known as the Judge. I refer to an old trader and mountaineer named Robinson, but passing always under the sobriquet of "Uncle Jack." He has been living on the frontier for nearly forty years, and has adopted many of the habits of the aborigines, several of whom he has as wives. During the summer months his abode is in any Indian lodge, and in the winter he is ensconced in a log cabin, a few miles from the fort. Uncle Jack, though for so many years without the bounds of civilization, has acquired none of that rudeness of manner, which it would seem must always necessarily follow his associations and mode of life. . . .

Fort Bridger, upon our arrival, was garrisoned by three companies of ex-rebel soldiers, who enlisted in our army, when prisoners of war, for duty on the frontier, fighting Indians. These troops are styled officially U. S. Volunteers, but are more generally known as "Galvanized Yankees," a term that seemed not at all offensive to them. The post has been most abundantly abused. Troops that have been mustered out of service shortly before our arrival, must have destroyed property from the mere desire to destroy; but in some instances there was apparently a little utility in their destructiveness, as they demolished buildings for firewood. Many of the officers just on the eve of leaving service, winked at the vandalism of their men, while others were unable to control them. . . . Everybody in this section of the country seemed to have become completely demoralized. Citizens and soldiers were alike in this respect. . . . Men stole and officers stole! That is their own testimony. . . .

Disciplined troops and honest officers were not sent to this country any too soon; and I fancy that Major Burt, when he assumed command at Fort Bridger, had not the easiest task in the world in attempting to straighten out things. . . .[10]

Elizabeth Burt resumes her narrative:

Dr. Waters was the only officer left with Major Burt, who was Commanding Officer, Adjutant and Quartermaster in addition to commanding two companies.

As there were no supplies in the Quartermaster's storehouse in the form of paint, calsomine, or even whitewash, we had our house cleaned as well as possible by Maggie.

The fatigue party soon emptied the one wagon and deposited the contents in our four rooms, two on each side of a large hall. On one side were two sleeping rooms and closets; on the other was a living room, dining room, and a pantry with a small kitchen and a tiny room for Maggie in the rear. All were plastered and looked very comfortable.

Three months of tent life had not made us critical of our new surroundings, although the post was not in particularly good repair and no quartermaster supplies were to arrive before the coming year. The only thing for us was to look on the bright side and be thankful that we were all together, in good health and sheltered in a substantial home.

An open fireplace in each room and an old cooking stove held together by wires was all the post afforded in the line of cooking and heating facilities. We were glad to have the stove, such as it was. The alternative would have been to cook with camp kettles and Dutch oven in the open fireplace of the dining room.

After the cleaning was finished and our household effects in place, there was quite an air of home comfort about the house. A Brussels rug was on the floor of the living room, while four army blankets sewed together made rugs for the other rooms. Bedsteads were found in the house with a few tables and chairs. Curtains were made of pretty material brought with us, which also covered packing boxes to serve as toilet tables and washstands. A few lamps we also had brought in the wagon, but the Quartermaster had no coal oil and it was too costly at the post traders to be used more than very sparingly. We bought candles from the Commissary.

A row of five sets of officers' quarters, like ours, but without any kitchens, faced a small grassy parade, through which flowed a clear mountain stream. This in former years had abounded in trout, but much fishing had now driven them away. The quarters for the soldiers were at opposite sides of the parade ground across the creek, over which were small bridges. In front of all was an irrigating ditch large enough for our three-year-old boy to fall into on all possible occasions, but as the water came from the mountains, ice cold, he soon learned to avoid it.

In all the valley there was no garden and consequently we had no vegetables, unless they were brought from Salt

Lake City, and this made them too expensive to indulge in, except on rare occasions. There was plenty of fresh beef, and our faithful Susy's milk, with eggs supplied by the chickens, which had borne the trip well, made our table comparatively luxurious. Mountain trout, young sage chickens, and mushrooms were often added to our bill of fare.

In addition to the usual supplies in the Commissary were dessicated potatoes and soup. Small squares of the vegetable were dried and compressed into cakes, supposed to be a good substitute for real potatoes and vegetable soup; but alas! they were a sore disappointment to us, and after one trial we never wished to add them to our larder. Doubtless they would have been hailed with delight by the army of four thousand soldiers under General Albert Sidney Johnston, who were sent against the Mormons in 1857. They built huts for themselves near where we now lived and had spent the winter there. The scurvy broke out among the men, who even chewed pieces of gunny sacks in which potatoes had been carried. The remains of the stone chimneys of their huts were very near us.

Fresh beef was purchased for us from "Uncle Jack Robinson," a white man with a squaw wife who lived in tents in the valley, where his large herd of cattle roamed. He was glad to have an officer keep a cow—or perhaps two —provided it and its calf were fed and cared for. In this way we were able to make butter and ice cream, as the ice house had been filled from a pond near the post by the volunteers.

There were no Indians in the vicinity, except occasional bands of Shoshones passing through on hunting trips. Thus fortunately we were relieved of fear of our red brethren, and at liberty to ride about the country in safety.

After his varied duties were over, hunting young sage chickens was a great pleasure for my husband, who often took my sister and me with him for the horseback ride. To be able to put my foot in his hand and vault into the side saddle for a few hours' dash up the valley gave intense pleasure.

Good roads led to the different streams full of trout. Often we went in the ambulance and took Andrew Gano, now growing old enough to be known by name, with some of Judge Carter's family, for a picnic. The trout fishing was a delight to the lovers of that sport, but I never became skillful in the art, though the streams were free from the tangle of undergrowth that so often present almost unsurmountable difficulties to women with skirts to manage.

"JACK ROBINSON" OF FORT BRIDGER, 1866.

Men who wear rubber boots and wade out into the rushing water rather rejoice in casting a fly under these difficulties; but I lacked the devotion to the cause.

One day on a trip of this kind we saw three white men who looked like prospecting miners. They had with them a fine pointer dog which at once attracted Major Burt's attention. He had a talk with the men, and the presumption is, made an offer for the dog. What the bargain was I never knew; but the next morning, bright and early, Jeff was brought to his new master and became exclusively his devoted companion for years, never caring for anyone else; but Beauty, our other house dog, was our constant attendant on all our walks. Jeff was an intelligent, well trained retriever, that had undoubtedly been some hunter's pet. Many times did he carry notes in his mouth to and fro between his master and myself, proving a reliable messenger. How those men had obtained possession of him we never learned, but he had certainly now found a good home. Beauty too became a good retriever after patient teaching by her master in the house and afterward in the field.

Judge and Mrs. Carter and their family proved most agreeable and helpful both by example and advice as they had an experience gained by years spent at Fort Bridger that had become a loved home to them. The Judge went there with General Johnston's army in 1857, spending that cold winter in huts when the men suffered from the scurvy and the hardships incident to terrible weather.

The arrival of the stages with the mails from opposite directions was the event of the day. In addition to receiving letters and papers, sometimes a friend passing through would have time to give us a brief, friendly greeting, as this stage station was one where passengers took their meals.

The greater part of our time was spent in the bracing, open air, giving us health and good spirits. In September, snow came but did not last long. In October we accepted an invitation to visit our friends, Major and Mrs. McClintock at Camp Douglas. Major Burt could not leave the post, as he was in command and had but two lieutenants who had lately joined. One of them he allowed to go with us. My sister, Judge Carter's eldest daughter, Andrew Gano, Dr. Waters and I completed the party.

We ladies, with our boy, rode in one ambulance and Dr. Waters and Lieutenant Wood in the other, each drawn by four mules. The start was made early one mild bright October morning. We were to be gone ten days. All that day we drove on a fine stage road, stopping at night at a stage station about forty miles from Bridger. The man who lived here with his wife kindly placed their one bedroom at the disposal of the ladies of the party. The house consisted of three rooms, built of logs forming a part of the stockade, which was also of logs, enclosing a space for the stage horses and stables. The supper was plain, but everything looked clean, which was really more than we had expected. The sleep of the party was disturbed by the coyotes, close to the door, whose dismal howls poured into our ears all through the night. This doleful, desolate sound was repeated every night, the woman told us. But the occupants of the house were not disturbed by it; so easy is it to become accustomed to the inevitable.

An early breakfast of a primitive kind enabled us to start by sunrise over the road, which now wound among canyons and grand mountain scenery. Fortunately for us the attention of the Indians was now concentrated on their affairs about Fort Laramie, relieving us of any fear on that score.

The narrow roads, sometimes high up on the mountain sides, filled us with dread at the possibility of meeting a stage coach or a team where there was no room to pass. When a wagon did actually appear in sight, Mason drove as close to the mountain side as possible, while all got out of the ambulances and the two men in the wagon held it on the slope while our ambulance was driven past. Many times in that western country have I had a similar experience, without my nerves becoming accustomed to these perilous drives. When at last the stage coach did come dashing along with six fine spirited horses, there happened to be room to pass without trouble. What a gasp of relief we all gave when the danger was over! We were very happy to learn that the stage from the East would pass us in the night after we had retired. Now we could enjoy the mountain views, the rugged canyons, the streams, far, far below in the green depths, the autumn tinted foliage among the evergreens and late flowers.

Signs of Mormon ranches began to appear. At last a fence enclosing a field gave us a sensation of delight, as six months had passed since we had the last glimpse of a fence far away in Kansas.

Another forty-mile drive and we had the novel experience of eating supper under the roof of a Mormon who kept a roadside house. The bracing mountain air and long drive had given us appetites to appreciate the simple and well-cooked supper. The house was substantially built of stone, the rooms immaculately clean and quite comfortable. Our curiosity was aroused to know if the woman who waited on the table was a wife! That we had a glimpse of the latest wife we felt convinced, as she was quite young and rather pretty. Across the road was a collection of old cabins whose weather-beaten condition showed that they had been there for years. Several women and children whom we saw in the yard interested us very much, as they were evidently part of the family. We only saw them from the windows and had no opportunity of acquainting ourselves with any items of the family life.

The next day, passing through Parley's Canyon, with its grand and ever-changing views, we crossed many sparkling streams which fed a fine irrigating ditch enclosed sometimes in stone, and extending through the valley, giving evidence, with the ranches along its banks, of the great industry and success of the Mormons. Late in the afternoon we reached the mouth of the canyon and feasted our eyes upon a memorable view. Salt Lake City lay like an oasis in a wide expanse of sand and sage brush. Camp Douglas formed a cultivated spot of green at our right, between us and the city. The river Jordan was a sparkling band of silver running through the valley. A chain of mountains loomed in the distance. Ranches dotted the valley, presenting a most welcome sight to us who had seen neither farm nor orchard since leaving Leavenworth. Truly the Mormons have accomplished a wonderful transformation in that distant land, proving that with the help of water industry can make all grains and fruits grow luxuriously in that dreary sage brush country. All honor to them for this great good!

We received a most cordial welcome from Major and Mrs. McClintock and our other companions of the march in their cozy homelike quarters at Camp Douglas, luxurious to us who had not seen anything allied to city life at Fort Bridger.

Many temptations here presented themselves at the stores of Salt Lake City, where all necessities and many of the luxuries of life were purchasable, at rates high enough to more than cover transportation by ox-team from the Missouri. It was a pleasure to visit the stores, but a greater one to go into the gardens and orchards, and above all to feast upon delicious fruits and vegetables, of which we had been deprived for so long. Peaches, apples, pears, quinces and grapes here grew in abundance in the gardens.

Our four days visit passed delightfully and all too quickly, we felt; but the result showed it had been far better if it had been limited to three days. The day before starting on our return, we ordered a bushel of peaches to be gathered early in the morning of our departure, fearing that they might spoil before we reached Bridger, as the weather was quite warm.

We parted soon after sunrise from our friends, to drive again through beautiful Parley's Canyon. Upon getting into the ambulance, we found on the front seat, with the driver, an addition to the party in the form of a white bulldog, looking especially ugly and fierce. I made no remonstrance, as Mason was a faithful man who had driven us over the plains and had always been a devoted friend to our dogs. It was he who never failed when a storm arose or the wind blew harder than usual, to be out in the night with his ax, driving the pegs of our tent more firmly, or to strive to protect us in every way.

A night was again spent at the inn with the Mormon family. Of their domestic life we again gained not an inkling, except to become convinced of their industry and cleanliness, two virtues that made their home far more attractive and comfortable than was to be expected in that lonely spot.

Upon starting very early next morning there was a decided chilliness in the air, making our wraps necessary. As we ascended higher in the mountains the cold increased, making the long drive much less interesting than when we had gone west, six days before. Glad were we to reach the stage station for the night. The dismal howls of the coyotes again deprived us of the sound sleep so greatly needed by our tired bodies.

In the morning signs of an approaching storm were unmistakable. Onward we hurried as fast as our teams could take us. About noon a cold wind was whirling a few flakes of snow about us. Upon reaching the last station, ten miles from Bridger, night was at hand, and the snow was coming down fast, while a strong wind had increased the cold.

Dr. Waters and Lieutenant Wood gave us their team, it being a better one. They told the driver to get us home as quickly as possible, fearing that one of those terrible western blizzards might catch us on the road unsheltered. To be caught out in a blizzard is the frontier plainsman's great horror for its wind and snow bring piercing cold. Indians are not more to be feared. Hundreds of our frontier pioneers have perished miserably in these blinding storms which shut out all landmarks guiding to protection and shelter. . . .

One can imagine our anxiety when old Mason mounted to his driver's seat on the ambulance saying, "Mrs. Burt, don't be feared if you bounce a little, I'm going to drive this team for glory every ounce that's in 'em to beat that blizzard."

My sister, Ada Carter and I all knew from hearsay what a fearful thing it was to be out in a western winter storm. Our fears and the jolting of the fast moving ambulance—for Mason was whipping the team along at a ten-mile gait—all made us cling to each other in fear and trembling. My baby boy I held in my arms.

After the first terrific blast of wind it lessened its force but the snow fell as I had never seen snow come down before. Darkness soon enveloped us but the snow-covered road was outlined by sage brush, and the friendly telegraph poles were a certain guide. We passed a butte that we knew was only a few miles from home. The wind now increased, filling us with fear that the ambulance might be blown over. Fortunately we had two buffalo robes and warm wraps to comfort us while the sight of the friendly poles assured us that without a doubt we would soon be gathered around a blazing fire at home; but it was not long before the ambulance stopped and Mason in a dismal voice said: "Madam, I am very sorry to tell you that I do not recognize the road at all, and I'm afraid we are lost."

"Lost! What in the world do you mean? We ought to be home by this time. How can we be lost? Aren't we on the road by the telegraph poles? We surely cannot be lost so near the post."

"We are on a road but it isn't our road. There are no poles that I can see."

"Why Mason, there is no other road. I don't understand you at all."

"See, Madam, for yourself! I don't know any other road and I don't know where we are, but we are lost, and only going in the wrong direction. I don't know what to do."

Ada Carter then helped us by telling how she had once been in a stage coach when a blinding storm made traveling impossible. The horses were tied to the wheels while the passengers and driver passed the night as best they could in the stage, and I remembered having heard my husband say when lost in a storm, and above all if night should come on, the wise thing to do would be to stop until the weather cleared and daylight came to show some familiar landmark. We all agreed we would profit by this example and advice. After the mules were securely tied and given forage that

Mason had for them, we laid one buffalo robe on the floor of the ambulance, and the other made a lap-robe for us all. Our little son was held under it in my arms. The blessed bulldog proved a veritable stove, keeping our feet warm all night. If it had not been for him our feet might have been frozen.

Thus was the night spent, while we longed for daylight to appear, oppressed with the continued fear of the howling wind threatening to overturn our shelter in the darkness which, added to the danger of possible attacks from wolves or other prowling beasts, struck terror to our hearts. Of all our party our little boy in my arms was the only one who slept through the night.

At the first peep of dawn the watchful Mason silently slipped out into the storm and again we heard the patient mules crunching their morning feed of oats. I, being on the watch for daylight, anxiously inquired, "Still snowing, Mason?"

"Yes, indeed, Madam, and coming down so thick and fast, I can't see two feet away."

"Where are we?"

A doleful reply came, "I can't tell anything about it."

Sure enough, upon raising a curtain of the ambulance slightly, there was nothing to see but the blinding snow. Where we were, we had not the remotest idea. "What are we to do?" was the cry from all lips.

The decision was to hitch up and drive on. This was done, but in a short time, Mason said he thought we had better stop and stay where we were, as we might be going away from the post, which would prove most disastrous.

It was not possible to make a fire. The lunch box was brought out but the contents were frozen hard; and the peaches which had been gathered so carefully from the trees in the warmth of the Indian summer of Salt Lake valley were found to be like balls of ice. However, the situation was so appalling that we had no desire to eat.

The mules were tied again to the wheels and we all seated ourselves as in the night with the bulldog to save our feet from freezing. Pete had become precious in our eyes above all of his kind. And now once more we summoned up our courage and patience to endure another spell of waiting. The slowly dragging time oppressed us so that we scarcely spoke to each other, enduring our misery in patient silence.

The storm did not abate, we were powerless to help ourselves, and our unspoken prayer was that some relief would soon come. Our greatest hope was that the other ambulance would reach the post when my husband, knowing that we must be lost somewhere in the storm, would lead a search for us at once.

Suddenly all our fears and misery were dispelled by the lifting of the ambulance curtain and the appearance of the cheerful face of Corporal Hudson of my husband's company, and his astonishing query:

"Why, Mrs. Burt, is that you?"

I could have embraced him with joy. Our cries of thanks and gladness overwhelmed him.

"Where are we, Corporal?" I asked.

He then told us he and his party were coming from the camp in the forest bringing the daily supply of fuel for the post. They knew nothing of our being lost and spending the night as we had done. They soon replaced our tired, half-frozen mules by fresh ones from their team and gladly we drove on to the fort. It seemed that when we reached the stream behind the guardhouse the previous evening, the mules, bewildered by the storm, turned a little and followed the wood road leading to the camp. None of us knew of this road which was, as Mason thought, taking us away from the post. We had spent the night less than a quarter of a mile from home.

The team of the officers had given out, necessitating Dr. Waters and Lieutenant Wood spending the night by the roadside, but within sight of the telegraph poles which guided them to the post in the morning.

It is easy to imagine what was the state of my husband's mind and the excitement in the post when it was realized that we were lost in the snow. He started out with as many men as could be mounted to begin the search. The party had all volunteered to go and this spirit of self-sacrifice was most deeply appreciated by us as their lives were endangered in the blizzard.

When we reached home others at once braved the storm to bring the searching party back, but the men were widely scattered and were not all found until night came and the blizzard began to lose its force.

A happy, thankful family were we upon my husband's safe return after his day's search for us. He had wandered about in the snow half crazed with the fear that a terrible disaster had befallen us. While urging the party to continue their efforts, it was necessary to observe that they all kept in touch with one another. A man separated from the party was a man lost.

The blessed bulldog, Pete, received his full share of caresses, as well as a good dinner, and would have been kept as part of our family had not Mason claimed him as his own. When we had calmed down, and my husband held our dear boy in his arms, he said to him,

"What did you think of, my boy, in the storm?"

The little fellow replied, "Why, Papa, I thought we were going to Heaven without dying."

In a few days the blizzard had passed, leaving the weather lovely again. In one way we suffered very materially. Wagons had been sent to Salt Lake City to bring a supply of potatoes, turnips, onions and cabbages for the soldiers and officers for the winter. Unfortunately the blizzard caught them in the mountains, and the vegetables, like our peaches, were frozen solid. In addition, my husband had ordered two barrels of apples for our own use. No appetizing baked potatoes for any of us for another year—nor an apple. The deprivation was keenly felt. However, with fresh beef and venison, apples dried — not evaporated — we at least had nothing to fear from scurvy. There were, besides these articles, large cucumber pickles sent to the commissary, in barrels. With sugar and spice added to them, Maggie made an appetizing relish for our table; so we could still smile and be thankful for many comforts. In addition we had bacon, salt pork, flour, coffee, beans, sugar and rice, the soldier ration, which we could purchase from the commissary.

General James F. Rusling, Inspector, Quartermaster Department, was dispatched in the summer of 1866 on a grand tour of western military posts, to inspect their condition, their bases and routes of supply "with a view to reducing if possible the enormous expenditures that then everywhere prevailed." He was gone on this mission twelve months, travelling over 15,000 miles, 2,000 of which were by stagecoach. The roughest coach ride of all, "a pretty fair test of one's power of endurance," was the 480 miles from Denver to Fort Bridger via Virginia Dale, Bridger's Pass, the Bitter Creek Basin or "desert of the mountains," Green River and famous Church Buttes. After four days and nights he reached Fort Bridger on October 8 in a half-comatose condition:

We halted at Fort Bridger two or three days, to inspect this post and consider its bearings, and so became pretty well rested up again. Some miles below the Fort, Green River subdivides into Black's and Smith's Forks, and the valleys of both of these we found contained much excellent land. Judge Carter, the sutler and postmaster at Bridger, and a striking character in many ways, already had several large tracts under cultivation, by way of experiment, and the next year he expected to try more. His grass was magnificent; his oats, barley and potatoes were fair; but his wheat and Indian corn wanted more sunshine. The post itself is 7,000 feet above the sea, and the Wahsatch Mountains just beyond were reported snow-capped the year 'round. Black's Fork runs directly through the parade-ground, in front of the officers' quarters, and was said to furnish superb trout-fishing in season. In summer, it seemed to us, Bridger must be a delightful place; but in the winter, rather wild and desolate. Apart, from the garrison, the only white people there, or near there, were Judge Carter and his employees. A few lodges of Shoshones, the famous Jim Bridger [sic!] with them, were encamped below the Fort; but they were quiet and peaceable. The Government Reservation there embraced all the best lands for many miles, and practically excluded settlements; otherwise no doubt quite a population would spring up. Sage-hens abounded in the neighboring "divides," and we bagged several of them during a day's ride by ambulance over Smith's Fork and return. We found them larger and darker than the Kansas grouse or prairie-chicken; but no less rich and gamey in taste. Maj. Burt, in command at Bridger, was an enthusiastic sportsman; but our ambulance broke down seven miles out, and we had to foot it back after dark. . . .

We left Fort Bridger October 12, at 10 P. M., in the midst of gusty winds that soon turned to rain, and reached Salt Lake City the next night about midnight; distance, 120 miles.

This stage ride to Salt Lake is of particular interest because of its curious coincidence with the adventure that befell Elizabeth Burt. It is apparent that she was visiting in Salt Lake during the time that General Rusling was making his inspection of Fort Bridger, and she and companions started back via Government ambulance the morning after the General's departure for Salt Lake. The General breakfasted at the stage station at the head of Echo Canyon, where Elizabeth Burt and party had spent their first evening outbound, "about forty miles from Bridger," so the two parties must have passed each other

Oct 30th 1866

Report of Public buildings at Ft Bridger UT

Officers Quarters
Six in number, — 82 feet front, 41 feet near — 4 rooms in each building — built of pine logs.

Mens Quarters
Nine buildings — 76 feet long, 21 feet wide 3 & 4 rooms in each building — built of pine logs.

Laundress Quarters
Two buildings — 12 rooms in each building — pine logs.

Hospital
100 feet long — 20 feet wide — 4 rooms pine logs

Commissary Store House
120 feet long — 32 feet wide — built of stone.

Stables
135 feet front. 2 wings each 210 ft long. 25 ft wide built of pine lumber

Corral
135 feet long. 125 feet wide — built of pine & cedar logs.

A. S. Burt
Capt 18" US Infy Bvt Maj
USA Comdg Post

REPORT OF BUILDINGS, FORT BRIDGER, OCTOBER 30, 1866.
By Major Andrew S. Burt.

somewhere between Echo Canyon and the city. Like Mrs. Burt, Rusling noted the pastoral charm of Weber Valley occupied by "a hardy, industrious, thrifty race, well fitted for their stern struggle with the wilderness. Everybody was apparently well-fed and well-clad, though the women had a worn and tired look, as if they led a dull life and lacked sympathy." Evidences of polygamy were noted without sermonizing. In Parley's Canyon the same blizzard which trapped the Burt party near Fort Bridger caught up with the Rusling stage-coach, making the descent a precarious one. The General was not consoled by realization that "only a week before, in a similar snowstorm, the stage-horses lost their foot-hold here, and a crowded coach—team and all—went crashing down into the creek below." Reaching Salt Lake House in one piece, and having a good night's rest, General Rusling shared Mrs. Burt's generous opinion of the Mormon capital: "Salt Lake seems like Rasselas's Happy Valley, or Paradise Regained."[11]

Rusling is a double-barreled informant, for he supplies us also with the official report on his inspection of "Fort Bridger, Utah Territory," dated October 11. In this, Brevet Major Burt came off very well:

> . . . Its military value consists in the fact that it commands all the eastern passes to Salt Lake Valley through the Wahsatch Mountains, and also the main passes to Montana and Idaho, the usual road to which branches off northwest from here. As such it has very justly been called *the key to Salt Lake*. . . . The post before the rebellion was built and regarded as a six-company post, but several of the buildings have been destroyed, so that its present capacity is rated at four companies. Its present garrison consists of two companies of the 18th Infantry, Brevet Major A. S. Burt commanding, in all about 135 men. . . .
>
> The only officer at Fort Bridger is Brevet Major Burt, who is now serving as commanding officer, adjutant, quartermaster, commissary, ordnance officer, etc. His duties are multiform, and it is needless to say he has too much to do. . . . He is an intelligent and efficient young officer, but he has little experience in quartermaster's affairs, and should be promptly relieved of part of his duties. If able to give his whole time to the quartermaster's department, he would have enough to occupy him for a year to come. . . . I recommend that he be supplied at once with at least three subalterns—one for each company, and one to serve as quartermaster and commissary, and even then the post will have no more officers than the condition of things here actually requires.

The post has been badly, not to say, shamefully, abused during the past few years. . . .

. . . Of the horses, fifty have been sent here for the use of mounted infantry by order of Major General Pope. Major Burt reports them as seldom used, and thinks twenty-five would be sufficient, as they are only required to mount a party occasionally in pursuit of deserters or criminals—the Indians here giving no trouble. . . .

The post proper consists of a quadrangular enclosure about the flag-staff, after the usual manner of our western posts. . . . The barracks are located on the north and south sides of the quadrangle, the officers' quarters on the east, the storehouses, shops, etc., on the west. . . .

The quarters, barracks, storehouses, etc., are built of logs, with board floors and shingle roofs. They are all chinked with mortar on the outside, and the officers' quarters are also lathed and plastered inside. The buildings have been placed on the surface of the ground, with no foundations, and as a consequence are yearly injured somewhat by frost. . . .

. . . There is now no chapel or reading-room at the post, nor any chaplain. One of the vacant buildings is now fitted up as a rough theatre, and Major Burt deserves commendation for thus trying to interest and amuse his men at odd hours. . . .

Major Burt is doing the best he can with the force at his disposal, and evidences of improvement are everywhere apparent. I have no doubt he will speedily reform various matters here in the way of repairs, policing, and general cleaning up of the post, as soon as his winter's fuel supply is secured. . . .

The accounts of Major Burt had been rendered for September, and in the main were correct. He makes no disbursements, except to employees. His cash on hand was $434.50; counted and found exact. He has no safe for his funds, but at present keeps them in the safe of the Overland Stage Company. This is bad, for obvious reasons, and I recommend that a small safe be sent here at once, for the proper keeping of such public funds as may come into his hands. . . .[12]

In November, 1866, Captain and Brevet Major Anson Mills, a war-time comrade of Burt, arrived on the scene and assumed command on the basis of seniority. He brought with him one other officer. These, together with Burt, Lieutenant Wood and Dr. Waters, made up the social circle of five officers referred to by Mrs. Burt. The deficiency in "subalterns" referred to by General Rusling was now corrected.

Mills' autobiography, *My Story*, is disappointing inasmuch as he made no reference to the Burts at Bridger. He showed a lofty respect for the Mormon character—"the best people in the country, and the only ones who would fill contracts fairly." He took pride in instituting a new system of punishing enlisted men, requiring them as a penalty for disorderly conduct to mount a mock wooden horse for a prescribed period, while shouldering a wooden sword about six feet long, "with its business end painted a bloody red." It was here at Fort Bridger that he devised a cartridge belt for which he obtained a patent and "eventually" made an independent fortune.

Anson Mills was quite an inventor and disciplinarian but he was not an entirely reliable reporter. He stated flatly that one day the Overland stage from Omaha arrived, disgorging an English-looking gentleman who announced that he wished to see Jim Bridger. Mills tells us that Bridger was the post guide, "reticent and hard to know," and that he obligingly took the traveller to see him. "Bridger" was living in one of the officers' quarters. "We found the old man looking grave and solemn." He then proceeded to relate a preposterous version of what purports to be Bridger's "most thrilling adventure," which ends with Bridger himself and companions getting trapped and killed by Indians in a box canyon![13] Anson Mills and General Rusling both made the egregious mistake of confusing Jim Bridger with old-timer "Uncle Jack Robinson."

5

Fort Bridger, Christmas, 1866 to Spring, 1867

Mrs. Burt remembers:

As winter drew nearer our lives were confined to a narrow routine. Captain and Brevet Lieutenant Colonel Anson Mills joined us and took command of his company, as well as the post, since he ranked my husband one file. They were war comrades and old friends, who had tented together in the 18th Infantry for a long time, had fought side by side in many battles and shared hardships together. He was a most welcome addition to our social circle which now consisted of five officers, Judge Carter's family, my sister and myself.

The daily walks, drives and horseback rides were continued until December when the cold weather became too severe. Sleighing proved a failure as the wind drifted the snow in high ridges, and laid bare other spots in the road, leaving no well defined track. Skating was also a disappointment as the ice froze roughly and was covered with snow. We soon concluded that sleighing in the solitary wilds was seeking pleasure under difficulties and this recreation as well as skating was abandoned.

Fortunately we found among the soldiers a Frenchman who had the Parisian accent, was quite a good scholar and glad of the opportunity to add to his income. With him as instructor my sister and I reviewed the French we had learned at school and made sufficient progress to encourage us to devote some time to this study. Household cares, sewing, writing letters, reading, playing whist in the evenings and exchanging a visit now and then with Judge Carter's family occupied our time during each week. Sundays passed without any special religious services. The best I could do was to gather together the children of the soldiers and employees on Sunday afternoons and teach them what I could of the Bible and the little Calvary Catechism. They learned quite a number of Bible verses. Our own three-year-old boy learned the 23d Psalm. Did it do any good, you ask? At least the mothers of the children dressed them up as neatly as possible and seemed glad to have them learn something for their good. Years after this, one day on the streets of Omaha, a tall man came to me saying, "You have forgotten me, Mrs. Burt?" I was obliged to confess that I did not recognize him. He then said, "I am W. H., who belonged to your Sunday School class at Fort Bridger, and I now have the Bible you gave me for learning the most verses." That he had kept the Bible all these years led me to believe some good seed had been sown. . . .

We were now receiving daily mails which kept us informed of the troubles Colonel Carrington was having with the Indians who refused to agree to the terms of the treaty offered by the Commissioners, at the Council held at Fort Laramie in July.[1] They were wily enough to appear amicable until the Government had distributed among them according to treaty, certain rations and clothing, consisting of flour, bacon, beef on the hoof, tobacco, sugar and other staples, cloth, blankets, beads and shoes for the men, women and children. The shoes were of no value to them as the stiff leather hurt their feet which had been encased in soft buckskin moccasins since childhood. After a distribution of goods by the agent I saw many pairs of their shoes that had been thrown to the roadside.

The Indians after the issue and with the property in their possession left the council in anger, refusing the terms of peace offered. At once their animosity was shown by their attacks on wagon trains, running off stock and killing every man found without protection. Fortunately for us we were too far from the seat of trouble to be molested. . . .

Through newspapers and the stage line, accounts came of increasing trouble at Fort Phil Kearny. The Sioux Indians had determined to unite in their efforts to drive the soldiers from their fine hunting grounds and to prevent a road being opened through the land that had always been exclusively their own. The depressing news was strong enough to cast a deep gloom over us; but as Christmas approached, for our boy's sake, we made as great an effort as possible to enter into the spirit of the season.

We made different kinds of candy, as we could buy as much sugar as was needful from the Comissary. Judge Carter had brought a small supply of gifts in his ox train. His present to Andrew Gano was the first mechanical toy we had ever seen. It was a boy who walked amazingly well and surprised even us older people.

The stockings were hung in the wide, open fireplace, down which Santa Claus could descend with ease. Plenty of snow made splendid traveling for his eight tiny reindeer. My six Sunday School scholars were made happy by homemade candy, ice cream, cookies and doughnuts.

A delicious Christmas dinner at Judge Carter's hospitable board helped greatly to make the day a happy one for us, so far away from friends.

The holiday time thus happily begun was of short duration for only a few days after Christmas we began to hear mysterious rumors of a fight which had taken place near Fort Phil Kearny in which the Indians had defeated our troops. We refused to believe them at first, but they continued. It was the Indian "underground" which carried the news from valley to valley, across mountain ranges, and delivered it in vague whisperings at the sutler's store through the "friendlies" who came in to trade. We hardly mentioned the subject except to say, "It can't be true. Surely it can't be true." Each tried to be hopeful before his neighbor but none succeeded in concealing his anxiety.

In our fear we little realized the actual truth, so when the official report arrived we were only partially prepared for the heartbreaking news—"Colonel Fetterman, Captain Brown, 18th Infantry, Lieutenant Grummond, 2nd Cavalry, and 78 men massacred near Phil Kearny"—this was a shock that reached the very soul of comradeship and from which it seemed we could not recover. These were among the friends from whom we had parted at the Platte River the previous June when they had separated from us to go with Colonel Carrington to build Phil Kearny in what is now Wyoming. Little did we imagine the horrible fate awaiting them when we said goodbye that peaceful June evening. Oh! the horrors of Indian warfare!

The version given by Mills could not have been fact, and like his "Bridger story" may also be ascribed to the garbled reminiscences of an older man. He has it that on "Christmas Eve, Judge Carter, the sutler, gave a dancing party. While the officers and ladies were dancing, I received a dispatch announcing the massacre of Fetterman and his command, partly of my regiment, at Fort Phil Kearny. I stopped the band and read the dispatch, which cast the garrison into gloom, and presaged a general war with the Sioux."[2] The fact is that word of the massacre did not reach the telegraph at Fort Laramie until Christmas night; the message was delayed in reaching Department Headquarters until a day or so later because of storm damage to the line, and Fort Bridger could not have had official word until several days after Christmas. Here is another demonstration of the reliability of Elizabeth Burt's knowledge of events.

Mrs. Burt was grateful for the Shoshones:

Occasionally the post was visited by some of the Shoshone Indians who were peaceful and who, passing on hunting trips, brought buffalo robes, beaver and otter skins to trade. This tribe had always been friendly to the white people owing to the fine control which their Chief Washakie exercised over them. Washakie came once to Fort Bridger before the severely cold weather set in. He was a man born to command, having strength and dignity, endurance, and a countenance expressive of fine character and determination. His features were strikingly like those of Henry Ward Beecher. More than once his order to some of his young warriors had prevented them going on the warpath. That his word was law in his domestic life as well as in the tribes is well illustrated by a story told us away back in the sixties.

Washakie was about to start on a hunting trip, to be absent a certain number of days. Before parting from his wife he told her he wanted the camp to be moved in his absence, to a place designated by him, and he would meet her on a certain day. At the appointed time he arrived at the place but no camp was to be seen. The mighty chief was very angry. Instead of a good supper and a smiling wife to greet him in a new, clean camp, he must continue his ride to the place he had left and upbraid his squaw for her unheard of disobedience. What excuses, he demanded, had she for the neglect of his orders? Her reply was her mother would not allow her to move camp. Such misconduct was unheard of in his family; and Washakie at once and ever after ended such rebellion by raising his gun and taking the life of his mother-in-law. Now it was easy to understand how Washakie ruled both family and tribe, literally with a rod of iron.

He spoke little English and consequently always had an interpreter with him when he came among white people. When in later years my husband once asked him to dine with us of course the interpreter came too. It was surprising to see how well they behaved and handled the knife and fork and napkin. Their keen eyes watched every movement of the host and evidently they tried to imitate him. They certainly proved to be apt pupils and seemed to enjoy the dinner very much. Women are such very inferior creatures in the estimation of an Indian that Kate and I engrossed little of their attention.

Among the few personal documents left by Major Burt himself is an account of this remarkable dinner with Chief Washakie. This was written by Burt as a retired Brigadier General in Washington, D. C., in 1903, while it must be remembered that Mrs. Burt was doing her "recollecting" in 1912. According to him the dinner was not "in later years" but was right then, on Christmas Day, 1866, at Fort Bridger.

Chief Washakie had a commanding figure; he was quite six feet high with a very dignified carriage; was powerfully built and had the reputation among his people for great endurance of hunger, thirst and fatigue. No man among the Snake Indians could outride him in a day's journey and repeat the performance day after day either in pursuit of an enemy or when being pursued. I first saw him at old Fort Bridger, Utah. I had been in the post several weeks before having a talk with this remarkable man. One day I said to Judge Carter, the post sutler, "Who is that very dignified Indian I have seen about the post; I never see him begging. He looks as clean as if he began his toilet with a bath."

CHIEF WASHAKIE, c. 1865-67.

"That must be Washakie," the Judge replied. "He is a remarkable man in his tribe and would be a notable one if he had been born a white man and had been educated."

"He certainly has a dignified carriage," I observed. "He is enough like Henry Ward Beecher for them to be brothers. Who is the Indian that's always with him?"

"Ah! That Indian is what Washakie calls his 'talk man,' sort of an aide-de-camp to his imperial majesty. Major, if you will, allow me to suggest that you send your orderly to Washakie with your compliments and say the Commanding Officer would like to see him."

"Will he understand that?"

"He will recognize your orderly and, knowing a little English he will understand what is wanted. He's a great stickler for form and ceremony. You have observed that while other Indians have hung around your house and office he has not been near either."

I acted on Judge Carter's advice and sent my orderly to the Shoshone Chief . . . Washakie came, accompanied by his aide or "talk man," a necessary adjunct to a formal "visit between kings." I saw from time to time a great deal of this old Indian warrior and discussed the Indian question with him in all its bearings. At first we used an interpreter. What he said to me came through his "talk man" and the interpreter, but finally I picked up some of the Shoshone words and that, with the sign language in which I was rather proficient, enabled us to talk to each other quite freely. I found him to be a very shrewd observer and close reasoner. At first I could not produce any astonishment from him when relating to him a wonder of modern civilization, such as the use of steam and the telegraph. The subject which was the most interesting to him was the number of our states ("Tribes" as he called them and the number of warriors in each "tribe.") That story had to be gone over and over with him and as he became intimate he would clamp his hands, throw back his head, and grunt his astonishment. I had talked so much to my wife about Washakie, she became desirous of seeing him and asked me to invite him to our quarters.

I invited him one day to call on Mrs. Burt and bring his squaw. At first he declined and when asked why he replied: "I got two squaws. You have only one. Your wife won't want to see one chief and two squaws. I bring one squaw other squaw get mad. I will have to lick 'em both make peace. I come bring 'talk man' when I come?" I told him I would consult Mrs. Burt and appoint a day and hour when he could dine with us. She selected Christmas day when we were practically alone. Of course, I had no Shoshone to mean dining. I used the Indian sign to eat and then the sign for sunset. . . .

At the appointed hour on Christmas Day, Washakie and his "talk man" rang the bell of the front door and were ushered into the parlor where my wife and I were waiting to receive them; of course, the Indians had no hats or overcoats to deposit in the hall before their entrance. I received the Chief, shook hands with him and went through the ceremony of presentation to Mrs. Burt. With extra elaborate politeness Washakie advanced, took her hand and said, "How. I like your man. Glad to see his wife." The talk man's keen little black eyes watched every move of his chief and his actions were as near like them as possible.

Mrs. Burt, Washakie and myself sat in the parlor chatting until dinner was announced. Upon acquainting Washakie with this fact, he arose in a dignified manner, turned and pulled his blanket around his shoulders, turning to do so in order that he might not expose his person, he being lightly clad in accordance with the Indian custom. He stood at complete ease until Mrs. Burt preceded us into the dining room, and upon a sign from me followed as if accustomed to such actions every day. In the dining room Mrs. Burt pointed out the seat he was to occupy and he stalked up to his chair but, to my utter amazement, he remained standing until Mrs. Burt took her seat at the head of the table and sat down. He remained perfectly passive awaiting Mrs. Burt's next move. She removed the bread from her napkin and placed it across her lap. He immediately did the same thing. Soup was served and I was anxious to see what he would do, for Indians have no regard for the silver and steel helps to eating in refined society, but again he did the right thing, picked up the soup spoon and ate as delicately as if he had been accustomed to it all his life. The same thing happened with his knife and fork as the turkey and other courses were served, and his dessert spoon came into use at the proper time. He took his after dinner coffee, used his finger bowl with a nicety and after Mrs. Burt had left the table joined me in a smoke and chat.[3]

Because of his sterling qualities, Washakie escaped the general condemnation Elizabeth Burt had for male Indians:

My first impression of domestic life among the Indians was intensely disagreeable and prejudiced me greatly against the lordly chiefs. I saw one of them walking in front of a squaw, whose back was bent under a heavy sack of something, probably flour, while he, with his tall strong body wrapped in a gayly colored blanket, carried nothing but a stick. We stopped to watch them. Did he offer to help her carry the load? Not he indeed; but on the contrary would use the stick to poke her in the back, to urge her on when, looking behind occasionally, he found her falling back with her heavy load. The brute! How I wished for a good strong soldier to knock him down but no one was there but my sister and myself. When I poured out my tale of outrage to my husband he said that if the Indian had been treated as I wished trouble would undoubtedly have resulted with the tribe; that the squaws were accustomed to this kind of treatment and my indignation was wasted.

Mills makes only fleeting reference to the Shoshone Indians at Bridger, the fact that a large band came in, camping near the post for a couple of months, and that he gave a demonstration of the mysterious telegraph to "the most intelligent of the Indians," who is not named. None of our reporters for 1866-1867, oddly enough, gave any space to the fact that Fort Bridger was a vitally important Indian agency, the principal rallying point of the Shoshones, whose dependable friendship for the United States was in marked contrast to the constant friction and warfare with other western tribes.

In 1858 the Utah Superintendency was established at Salt Lake; in 1861 the Eastern Shoshone Agency was established at Fort Bridger. Luther H. Mann, the first appointed Indian agent there, held his post until 1869, a remarkably long tenure. In July, 1863, an important treaty was made with the Eastern Shoshones at Fort Bridger, the chiefs in council representing up to 4,000 tribesmen. "These bands," wrote O. H. Irish, Utah Superintendent, "are under the control of Wash-a-kee, the finest appearing Indian I have ever seen. He is justly regarded as a firm friend of the government and the whites, and steadily refuses to hold communication with bad Indians." In 1865 Agent Mann reported that the tribal hunting grounds of the Fort Bridger Indians were "bounded on the north by Snake River, east by the Sweet Water and North Platte Rivers, south by Yampa and Bear Mountains, and west by the valley of Salt Lake."

Records of the Commissioner of Indian Affairs indicate that Washakie was a frequent visitor to Fort Bridger in 1866. In June the tribe came in to receive annuity goods. In mid-August, after the Burts arrived, Washakie came in "with some 300 of his men just for a visit." Reported Mann, "He wears about his neck the medal which you sent him by Judge Carter, and with which he is exceedingly pleased." Agent Mann felt that the medal was deserved for Washakie's record "is untarnished by a single mean action."[4] Evidently the chief's summary execution of his mother-in-law, reported by Mrs. Burt, was an incident of small account!

Following news of the disaster inflicted by Red Cloud on Carrington's forces, Elizabeth Burt's idyllic stay at Fort Bridger was doomed:

> Doubly thankful were we that orders had taken us to Bridger instead of Phil Kearny. . . . This peace of mind was sadly dispelled before long by an official document directing Major Burt's transfer to the 2nd Battalion, and that he take station at Fort C. F. Smith in Southern Montana, about 100 miles northwest of Phil Kearny. We were in the midst of winter, with frozen snow in every part of the country. Appalling news, indeed!

> To reach this new post, it was necessary for an officer to go in the coach as far east as Cheyenne, there leave the railroad [there under construction], go to Fort Laramie as best he could, and from that point reach Fort Smith through deep snow by any means that were presented. To take his family was an utter impossibility. Oh! To be back in my mother's comfortable home; little had I dreamed of a situation so dreadful.

> After days of torturing thought, a happy relief came with a telegram, ordering my husband to stay at Bridger until an empty wagon train arrived from Salt Lake. Then he was to join and command it until it reached Fort Sanders. That the train could come before the snow had melted the officers assured me was impossible; so my mind was relieved on that score for the time being.

> This transfer was heartbreaking to my husband, as it meant separation from his beloved Company F, 1st Battalion, 18th Infantry, which he had commanded since his promotion to a Captain in '63, at which time he resigned his position in the Inspector-General's Department on General Thomas' staff, to be with his company. Many of the men were bronzed veterans who had been with him in every battle, had marched with him and shared with him all of the trials, hardships and dangers of the war. He was very proud of the record of his company and personally attached to his men. To be forever separated from them was a great wrench at his heart strings, and the men seemed equally loath to be parted from their old captain. Then, too, he

would cease to belong to the dear 18th, as the 2nd Battalion was destined to become the 27th Regiment.[5]

The cold increased and the snow became so deep that weeks passed without bringing letters or papers to us, for the mail bags were often left behind at stations when their weight, added to that of the passengers, became too great.

One morning we wakened to find ourselves in complete darkness, which was not relieved until the men had cleared the snow from the windows and doors; after which they dug paths from house to house. That snow did not thaw until April, compelling us to confine our walks for health to a very limited space.

A great hardship of this winter resulted from the fact that no fuel had been stored. At times the mercury froze, and the thermometer stood below zero for weeks. We had arrived too late in the season for a contract to be filled for a supply of wood. The consequence was that each day the wood party brought us only enough fuel to scantily supply the post for twenty-four hours. Of course, each person felt obliged to burn as little as possible. The fire by which our toilets had been made in the morning at once became extinct, while we lived in our combined sitting and dining room during the day and evening. I love a sparkling wood fire in an open fireplace but there we surely learned that it is not to be relied upon in all kinds of weather. My deep sympathy was appealed to each day when the men brought the water from the river in the wagon sheathed in ice. Of course the water froze as it spilled on the men. However, as a result of this severe duty, I am glad to say that no one had pneumonia, nor even bad colds.

As spring came on we made what small preparations were necessary for leaving the garrison when the expected wagon train should arrive early in June. The melting snows made the roads impassable for so large a number of wagons during May. Finally on the second of June when the train did arrive we found it in charge of a lieutenant and a company of infantry from Camp Douglas. The Government could not afford to send so large a number of animals and such valuable equipment through the Indian country without adequate escort. A large number of ex-Mormons and some other civilians had received permission, before the train left Salt Lake City, to return East in the empty wagons, 100 in number.

Among our preparations for our journey was the shoeing again of our beloved cow Susie, who like an old campaigner, was ever ready to accompany us, and also the repairing of the coop for the same Buff Brahma rooster and his eleven hens that started from Fort Leavenworth with us.

Parting with much regret from our friends at Fort Bridger, we left our first frontier home.

Following the Burts' departure in June, 1867, important events followed rapidly. That very summer the discovery of gold in South Pass brought a sudden increase in population to the Fort Bridger region, and a great boon to businessman Carter. The Dakota legislature in far-away Yankton finally took cognizance of this southeast corner of that oversize territory, and on December 27 took Green River County away from Utah, calling it Carter County. On July 3, 1868, another peace treaty was concluded at Fort Bridger by which the Shoshones relinquished their land claims and retired to their present Wind River Indian Reservation and a new agency called Fort Washakie, where the Burts and the old chief would one day again cross trails. On July 25 Wyoming became a territory in its own right, definitely ending Utah and Dakota claims to the region. The Green River strip now became Uinta County, the first county seat being located at Merrill, a small mushroom settlement adjacent to Fort Bridger named in honor of Colonel W. W. Merrill, who resurveyed the post reservation. In 1870 the county seat was moved to Evanston. During 1868-1869 the Union Pacific Railroad was under construction through western Wyoming, and units of the 36th Infantry at Fort Bridger, under Colonel H. A. Morrow, saw a lot of action in escorting engineering parties and guarding what was left of the overland stage route. The railroad would be eleven miles north of the historic fort, and the nearest station would bear the name of Carter.[6] The completion of the transcontinental railroad on May 10, 1869, at Promontory, Utah, signalled the end of Fort Bridger's historic period, though it would continue in a useful role as a territorial police station for two more decades.

An excellent pen sketch of Fort Bridger in 1867, which conforms to the descriptions of Elizabeth Burt and General Rusling, is reproduced here.[7] It was made by General Grenville M. Dodge who arrived there shortly after Major Burt's departure, to pick up Major Mills as escort on his Oregon survey. This is substantially the same post built by troops under Captains Hoffman and Canby in 1858-1859. Not pictured is the "cobblestone fortification" of Mormon origin which, according to A. K. McClure, a visitor of 1867, then served as "stable for the garrison."[8]

FORT BRIDGER, UTAH TERRITORY, 1867.

Drawn by General Grenville M. Dodge, from his *Biographical Sketch of James Bridger*, New York, 1905.

Fort Bridger became a state park in 1929, when it was acquired with funds provided by the Wyoming State Legislature, and placed under the management of the Wyoming Historical Landmarks Commission. It is now administered by the Wyoming Historical Department. Structures still preserved include the Pony Express station and stables, sutler's store, the old Carter home, store-houses, barracks, jail and a remnant of the Mormon wall. One of the store-houses has been converted into a museum. The log building which was Elizabeth Burt's "first frontier home" is gone, along with all trace of Jim Bridger's original trading establishment; but, regardless of its degree of preservation, Fort Bridger will be long remembered as an important outpost of civilization during the fur trade, the covered wagon and the stage-coach frontiers.

6

Getting Into Red Cloud's War

In June, 1866 the overland route across southern Wyoming had been something akin to virgin wilderness. Now, one year later, the map was being drastically revised. Elizabeth Burt ran head on into the new Fort Sanders, new Cheyenne, and the advancing Union Pacific Railroad:

> The Fort Bridger valley was beginning to appear beautiful in its fresh spring garb, making us sigh for the lovely summer days we had expected to spend there after the tedious winter; but the order said move, so move we must, retracing the steps of last year's journey as far as Fort Sanders, Wyoming.

Dr. Waters urged me to stay at Bridger. If I did, how could I ever join my husband in Montana, and how could my sister and I, with Andrew Gano, ever reach Ohio by ourselves? A very important consideration was the expense of the stage; the fare from Fort Bridger to Kansas City was about $200 for one person, not including meals for eight days. Then riding in the coach day and night at breakneck speed was very hard even for a strong man. How could women and children stand it even if in good health? The stages, when crowded, carried fifteen persons, in addition to large quantities of mail and express. How could the purse of a captain in the army bear this expense? To go to Fort Smith was my decision and my husband heartily acquiesced.

To reach southern Montana would not have been a very long journey in a direct line; but there was no way for us to go except to return on the stage road until we reached the one going northwest through Fort Fetterman, making a long journey.

My husband who was now in command of the train divided it into three parts, each in charge of an experienced wagon-master, and all under a head wagon-master, Pearsall, who was a most competent man. Scouts were placed constantly on duty to the front, rear and flanks to watch for signs of Indians.

We passed now and then a ranch that had been lately burned by them but fortunately the inmates had apparently been able to find safety in flight. Again we camped on the same ground as in the previous summer along Bitter Creek, where the water still was most undrinkable; the wind blew as hard as ever, depositing the same amount of sand in our food, in spite of the recently melted snow; the streams were the same raging torrents as then, always highest in June; but the ferries were better equipped with cables than when we had met with the terrible disaster a year ago. We crossed the Platte safely after many detentions, all of which prevented our reaching Fort Sanders in the Laramie River Valley until the 3d of July, 1867. Our trip of 350 miles took twenty-three of our summer days.

At Sanders we found the beginning of the post that Captain and Brevet Lt. Colonel Mizner began when he hauled to that site all that was considered of value of abandoned Fort Halleck, and we met a new regiment, the 36th Infantry, with its Colonel, General John Gibbon, his wife and three children.[1] Some of the officers we had known before, but the greater part were strangers to Kate and me.

They were, however, old comrades of my husband as this regiment had been organized from the 3d Battalion of the 18th Infantry. There were several ladies in the garrison, none of whom we had ever met. However, their reception was most cordial. Major Burt was now ordered temporarily for duty under General Gibbon.

Not until we were safely settled in this new abiding place did I know of additional trials borne by my husband during the trip. I knew of the danger to our lives from attacks from Indians, and the responsibility of the train commander for the preservation of Government property, including the valuable mules which the Indians were very likely to try to stampede, but I did not know that a citizen was in one of the wagons in irons by order of higher authority, and that among the wagon passengers a party friendly to the prisoners sent my husband a round robin threatening his life. How far this hostile feeling extended he did not know, but he realized the only way to meet it was with a bold front. With quick determination he had made it understood that he was head of the command and would stand no insubordination. The better part of the men stood by him and the cowardly villains afterward obeyed his orders without further complaint. The prisoner was landed safely at Fort Sanders, where the Major's orders relieved him of this disagreeable and trying responsibility.

My health was not good. I was glad to rest after the hard trip and it became necessary for me to find some sort of an additional servant, even in that country where of servants there were none. Among the ex-Mormons in the wagon train who were leaving Utah was a family consisting of a poor man, his wife and children. One of the latter was a girl of twelve years, Christina, who was glad to stay with us on condition that she was to try to learn to do anything that I might teach her. Her parents could spare her from their large family and seemed glad to leave her with us, while she appeared pleased with the arrangement.

The only houses yet built were one for General Gibbon, one for his Quartermaster and another for the Adjutant's office. Everyone else was living in tents. A block house built by Colonel Mizner was the most conspicuous building. It was a large square structure of hewn logs, with a firm foundation upon which the upper part or story was set at right angles, enabling soldiers, in case of attack, to fire from above through the loop holes and cover all the faces of the lower part. Double rows of loop holes above and below with two square openings on each side for two cannon permitted its

EDITH BURT.

occupants to fire from all sides and withstand any sudden rush of hostile Indians.

General Gibbon gave orders to the Quartermaster to make this block house as comfortable for our occupancy as possible. Canvas was stretched over the roof to keep out the rain, wind and snow, and inside to cover the loop holes. Half window sashes were placed in the large openings that were intended for cannon. The space inside the upper part was divided by upright unplaned boards, into four large rooms. The boards, of unequal length, extended about half way to the pointed roof, leaving space for freer circulation of cold air than we cared for. However, there was a good stove in each room. In the dining room the two cannon were left as armament all during the three months we remained in this summer home.[2]

To enter our abode it was necessary to step over a hewn log at the door. Just within was a large space of bare ground where in one corner Maggie, the cook, was installed with our camp stove and the remainder of our cooking utensils. The stairs were of rough boards. Susie and the chickens were taken care of outside. Thus we were made comfortable as possible by the Quartermaster, Lieutenant Wands. All went well until one stormy day when the wind puffed the smoke down the stove pipe, filling the rooms with smoke. Then the good Quartermaster, as a remedy, had an additional stove put up on another side of my bedroom so if one stove smoked we could have a fire in the other.

Each pleasant day General and Mrs. Gibbon, with the children, came for me to drive in the ambulance with them. He took his gun to be prepared for game which he often found. We gathered violets, wild prim-roses and other flowers, and sometimes we fished.

One morning in August our four year old boy was brought to my bedroom to see his wee baby sister [Edith], left by the stork in the night. All went well with us though we had no nurse but my young sister and Christina learning under the watchful eye of Maggie.

I remember often watching, from my bed, the moon pass over the end of my room. It shone through the cracks as it passed from board to board of the upper story above the logs. For amusement by day sometimes the long ox trains plodding east or west on the Black Hills road, interested me; oftentimes teams of thirty oxen slowly wound their way from view drawing heavy loads of merchandise, or perhaps logs from the wood camps.

Block House — Fort Sanders

Courtesy, Burt Collection

FORT SANDERS BLOCKHOUSE, 1867.
Contemporary sketch, artist unknown.

At this time also work was begun on the Union Pacific Railroad in the vicinity of Sanders. With a field-glass I could see men plowing and grading the ground. Tents were put up, starting the city of Laramie. Soon great gangs of men were working on the road about three miles from my window, which gave me something new to watch.

The "iron horse" was about 100 miles east of Fort Kearney in May, 1866 when the 18th United States Regiment of Infantry left there to garrison the western outposts. Inspired by the brilliant and energetic Chief Engineer of the Union Pacific, General Grenville M. Dodge, and supervised by the hard-driving Chief of Construction, General J. S. Casement, the construction crews performed miracles, laying track to just short of Julesburg by the end of 1866. Advancing construction and operating crews were frequently attacked by Sioux and Cheyenne Indians, and preyed upon by mobile saloon-keepers, gamblers and strumpets. The need for collaboration of the army with the railroad, to ensure the success of the enterprise, was clear. The Department of the Platte, already bedevilled by Red Cloud's warriors on the Bozeman Trail, hummed with renewed activity. Cavalry units were sent to protect the Union Pacific workmen from savage raids, and to police the dives that had sprung up successively at Fort Kearney, North Platte, Julesburg and intermediate points. In 1867 the track reached Cheyenne. West of the Laramie Mountains or "Black Hills," which offered the Union Pacific its first real engineering problem, lay the Laramie River valley, and new Fort Sanders. Despite furious construction efforts, tracks did not reach here until late in the spring of 1868.

The log block house in which the Burts were sheltered in the summer of 1867, and from which Mrs. Burt observed rail grade construction, appears in an official post description of 1870.[2] The pencil sketch of the block house reproduced here, artist unknown, was found among the Burt family papers.

Important events were transpiring at Fort Sanders which Mrs. Burt failed to mention, perhaps did not even know about as the result of her confinement. Two weeks after presiding at a rip-roaring Fourth of July celebration at Cheyenne, General Dodge, accompanied by Grant's Chief of Staff, General Rawlins, started westward to inspect the progress of his graders and survey crews. About August 1 they were in conference at Fort Sanders with General Gibbon, one of Grant's most trusted officers during the Civil War. A rider, with foaming horse, galloped up with news that the Percy Brown engineering party had been attacked by Sioux near Bridger's Pass, Brown and another man being killed. This culminated a long series of Sioux outrages, and Dodge was urged by his advisers to halt all work for six months, pending arrival of new troops. With a strong escort supplied by Gibbon, Dodge pushed westward to strengthen his badly demoralized engineering parties. Finding the North Platte swollen with heavy mountain snows, he and his party nearly met the sad fate of Sergeant St. John of the Burt party in a desperate horseback crossing. On the west bank he selected the site of new Fort Fred Steele. The townsite of Rawlins then received its name, and in late August the Dodge party reached Fort Bridger, two months after the Burts had departed from that post.[3]

Elizabeth Burt was not concerned with these epochal events:

> My chief thought was to get well and be ready to start when the order came to go north. Had we been in a

city with no more comforts than I had here, it would have seemed impossible to get well, but Providence certainly watched over baby and me in answer to my prayers.

Kind friends sent unexpected dainties to tempt my appetite. Never had I expected to enjoy eating frog legs; but when General Gibbon sent some, surrounded by small lettuce leaves, which he had raised in a cold frame, they proved delicious. An officer on duty on the road sent young sage chickens that were almost equal to the quail. An occasional squab from the wife of the sutler proved a great delicacy. Thus everything possible was done for me by my own dear ones and by many kind friends.

One day a man appeared with a load of something to sell. Visions of fresh vegetables floated through my brain. Alas! These hopes were speedily dispelled, when Maggie announced that it was a load of turnips.

"Turnips, Maggie! I could never eat turnips."

"But them's young, and I can cook 'em so you'll like 'em."

"Well, Maggie, we will try some." And we all actually enjoyed those hitherto scorned vegetables. However, when one has lived without anything fresh except wild lamb's quarter greens for eighteen months even turnips taste delicious.

At this time my little boy came to me, his face beaming with joy, carrying a little white roll of fur:

"Beauty's dear little pup, Mama," he said, "and this is my own, and there are ten more. Can't we keep them all, Mama, please? They are so pretty. I love them and want to keep them every one. Beauty lets me play with them."

"Well, dearie," I replied, "we will see about it when I am well." It was useless to say "No" to the little fellow. Gradually he would realize that our household could not harbor ten more pets, but for the time being he could be allowed to keep them.

When baby was three weeks old an order came for her father to proceed to Omaha and take command of recruits going to Forts Reno, Phil Kearny and C. F. Smith. The question of his absence was a serious one for we knew that he would be gone about a month at least, and would not return to Sanders. Kate and I would be left alone to arrange for joining him or going East as might seem best. It is true that the entire garrison at Sanders was most pleasant and cordial toward us, proferring their assistance as is customary in the army where one finds the closest ties of friendship. Especially is this true when formed at frontier posts where people are dependent upon each other for companionship, day after day, month after month.

Had my health permitted, my husband would have taken us with him, to [continue on from Omaha and] stay with my mother in Springfield, Ohio. In discussing the question he told of the serious trouble with the Indians and of Major Powell's fight near Fort Phil Kearny that had lately taken place [the Wagon Box Fight], and he added: "If you were well enough I would take you east as far as Omaha without doubt. The next plan is for you to go home as soon as you are able to travel. You cannot stay much longer in the block house as it will be too cold. I will make arrangements for you to go home as soon as the doctor pronounces you ready for the stage trip."

My heart was heavy indeed when he left us. Oh! that I could go with him! It certainly seemed wiser to go East, but the prospect of a long separation was very dreary. There was no time to hold my hands and weep. I must do all in my power to grow well and strong enough as quickly as possible, to be prepared for a hard journey east or north.

A short time after my husband's departure an orderly brought a note from General Gibbon saying the Department Commander, General Augur, was in the post, and would come with him to see me, if I could receive them. My reply was a courteous "Yes," while all the time my heart was filled with misgiving, for I felt sure that General Augur agreed with all the other officers that it would be unwise for me to attempt to go into that hostile northern country.

He had the reputation of being a most efficient officer and just Department Commander. To me he proved a delightful, courteous gentleman, winning my heart when he asked to see the baby. After admiring her he said: "I do not see, Mrs. Burt, how it is possible to take this beautiful baby on that long trip to Montana. Think seriously of it, for in addition to the cold, the Indians may attack the command. What could you do then? My advice is for you to stay here under General Gibbon's care until you are able to go home to your mother."

He might have forbidden my going with my husband's command, but left it to my decision. Why he asked to see the baby I did not understand, as children were no novelty in his unusually large family. I cannot vouch for the truth of the following story, but it was considered true at the time. Cheyenne was then in its infancy and General Augur was asked to name it. He replied it was as much as he could do to name his children. "Let some one less favored than I, in this respect, name the embryo city."[4]

One day in September, when snow was on the ground, an unusual sight was to be seen from my window. With the aid of the field-glass I saw a long column of soldiers coming down the hill before our house. They proved to be a battalion of the 18th Infantry, commanded by General Wessels, going to Fort Fetterman, a post just being built between Forts Laramie and Reno in a dangerous part of the Indian country. The General came to see me and told me he heard there was a possibility of my going beyond his post with my husband. He also joined in the cry of disapproval and advised me to go East, but added, "If you do come to Fort Fetterman, I hope you and your sister will make my house your home, and I will do the best I can for you."[5]

It was lovely of him, and we assured him his invitation would be gladly accepted should we arrive there. His white hair and delicately built frame made me feel that he ought not to be required to make that march, and he, in turn, thought a young woman with a wee baby had better go to a good home with her mother.

Letters came now from the Major saying it must be decided at once what I was to do, as his orders were to leave Omaha soon with a large number of recruits. He also thought it better for me to go East. Part of the trip could now be made by rail, lessening the fatigue of the journey.

As my strength returned, my courage came also. The temptation to go with him was too great, and I decided to join him. Long before this I had told my sister that it was not possible for me to go without her. She agreed to go, with our mother's consent, which was at length given very reluctantly, as she had little patience with this lack of judgment on my part, as she thought it.

My problem now was to go as far east as Fort Russell at Cheyenne near which we would be able to meet my husband and his detachment. General Gibbon again showed his great kindness by offering to escort us, with his adjutant, Mr. Starring, Quartermaster Major Male, and a few soldiers, as far as Russell. This was an unexpected attention.

Again the packing began, making the block house most dismal and comfortless. The cannon were more formidable in appearance than ever, so gladly we accepted an invitation from the adjutant to occupy his one living room that was attached to his office. There were no luxuries other than a bare floor, a bed, a few chairs and a box for toilet table but the walls were plastered, which at least prevented the snow and cold wind penetrating through to the bones. Better than all was a large wood stove that made the place seem a paradise compared to the wind-chilled rooms of the block house. Friends invited us to their hospitable tables for our last meals but they had no place in which to keep us at night. Mr. Starring's kindness at that time is one of the bright spots in my memory. He even sat behind the stove and held baby while Kate and I did our last packing at the block house. . . .

About the middle of October, on the morning appointed for our leaving Fort Sanders, we wakened to find a lowering sky and fast falling snow. General Gibbon said we could not start in the storm. However, we were obliged to leave the next morning as we had only two days in which to make the journey to meet Major Burt's marching column, which of course could not be delayed for us.

Fortunately the storm ceased and the morning broke clear, enabling us to make an early start on a trip of about 450 miles [to Fort C. F. Smith]. The bottom of the ambulance was roomy enough for baby's bed, a champagne basket padded on the bottom and sides with cotton, making a safe and warm bed for the little one, where she was more comfortable than Kate and I could have made her in our arms. Back we went over the Wyoming Black Hills road to Cheyenne. Here we found every indication of a town starting into existence, men in dress of the frontier, railroad employees, miners, store keepers with their supplies in tents, and "hangers on" of every new born western town.

The city of Cheyenne owes its existence to General Dodge, who personally selected the site at the head of Lodge Pole Creek as a major railroad base, and thought to mollify the hostile Cheyenne Indians by conferring the name. General C. C. Augur, Commander, Department of the Platte, followed up with the establishment of nearby Fort D. A. Russell. Beginning in July, 1867 the rush to Cheyenne was on, with town lots rather than gold being the object. Its rapid transformation from a sprawling hell-roaring tent camp to a community with hundreds of substantial buildings, 10,000 inhabitants and a sober city government earned it the title of "The

Magic City of the Plains." In November of that year, soon after Elizabeth Burt passed through, the track reached town and the arrival of the first passenger train was celebrated.[6]

General Stevenson, who was at Fort Russell in command of his regiment, the 30th Infantry, placed tents at our disposal for the one night we were to remain there, and entertained us at dinner and breakfast in one of his tents. His entire command was under canvas while quarters were being hurriedly put up for them.[7]

Here we were met by Lieutenant Thomas Brent who had been sent by Major Burt to escort us to his camp on Lodge Pole Creek, where we were to meet him. Being in command, he would not leave it to come for us but sent a reliable and agreeable representative, who was going to Fort Fetterman to join his regiment. Neither of the other three officers with Major Burt had ever been on the frontier before.

Farewell now to the friends who had been so kind to us while we were detained at Fort Sanders. After we were settled in the ambulance ready to leave Fort Russell, General Gibbon came with a bottle of gin, saying it was for baby when she had the colic.

"But General, I have never used gin."

"Then you don't know what a blessing it will prove. I have raised a large family out here in the West and know."

Of course I had to thank him especially for his kindness and thoughtfulness. Major Male came too with a leg of mutton that indeed was a treat to be enjoyed on our march.

"Think of us at Fort Sanders when you are enjoying this change from beef," he said. How could I refuse his kindness?

The bottle of gin was put away for baby, but she had no colic and when we looked for the bottle, Lo! it had disappeared. And though we never learned how, nor where it had gone, we felt morally certain it had not taken flight without assistance. However, baby did not need it and no one suffered from its disappearance as far as we knew.

That afternoon we joined my husband and his command on Lodge Pole Creek. When he saw that I looked pale and thin he said: "I fear this is a mistake and the trip is going to be too severe for you; I ought to have insisted on you going home."

106

"Don't worry about me," I told him. "I am gaining strength every day and will soon be perfectly well. I feel it is all right. If not, it is my own fault, so please do not worry. You have enough care upon your shoulders in watching over the safety of the column in general, but especially your raw recruits and the mules."

The subordinate officers with my husband had no experience in Indian warfare so his responsibility was doubly great. Realizing that to lose our herd of animals in such cold weather would be an appalling calamity, he gave particular orders in regard to the care of the herd and had impressed it upon all that when the mules out grazing showed signs of restlessness the bell mare should be instantly started by the herders at a run for the wagons, then the rest of the mules would quickly follow.

My confidence in my husband's ability to carry the command safely to the journey's end prevented my worrying on our own account. Sometimes I thought he often wished to be released from the responsibility of having us there, but if he felt it he never said so, nor made us feel he was not always glad to have us with him.

With the command were Dr. Frantz and three lieutenants, one of whom, Mr. W. H. Miller, had his wife with him. For this we rejoiced as Kate and I would not now be without a lady companion. Besides a large number of recruit companies the column consisted of a long train of wagons each drawn by six mules, under the famous Bill Reed as wagon master.[8]

All shared with us the desire to reach the journey's end as speedily as possible, especially as the weather each day grew colder; the fatigue party often shovelled away the snow before the tents could be pitched and water froze solid in the buckets at night.

My husband determined to follow a trail west of Fort Laramie, thereby shortening our distance some miles.[9] We soon reached a rolling country scattered with trees. For days then we travelled round the base of Laramie Peak which loomed grandly at our left. Glimpses of picturesque views gladdened our eyes as the road began to be rough, taking us over lower foot hills of the Peak.

You ask how baby bore this strenuous life? The little soul was the most comfortable member of the party. Rolled in furs she slept the hours away, never requiring the pain killer.[10] After we became well acquainted with Dr. Frantz he said to me: "How you had the courage to bring that tiny baby to this country at this time of year is a wonder to me. When I heard in Omaha that an officer's wife was coming with him on this winter trip bringing a young baby, I thought it monstrous and supposed my services would be required day and night to care for them. It is amazing how you both endure the trip."

Mrs. Burt's decision seems incredible to us today. It would also have been marvelled at by M. Simonin, a French gentleman observer accompanying the Indian Peace Commission which arrived in Cheyenne in early November, 1867, but a week or two after Lieutenant Brent escorted her by ambulance to Major Burt's camp on the Lodgepole. Simonin noted at Fort D. A. Russell the presence of officers' wives: "These courageous women have said farewell to New York or Boston, and have come without a word of complaint to settle at the end of the desert with their husbands and children. After all, they are only a thousand leagues from their native land."[11]

It had been over 400 miles overland from Fort Bridger to Cheyenne, with time out at Fort Sanders for urgent family business. Another 400 miles of travel confronted Elizabeth Burt, in delicate health, with two small children, through a wilderness infested by enraged Sioux, and with winter ominously approaching. The fact that the expedition arrived at its destination with the Burt family in excellent health is a tribute to her youthful resilience and the Major's highly efficient and vigilant management of the train. Also, conditions along the Bozeman Trail were somewhat less grim in the autumn of 1867 than they had been for over a year. In August Red Cloud and company had taken a fearful drubbing at the Wagon Box Fight near Fort Phil Kearny and the Hayfield Fight near Fort C. F. Smith. The Sioux were still angry but they had lost much of their sting.

The winter of 1867-1868 that the Burts occupied Fort C. F. Smith was epilogue to the epic story of the Bozeman Trail, known also as the Powder River Road or the Virginia City Road.

In 1862 gold in paying quantities was discovered in southwestern Montana Territory, resulting in feverish migration to that neighborhood, and the rise of Bannack and Virginia City. Up to this time there had been two routes of travel to the Northwest, both circuitous. The steamboat route up the Missouri to Fort Benton was slow and expensive. The wagon road up the North Platte via Fort Laramie and South Pass to Fort Hall, Idaho, thence to the mines, was long and toilsome. A more direct overland route would take off northwestward from Fort Laramie into the Powder River country along the east side of the Big Horn Mountains, across the South Fork of Cheyenne River, Crazy Woman's Fork and other branches of the Powder, across Tongue River to the Big Horn, thence west over Pryor Creek, Clark's Fork and other streams to the Yellowstone; thence over Bozeman Pass to the Gallatin and Madison River valleys. This general route was not unknown to old fur trappers like Jim Bridger, but its effective rediscovery and pioneering was accomplished by an adventurer named John Bozeman, who is honored today by the pass and the thriving city of that name.[12]

Popular enthusiasm for the new route, which chopped off several hundred miles of wagon travel to the diggings, was quickly dampened by the violent reaction of Sioux and Cheyenne allies to this invasion of their hunting grounds, held by them to be sacred by the Fort Laramie Treaty of 1851. The Bozeman Trail, littered with burned wagons and scalped corpses of luckless emigrants, thus engaged the special attention of the War Department which, following Appomattox, was free to look after affairs in far-off Dakota Territory. The 18th U. S. Infantry had an illustrious combat record in the Civil War, and it seemed just the outfit to straighten out the troublesome Sioux situation. Colonel Carrington had a force of 2,000 men, which must have seemed formidable enough when it paraded out of Fort Kearney on May 19, 1866. But army strategists sadly miscalculated. The bulk of the regiment was made up of raw recruits and these were distributed at forts so widely scattered over the Plains that no effective single fighting force was left. On the other hand the Sioux fought on familiar ground, and with all the fury of patriots threatened by a foreign invader. To make matters infinitely worse, the Government was suffering from bureaucratic schizophrenia, for while the army was contemplating military occupation of the Bozeman Trail, the Indian Bureau was organizing a peace movement. The net result was a misunderstanding of the true state of affairs on Powder River, a weakening of the military effort, and disaster.

On June 6, 1866, while the Burt family, with cow, chickens and Company F, First Battalion, 18th U. S. Infantry, proceeded up Lodgepole Creek to Fort Bridger, the main contingent under Colonel Carrington crossed over to the North Platte, following the well worn Oregon Trail via Mud Springs, Chimney Rock, and Fort Mitchell at Scott's Bluffs, where another company was detached. The arrival of the troops at Fort Laramie on June 13 upset negotiations there under way between the Sioux and Cheyenne and peace commissioners, including Colonel H. E. Maynadier, the post commander. When the regiment marched westward on June 17 Chief Guide Jim Bridger knew that it was entering enemy territory.[13]

The heavily laden column of over 120 wagons and 700 men crossed the North Platte at Bridger's Ferry, which the old guide himself had instituted a few years earlier, followed the north bank to the vicinity of present Douglas, Wyoming, then went north to the head of Sage Creek, a country barren of all but sage, cactus and buffalo chips. Some grass and timber was found at the crossing of the South Fork of the Cheyenne, and from here the great landmark of Laramie Peak still loomed to the southward. Arriving at Dry Fork of the Powder River the soldiers got their first good view of the magnificent Big Horn Mountains, while to the northeast they could discern the four columns of Pumpkin Buttes. A march down the bed of Dry Fork brought them to Fort Connor, established the year previous by General Connor of the ill-starred Powder River Expedition. Here volunteer troops were happy to be relieved by two companies of the 18th U. S. Infantry under Captain Proctor. The desolate post, re-named Fort Reno, was soon to be reconstructed of logs and adobe. It was here that Carrington's men had their first exposure to Sioux strategy, when mounted warriors swooped down and stampeded the post sutler's mule herd.[14]

The intense July heat played havoc with wagon wheels, and camp had to be made at well-timbered Crazy Woman's Fork of the Powder to improvise repairs. At Big Piney Fork above Lake De Smet, north of present Buffalo, Wyoming, the troops rested, gazing in awe at Cloud Peak of the Big Horns towering grandly to the west. After a reconnaissance of the Tongue River Valley, where modern Sheridan is now located, Colonel Carrington accepted Bridger's advice and located Fort Phil Kearny on a strategic plateau at the junction of the Big and Little Pineys. This soon became an impressive log-stockaded post, 600 by 800 feet in size, which Inspector-General W. B. Hazen pronounced "the best he had seen, excepting one in British America, built by the Hudson's Bay Company." It served as Headquarters for the new Mountain District, Department of the Platte.[15]

On August 3, 1866 Carrington sent Captain N. C. Kinney with two companies to the crossing of the Big Horn River, to establish Fort C. F. Smith, the third in the chain of posts designed to keep the Sioux peaceful. A fourth intended "post on upper Yellowstone" was never built.

The route from Fort Phil Kearny northward crossed and re-crossed Peno Creek, Goose Creek, Tongue River near present Sheridan, to Little Big Horn River above the present Montana line, swinging westward to the head of Grass Lodge and Rotten Grass Creeks, and over a hogback to the C. F. Smith site. This was on the east bank of the Big Horn River, two miles north or downstream from the mouth of Big Horn Canyon, between Spring Gulch and Warrior Creek. From here the trail continued westerly to Gallatin Valley and Virginia City.[16] By odometer measurement in 1866 the distances between major points on the Bozeman Trail were as follows:

Fort Laramie to Fort Reno	169 miles
Fort Reno to Fort Phil Kearny	67 miles
Fort Phil Kearny to Fort C. F. Smith	91 miles
Fort C. F. Smith to Clarke's Fork	63 miles
Clarke's Fork to Yellowstone Ferry	90 miles
Yellowstone Ferry to Bozeman City	51 miles
Bozeman City to Virginia City	70 miles

Far from keeping peace with the Sioux, Carrington's thin command was almost immediately placed on the defensive, fighting for its life. Construction of Fort Phil Kearny, Dakota Territory, had been started on July 15. Cheyennes under Black Horse arrived on July 16 to smoke the peace pipe; momentary illusions were shattered the following day when Captain Hayward's men guarding the herd were ambushed and two of them slain by Sioux; and Louis Gazzous, a trader, and four others were massacred. Thenceforth the Sioux kept up a relentless campaign of harrassment and extermination against hay and wood-cutting details and supply trains, chasing off stock, picking off sentries with bow and arrow, and defying the garrison to come out and fight. This culminated on December 21 in a Sioux-Cheyenne ambush within a few miles of the post which resulted in the annihilation of eighty men under impulsive, glory-hunting Captain W. J. Fetterman.

The resultant upheaval in the Department of the Platte, which prompted Major Burt's move from Fort Bridger, had two notable and ironical results. Although Captain Fetterman clearly disobeyed Carrington's orders in getting himself trapped, the latter became the official scapegoat and was sent packing with his entourage in sub-zero weather, first to Fort Casper and then to Fort McPherson. In his stead came General Henry Wessels and troops from Fort Laramie. Meanwhile, having taken himself and others to sudden death, Captain Fetterman was honored by having a new fort named after him.[17] This was started in July, 1867, on the south bank of the North Platte, at the mouth of La Prele Creek and opposite Sage Creek Basin where the Carrington expedition had turned north a year before. In time this would become a substantial military post and supply

CAPTAIN WILLIAM J. FETTERMAN, 18TH U. S. INFANTRY.

base for troops campaigning northward, but in November, 1867, when Elizabeth Burt paused there it was a sorry affair. She wrote:

> For a few days before we reached Fort Fetterman we talked of the pleasure of reaching General Wessel's hospitable roof. Luxury we did not expect but a comfortable warm house at least as good as Mr. Starring's. Alas! how our modest hopes were blasted! The poor general came to us with a sorrowful countenance, regretting it was not possible to receive us at his house as he had expected to do. There was no house! He was living in a dugout cut in the river bank. In his courtly manner he expressed deep regret at his seeming inhospitality, which was entirely unnecessary as we understood exactly the miserable state of affairs. His officers were living in tents.
>
> Major Burt delayed the command here one day while he superintended the transformation of an army wagon for me and the family into a prairie schooner. The sides of the wagon were raised and canvas stretched over the top high enough to enable us to stand erect. A half window sash was set in the front and a small door in the rear. To reach the ground a short ladder could be removed from the side of the wagon and quickly adjusted at the door. In one corner a camp kettle was imbedded upside down in a small bed of mortar for a stove, and a tiny pipe carried the smoke through the zinc-encircled opening in the top. By this stove I sat on a pile of buffalo robes with a gunny sack of charcoal at hand for fuel, and baby in my lap or in the champagne basket. My sister's place was at the window with Andrew Gano on buffalo robes, while the Mormon girl, Christina, sat in the middle of the wagon on a pile of bedding.
>
> Maggie filled us with dismay at Fetterman by announcing her intention to stay there. "Too many Indians" was the reason given. She had heard harrowing tales of the dangers in store for her if she went on with us. Offers of higher wages had no effect. Go she would not. There was no time nor prospect of making any other arrangement so we started the next morning, with a comforting fire in the stove puffing smoke out of our prairie schooner to keep up our spirits.
>
> Twice a day we left our wagon and gathered with the officers and Mrs. Miller round a camp fire for breakfast and dinner, when a soldier cook gave us coffee and whatever the meager larder provided. Beans, one of our staples from the Commissary, we could not have in that high altitude as it

took too long to boil them. Sometimes the hunters brought us game when they were fortunate enough to kill any near camp. As we were now in a dangerous Indian country, strict orders forebade any one going far from the command.

In June, 1866 Margaret Carrington had exulted in the beauty of cactus flowers and the grand scenery of the Big Horns. Some months later, after a few skirmishes with the Sioux, things wore a less rosy aspect. When Frances Grummond travelled with her husband to Fort Phil Kearny that autumn she confessed that "contemplation of beautiful mountains brought no corresponding uplift of spirit, for mountains, hills, canyons and ridges suggest a hidden foe." Far more beautiful to her was the sight of Fort Reno, which promised shelter from harm and relief from camp cooking.[18] One year later Mrs. Burt had little comment on the scenery either, but her recollections of Fort Reno reflect a warm glow:

Upon reaching Fort Reno we were cordially welcomed by Major and Brevet Colonel James Van Voast of the 18th Infantry, from whom we had parted at the Platte River the year before.[19] We found but one lady there, the wife of Captain Ogden. She had made her log cabin very attractive and entertained us at a delightful dinner. How we wished we could stay in this comfortable little post, though it was in a dangerous part of the country! But hurry on was the order.

Soon after starting at the peep of dawn the next morning, the wagon halted and a cheery voice said: "Good morning. Can you open the door?"

"Who are you?" I replied.

"Friends who want to see you." Upon opening the door two figures clothed in fur from head to foot said, "How do you do," in familiar voices. Then we saw the faces of our friends Major Henry Noyes and Major Edward Spaulding of the 2nd Cavalry.

"Where did you come from?" we asked. "Fort Smith, where you are going," was the reply. "We escorted there a train of supplies to add to your comfort this winter. We are now hurrying back to God's country before we are frozen stiff." A few kind messages to their wives, a hurried goodbye and on we went.

I afterward learned from my husband that they warned him that Indians were watching us closely and would without doubt try to drive off our mules at Crazy Woman's

Fork which we were approaching. These officers had camped within a few miles of us without knowing it.

After leaving Fetterman, Major Burt had ordered the corral to be formed around my wagon every night. We were placed in the middle with the other wagons in regular order about us, their tongues pointed toward our wagon. An opening for passage was left at one end.

These were the short days of November; camp was made each afternoon only a short time before dusk when the mules were turned out to graze for a while under the careful watch of herders and the officer of the day. Their safety was one of the greatest responsibilities of the commanding officer, as their loss would have left us helpless in the wilds. The Indians realized this.

When our mules were driven in each team was tied to the tongue of the wagon to which it belonged. That they ever slept was doubtful for the continued crunching of oats seemed to me to last through the night; but this, with a feeling of safety, brought slumber in spite of the surroundings.

Inspector-General Hazen recommended that a blockhouse be built at the crossing of Crazy Woman's Fork, twenty-six miles beyond Reno, and for good reason.[20] Except for the immediate vicinity of Fort Phil Kearny itself, no other place on the Bozeman Trail received more devoted attention from the Sioux. Supply trains and mail carriers could almost depend on being assaulted there as the result of a terrain that favored ambush. The Indians would dig up the graves and scatter the remains of their hastily buried victims; re-burying the dead at Crazy Woman's Fork became standard practice. Mrs. Grummond's party had no trouble there but found a stray white cow with an arrow in its flank; the creature was executed for an evening meal. However, two months earlier (June 25, 1866) an escort party, which included the wives of Lieutenant A. H. Wands and Sergeant Fessenden, ran into a hornet's nest. With this train there were twenty-six men, en route from Fort Laramie to Fort Phil Kearny, under Lieutenant Wands, and including Chaplain David White and Lieutenants James H. Bradley, George H. Templeton and Napoleon H. Daniels, all going to new assignments. At Dry Creek they had ample warning, finding the body of a white mail carrier pin-cushioned with arrows. At Crazy Woman, Daniels and Templeton were riding ahead when the Sioux struck, killing Daniels instantly. Templeton raced back to the train reeling from his saddle with a gaping wound in his face and an arrow imbedded in his back. There was barely time for a wagon

CAPTAIN GEORGE H. TEMPLETON.

train corral to be formed before the group was under desperate siege. Another man was killed and several others wounded. It was agreed to kill the wounded and the women if the corral was overrun, for the Sioux notoriously tortured their captives; meanwhile, according to one participant, "the two ladies were angels of mercy and tenderness and looked after the wounded most heroically." The day was saved by the chance arrival of a strong detachment from Fort Phil Kearny under Captain Burrowes, escorting an empty supply train to Fort Reno.[21]

Over one year after this harrowing incident Major Burt's wagon train was also attacked at the Crazy Woman, but Elizabeth Burt was spared the crisis that confronted Laura Wands:

At Crazy Woman's Fork, as had been predicted, we met our first attack. The camp had settled for the night although all the officers and soldiers were on the *qui vive* on account of special alert orders which have been given them in this dangerous locality.

Early in the evening we were all startled by the sudden rush of the herd following the bell mare into the corral on the run. The Indians were on us. Some of them were even among the herd waving buffalo robes endeavouring to bring a stampede. Their wild whoops pierced our ears and then bang, bang, bang went the rifles of our men. The attack was on in earnest. My boy, my boy! was my first thought, for he slept outside the corral in his father's tent among those of the other officers and men. My anguish was greatly relieved when Dr. Frantz appeared at the door with our dear boy in his arms, and said, "The Major said not to be frightened, no one is hurt. It was the mules the Indians wanted and they are all safe."

The shots still continued, however, so my sister and I and Christina lay flat on the mattress trying to present as small a target as possible. Trembling with fear and uncertainty, with both children held closely in my arms, we waited to know the result. At last the firing ceased but our anxiety and fears in the stillness were only relieved when my husband opened the door saying: "It is all over, no one is hurt and the herd safe in the corral. There is no danger of another attack."

Tears of thankfulness were mingled with our prayers and my husband added: "Those were sure enough war whoops—how did you like them?"

"God grant I may never hear another," was my response. After the excitement had passed the sentinel's cry

of "All's well" ringing through the night was indeed sooth-
ing balm to our quivering nerves.

A search of army records reveals Major Burt's official version
of the affair, dated December 21, 1867, addressed to Col. H. G.
Litchfield, A.A.A. General, Department of the Platte:

I have the honor to submit the following report of an
affair with the Indians on the 13th Nov 1867 near Crazy
Woman's Fork DT while en route to Fort Philip Kearny DT
with detachment recruits 27th Inf: I put my command into
camp that day at dark, corralling the wagons, and pitching
tents around them; also posting the guard in rifle pits
around the entire camp, three men in a pit the one on post
to sit on his haunches, his gun across his knees; up to this
point I had herded my stock all night without hobbles with
five herders who were cautioned to remain mounted during
their tour of half the night. I sent no guard with the animals
believing that if the herders were vigilant they would be as
well able to drive in the herd as a large party; also, that the
firing of those defending served as much to frighten the
mules as the manoeuvers of the Indians, and that the fight
for the herd should be with the animals inside the corral and
not out: I am particular in these details for I believe that it is
owing to them that our affair terminated so quickly, and
without the loss of a man or an animal.

About half past one AM the Officer of the Day Lieut
Miller 27th Inf observing the mules restless, and the herders reporting that they (the mules) had not been eating for
the last half hour, ordered the herd in which was done immediately; all had been secured save ten or fifteen when a
number of Indians variously estimated from fifty to two
hundred made a sudden rush upon all sides of the camp
shooting and yelling; owing to the warning of the OD the
guard was not surprised and received the enemy with a
willingness that drove him out of range; the entire command then turned out with little noise and were stationed
in and between the rifle pits in single rank as skirmishers,
each man lying down; this disposition had just been made
when the enemy renewed the attack seemingly with an increased force (although it was a bright moonlight night I
could not give an accurate estimate of their numbers), and
certainly with more persistence and determination.

During this last attempt occurred an incident I wish
to particularly call the General Commanding's attention to.
The mules spoken of as still loose stampeded and broke for
the mouth of the corral. Lieut. Miller being at that point

turned his portion of the line quickly from the fight and clubbed them back and then resumed the action.

The fight continued about an hour, during which time the enemy's attack decreased in daring to desultory effort to obtain close shots; they finally retreated and were followed a short distance by a small scouting party in command of Corporal White. At daylight we moved on, and from there to Phil Kearny DT were not troubled again. But once did the men let loose a stampede volley; they fired individually as if shooting to kill, and not in the air; this was owing to the repeated injunctions of myself and officers to the men previously during the march up and in the fight.

We lost neither a man or animal hurt or captured. The enemy lost two ponies; I can not state that we killed or wounded an Indian, but I am fully convinced that we hurt somebody.

I owe my thanks to J. H. Frantz, Assist Surgeon, Bvt. Lieut. Col, U.S.A., Lieut Stephenson 27th Inf, for their able assistance in directing and encouraging the men. I have the honor to be sir very respectfully, your obedient servant,

A. S. Burt
Bvt Major U.S.A.
Commanding Detachment.[22]

Elizabeth Burt resumes her narrative:

In a short time the command reached Fort Phil Kearny and on a pleasant day of November camped on a grassy slope near the post where a mountain stream supplied us with pure cold water, and its wooded banks, fuel in abundance.

Colonel Carrington and his command had been ordered away. None of our friends of the 2nd Battalion were there but we were cordially received by Doctor and Mrs. Horton. This was now the headquarters of the 27th Infantry, my husband's new regiment, of which Colonel John E. Smith was in command.[23] Glad indeed were we to meet again Captain and Brevet Major David Gordon of the 2nd Cavalry, and his wife and boys. Not less pleased were we to find with them an old friend, Lieutenant Thomas Gregg, who belonged to Captain Gordon's troop.

The Quartermaster, Lieutenant Warren, had his wife with him, a charming lady, as was proved when we lived side by side in after years. We were invited to dine with them,

General Smith and his adjutant, Lieutenant Bowman. The immaculate linen, pretty china, and the varied menu, served in a real house, though built of logs, delighted us beyond measure. It was a most pleasant contrast to the dinners we had been serving in camp for so long.

At Fort Phil Kearny the Burts, among old regimental friends, heard in detail of the Fetterman disaster, and the heroic Wagon Box Fight of August 2, 1867, when a party of wood-choppers and armed escort under Captain Powell successfully withstood the massed attack of Red Cloud's warriors. Their principal informants, Chief Surgeon and Mrs. S. M. Horton, were the only ones in the officers' circle remaining at the post who were present on that dreadful night of massacre, when mangled and frozen corpses were brought in like cordwood. At that time five officers had their wives at the fort—Carrington, Horton, Grummond, Bisbee and Wands, Mrs. Grummond being widowed by the affair. In addition there were some children and female servants, and at least seven noncommissioned officers and civilians had their families along, all getting a lot more of Red Cloud's medicine than they had bargained for. John Bratt, who stayed with the wood contractors during November, 1866, pays gallant tribute to "the brave wives of officers at Fort Phil Kearny."[24] Margaret Carrington's *Absaroka* reflects the quiet heroism of these women, who made their homes amid scenes of terror.

Elizabeth Burt continues:

Now that I was on the ground where these horrors had so lately taken place, I began to question the wisdom of my decision in coming among such scenes; but I was there and could not go back, so tried to banish the thought of danger and prayed to be spared from any further trials. To try to look on the bright side of everything was certainly my duty; but I could not help thinking that it was no wonder that General Augur and General Gibbon thought I ought not to go to this land of warfare.

After three days spent at Phil Kearny the recruits were divided, the quartermaster and commissary supplies destined for that post were taken from the wagons, and our command started, hoping to reach its destination while the pleasant days lasted.

Counterpoint to Mrs. Burt's recollection is the official record of Major Burt's arrival at and departure from Fort Phil Kearny:

16th [November] Bvt. Major A. S. Burt, Captn 27th Infty, 2nd Lieut. William Stephenson and 2nd Lieut. Wm. H. Miller 27th Infty arrived at Regt. Head Qrs. in charge of 181 Recruits from General Recty. Depot, 16 of which were rejected at this Post, leaving for assignment 165 present, since leaving Governor's Island, 17 Deserted, 1 was left sick and 1 died en route, these (the 19 last mentioned) were assigned to Companies and accounted for, making the total number accounted for one hundred and eighty four (184)—Detachment left Fort Sedgwick C.T. October 20th, 1867, marched by way of Cheyenne and Fort Fetterman, arriving at Fort Phil. Kearny Novr 16, 1867. The detachment had an encounter with Indians, near Crazywoman's fork of Powder River, D.T. on the 13th inst. No casualties.

21st. Bvt. Major Burt and Lieut. Miller, 27th Infty, left Post for Fort C. F. Smith, M.T. in charge of recruits assigned to Companies at that Station.[25]

Elizabeth Burt remembers:

The country through which we were now passing was valued by the Indians as their most precious hunting grounds and abounded in elk, deer and antelope. Evidence existed of buffaloes having roamed there in vast herds, but at this time of year they had gone further south. We feasted upon game and trout fish from the clear mountain streams, and enjoyed the beautiful fall days even though our scouts were constantly on the alert and guards kept strict watch over the camp.

On the second day out from Fort Kearny an alarm was given that a large party of Indians was approaching. At once a corral was formed and every preparation made for an attack; our fears were soon allayed, however, when a good field-glass showed them to be a band of Crows who were known to be friendly to the white men.

Upon near approach they looked very picturesque in their gay blankets and decorations. Squaws and papooses added to the scene. They camped with us, making an interesting addition to our party. They were inclined, however, to be more sociable than we cared to have them, impressed as we were by their reputation for thievery. The curiosity of the squaws about us was made apparent by their gestures and conversations among themselves, expressed in a modest way.

The greatest source of interest to them was our baby girl, whom Crazy Head's squaw made me understand she wished to hold in her arms. As she seemed dressed in clean garments, I consented, though with reluctance. Soon the baby was the center of admiring squaws, who held a great pow-wow over her.

Crazy Head entered into it, too, with apparent interest. Our curiosity was greatly aroused to know what this animated discussion meant. The mystery was solved when Crazy Head made an offer to my astonished husband to buy our blessed baby. "Ponies—twenty," he expressed on his fingers. "No!" "Thirty." "No, no, no!" most emphatically pronounced by my husband, with signs to leave camp at once, partially to soothe my fears. If in addition to danger of Indian attack we were to be harrowed by the thought that our children might be stolen, what was to be the state of my mind? Then, indeed, had it been better that I had never come among them.

The Indian's [next] proposition to trade his squaw [for the baby], it seemed to us, could only be explained by the thought that after the trade was made, she could easily join her tribe and still have baby. All the time we were among the Indians I could not divest my mind of this harrowing fear that some day they would try to steal the children.

At the close of the fourth day we were nearly at the end of the 91 mile trip from Phil Kearny. As there was a steep hill to descend, we went into camp towards dark, with the pleasant feeling that it was for the last time.

An early morning start was gladly made and soon brought us within hailing distance of a party of officers and a company from the fort who gave us a joyous welcome, for did we not bring them supplies and news, and mail from home which they had not received for so long? There were no martial strains, however, to greet us as Fort C. F. Smith was not headquarters of the regiment and consequently did not possess a band. Most of the officers were war comrades of my husband. All were strangers to us ladies but most cordial in their greetings. Some of them were newly appointed in this regiment, the 27th Infantry, formed from the 2nd Battalion of the 18th.

It was now near the end of November and after almost two months of marching this dreaded journey was happily ended with the safe delivery at their destination of officers, enlisted men and, what was almost as important, the mules and wagon train, a cause of sincere congratulations to my husband. I felt justly proud as the Indians had driven off so many mules from different parties making the trip during the summer.

The diary of the journey kept to send to my family was thankfully completed and delivered for mailing to the returning wagon train, with the good news that we were all well and no one had suffered greatly from our experiences.[26]

7

Fort C. F. Smith, 1866-1867

Much has been written about Fort Phil Kearny and the spectacular Indian fights centered there. In contrast, Fort C. F. Smith is an historical orphan, except for space given to the Hayfield Fight of August 1, 1867, in Hebard and Brininstool's *Bozeman Trail*. Even the Hayfield Fight is ignored in basic Indian war histories such as Dunn's *Massacres of the Mountains* and Grinnell's *Fighting Cheyennes*.[1]

There are perhaps three reasons for this undeserved obscurity. First, the site is in a remote region, inaccessible to pavement-bound tourists, seldom visited except by sentimental cowboys and stray Indians. Second, it is of little interest to Wyoming historians because it is in Montana; while at the same time it is of small concern to Montanans, apparently under the impression that its history is linked

primarily with that of Wyoming! Third, during its two-year occupancy communications were so frequently disrupted by the Sioux
that it was virtually isolated, becoming a lost island of history.
Margaret Carrington asserts that her husband, "Commanding Officer
of the Mountain District," was quite conscious of "some responsibility
for helping Fort C. F. Smith to communicate with the outer world,"
but he was so harassed by Sioux at Phil Kearny that he was practically
in a state of siege himself. One soldier recalled that Fort C. F. Smith
was "an unknown quantity" during the period of nearly one year
that he was stationed at Fort Reno. Private William Murphy, for all
he endured at Phil Kearny, figured "we were not as badly off as the
men at Fort C. F. Smith. They were abandoned from the middle of
November, 1866 until March, 1867 and corn was about all they had
to eat. I am of the opinion that the officers thought that the men
were all killed at the time of the massacre and no one was left." Even
Hebard and Brininstool admit to "scant information on the history
of C. F. Smith which, by the fact of its distance from help, made
officers and soldiers work out their own salvation."[2]

The scantiness of information has been remedied somewhat by
the appearance of the Burt journal, coupled with the unearthing of
post records in the National Archives. Fort C. F. Smith was and
still is remote, but it did function effectively as an outpost of the
United States Army during the strange defensive war with Red
Cloud's warriors. It deserves better recognition by historians and
historical preservation groups.

The name of "C. F. Smith" itself should be enough to tingle
patriotic blood. This was, in fact, General Charles F. Smith, an old
army regular with thirty-five years' service, commander of cadets
when U. S. Grant and W. T. Sherman were at West Point, described
as "tall, slim and straight, with great piratical mustachios, a man
with ruddy pink cheeks and clear blue eyes, a strict disciplinarian
and a terror to volunteers." As division commander under Grant
at Fort Donelson, "old Smith" contributed mightily to that brilliant
Union victory by personally leading his green and hesitant troops
on a successful charge of the Confederate works. A few months after
the Battle of Shiloh he died from a gangrenous leg.[3] Fort C. F. Smith
was named for a great fighting general; it was a good name for an
army post surrounded by hostiles, where willing fighters would be
at a premium.

In early August, 1866 Captain (Brevet Lieutenant Colonel)
N. C. Kinney dutifully proceeded from Phil Kearny with Companies
D and G, 27th Infantry—about 165 men—to set up this post on the

Big Horn. He was accompanied by Captain Thomas B. Burrowes, "Major Bridger, District Guide," and Henry Williams, assistant guide, who were instructed to reconnoitre the situation regarding hostile Indians on the route to Virginia City. They encountered 600 Crows near Clark's Fork who were disposed to be peaceful. From them they learned, however, that hostilities could be expected from "Sisseton, Bad Faces, Ogillallas, Minnecongous, Unkpapas, some Cheyennes and Arapahoes as well as Gros Ventre of the Prairie," perhaps some 1500 lodges in all, encamped in the Tongue River Valley. This was ample warning of things to come.[4] The Captain concentrated on the selection of a suitable site and the construction of a strong defensive works. These circumstances are vividly described by eye-witness James D. Lockwood in a nearly extinct little volume, *Life and Adventures of a Drummer Boy*:

> At length, after several days of severe marching, the high bluffs overlooking the valley of the Big Horn were reached, and a view was afforded of the locality. . . . The valley seemed to be about 2 miles in width, with the towering peaks of the Big Horn Mountains standing in awe-inspiring majesty at the head of it; with the river issuing from its protecting shadow, through a mighty, rugged, walled cleft or canyon, and then flowing peacefully upon its course, taking nearly the center of the valley and shimmering like a stream of silver in the sunlit distance. . . .

> After some delay and difficulty in getting the heavily loaded wagons down from the rugged bluffs into the valley below, a march of eight miles further brought the little expedition upon the ground chosen for the erection of Fort C. F. Smith in Montana Territory. . . .

> A spot was selected upon the point of a large plateau of land near the river and which might be designated as the second bank of the same, for the fort—a place which the savages could not approach, within a mile, from any point of the compass, without being discovered. . . . Volunteers were called for to perform the labors of digging trenches, cutting logs, etc., for the new fort, at extra wages of forty cents a day, for the winter was not far distant and in that section is very inclement. . . .

> A trench was dug about three hundred feet square, two feet wide and three feet deep; and while this was being done, a party was sent to the mountain each day to cut pine logs ten or twelve feet long, to stand upon end in it, to make a palisade or wooden wall all the way around the square—these logs having been placed in the trench with

the earth packed securely around them. At the southeast and northwest corners of this enclosure were little places built out like the bay windows of a house, to receive the two small cannon which they brought with them; portholes were made through the wall or stockade, so that each cannon could rake two walls on the outside, in case of assault. Log quarters or houses were built on the inside of this stockade for the two companies of soldiers and their officers. A flagstaff was planted in the center of the enclosure, the flag was hoisted at sunrise and hauled down at sunset daily, accompanied by the sound of drums beating, and morning and evening salutes of a single cannon shot, which certainly startled the natives.[5]

To Carrington's complaint that there were not enough troops to man the three Bozeman Trail forts, Headquarters suggested the abandonment of C. F. Smith. To this Carrington pointed out the absurdity of leading emigrants to Fort Phil Kearny, "the heart of the Indian hunting grounds," and then abandoning the protection of the road to their destination, Virginia City. He wrote: "To refuse to advance to Big Horn River was the surrender of the purpose of my entire movement."[6]

Early in September, 1866 there were some notable visitors. While General Rusling was visiting the Burts on his survey of posts on the Overland Trail, General Hazen was sent to inspect posts on the Bozeman Trail and Upper Missouri River. On September 3 this dignitary arrived at Fort C. F. Smith, escorted by Lieutenant James Bradley, with twenty-six mounted infantrymen and pack mules. His guide was young Jim Brannan, but his approach was heralded by an aged mulatto who was a wilderness celebrity. This was Jim Beckwourth, fur trapper and explorer, wagon train guide, Blackfoot killer, squawman, onetime Chief of the Crows. After a quick inspection of the brand new fort, and noting its unsatisfactory state of isolation, General Hazen, with scalp intact, moved north along Big Horn River to the Yellowstone, then continuing north to Fort Benton at the head of the Missouri River navigation. Beckwourth and Brannan did not make out so well.

In late October Lieutenant Bradley and the escort party returned from Fort Benton without mishap until a short distance from Fort C. F. Smith. Brannan and Surgeon McCleery were riding ahead when they were set upon by some sixty Sioux, Brannan being killed outright. McCleery saved himself by galloping furiously back to the main party.[7] Meanwhile Beckwourth and Captain Templeton, who had but recently arrived at the fort in lame condition after stopping

126

Sioux arrows in the aforementioned ambush at the Crazy Woman, were nearly cut off and killed by "20 Crows who turned out to be Sioux." The Indians wreaked their vengeance on a miner innocently camped nearby.[8]

Accompanied by only one soldier, old Jim Beckwourth went off to the Crow villages on Clark's Fork, with the object of persuading that tribe to go on the warpath against the Sioux and take the pressure off the Bozeman Trail forts. He was a Crow hero himself and might have succeeded in his mission, but death intervened. He was a sick man when he left the fort and upon arrival he soon died in an Indian lodge and was buried with ceremony. A few days later the entire Crow village of some 1200 lodges moved over to the fort to report the tragedy, and camp for a spell. These peaceful but wholesale visits were to become commonplace, and Fort C. F. Smith became a virtual headquarters for the Crow nation.[9]

On September 23 Carrington received word that one of the C. F. Smith contractors named Grull and two of his men had been attacked and killed by Indians.[10] An entry in regimental records for September 29 reads:

Cos. D and G, at Fort C. F. Smith, under Bvt. Lieut. Col. N. C. Kinney, have been employed escorting mails, erection of their Post, and frequent operations against Indians; laboring under great and frequent annoyance, their work has been severe. Corpl Alvah H. Staples and Thos. Fitzpatrick, D. Co. were killed by Indians near Fort C. F. Smith Sep. 20—Pvt. Charles Hackett, D. Co. wounded by Indians same place. Sep 21.[11]

As a result of these hostilities, Kinney reported that he had but ten rounds of ammunition per man, each equipped with obsolete Springfield single-shot rifled muskets. Presumably this situation was remedied, for ordnance stores did go forward at least once that fall.[12]

In November Mrs. Carrington expressed concern that "we shall not soon hear from Fort C. F. Smith," as Lieutenant Bingham had just returned from that post with twenty-five men who had escorted a supply train, the last one that could be sent for several months. At the same time Captain Kinney, "who has just made us a week's visit," returned to his duty station, advising Carrington that it would be unsafe to undertake the trip with less than fifty men.[13] One-third of the man power in the C. F. Smith garrison would barely fill this prescription for a wagon train escort.[14]

Winter closed down, Fort Phil Kearny underwent its trial by fire which culminated in the Fetterman massacre, and in the ensuing official uproar, Fort C. F. Smith was nearly forgotten. The first few months of 1867 are the most obscure period at this outpost, but a few facts have now filtered through the time barrier.

Drummer boy Lockwood reports the advent of some "Indian runners," a short time after the Christmas holidays:

> . . . they brought news of a "big fight" at Fort Philip Kearny, with great slaughter to both the Indians and soldiers. They signified that there was much weeping in the Sioux lodges. . . .
>
> After this the guards were doubled, and there were no Indians allowed to enter the stockade, unless a few individual visitors, who were vouched for by the chiefs. The rations were getting low, and matters were looking very gloomy. There was no way of obtaining news from the outside world, and the officers caused a bulletin board to be erected in a public place in the barrack square and upon this they would daily post clippings from newspapers, which they happened to have in their baggage; this served to break the dull, gloomy monotony which seemed to pervade everything, and in some measure to distract their attention from their desperate situation. The snow was very deep and the weather remained bitter cold; the rations gave out entirely, and they were compelled to take the grain which was brought for the animals and boil it to make food with which to sustain the lives of the garrison.[15]

Worried about the situation up north, the Phil Kearny commander, General Wessels, asked for volunteers to make the perilous journey through heavy winter snows to see if the garrison was still alive. Sergeants Grant and Graham made it safely, arriving at the stockade on the evening of February 7. They delivered a message dated January 23 from Lieutenant Brent, "Acting Assistant Adjutant General, Mountain District," which constituted the first official notice of the Fetterman massacre. Two days later the sergeants started back, furnished by Captain Kinney with "a guide experienced in frontier life" who is not identified.[16] Returning, they were intercepted by Indians and managed to save themselves only by hastily abandoning their animals, rifles and provisions and losing their pursuers in the mountains. Recalls Sergeant Fessenden: "Their sufferings were indescribable. They evaded the Indians but, without food, their lot was indeed a hard one. They managed to kill one rabbit, and this they ate raw. Their shoes gave out and they were obliged to take their coats and wrap them about their feet. Their indomitable pluck saved them, however, for about eleven o'clock one night they reached the fort, but they were in a frightful condition."[17]

Having no faith that these messengers returned safely, Kinney engaged Bad Elk or "Absarrookee Jim" to carry dispatches. Bad Elk, after thinking things over, changed his mind about going. In late February sixty lodges of Crows, fresh from a battle with the Snakes, arrived and Chief Crazy Head agreed to send three young men on the mission. The braves must have made it, for they jointly received pay of $186.96 in goods. Two of these hardy messengers are identified as Iron Bull and Feather-in-the-Hand, and their trustworthiness was rewarded by an offer of steady employment, "the compensation of each to be $50 per month." At the same time Mitch Boyer, who would one day be slain with General Custer's command, was hired on as "courier, guide and interpreter," to receive $5 and one ration per diem while at the post, and $10 "while traveling during the present interrupted state of communication," a chronic condition between the two forts.

In a series of February communications to the Mountain District, Kinney passed along information received from Bridger and Boyer about the detailed disposition of hostile tribes, estimating 2,720 lodges in the general vicinity of Rosebud and Tongue Rivers, "where they are fortifying themselves." For defense he reported "93 rounds to the man for Springfield rifled muskets; 60 rounds of 12-pound Howitzer ammunition, and a total of 200 rounds for Spencer carbines."[18] The fate of these Indian-carried messages is uncertain. Regimental records indicate "no communication" with Companies D and G at Fort Smith during December, January and February. Finally, on March 15, it is recorded that "Crow Indians arrived from Fort C. F. Smith, Montana Territory, bringing dispatches from the Commanding Officer. . . . During the entire month the weather was extremely cold and snow storms almost constant."[19]

In mid-April, 1867 trail-blazer John Bozeman and Tom Cover, enroute to Fort C. F. Smith from Bozeman City to secure flour orders for their new mill, were intercepted at the Yellowstone crossing by a small band of horse-stealing Blackfeet who shot and killed Bozeman. Cover made his escape but there is no record of his ever again attempting to reach the fort.[20]

In May, Boyer accompanied John Richard, or Reshaw, a half-breed farmer who had contracted to supply the post with hay and vegetables, back to his home in Gallatin Valley. According to Granville Stuart, they brought news to Bozeman that Fort C. F. Smith was in a desperate condition: "There were only two hundred men at the post; the horses had all died, or had been run off by Indians, and the post was short of provisions and must have help at once." They also stated that the Sioux were holding their Sun Dance on Powder River and would start out in force on the warpath about June 1. A party of volunteers guided by Boyer and Reshaw set out to relieve the post and slipped safely through the hostile country, probably because the Indians were still dancing.[21] Almost nothing is known of the activities of these volunteers. That they may have provided escort service between the fort and Bozeman City during the summer months is suggested by a Special Order of September 29, 1867: "First Lieut. R. H. Fenton will proceed with 24 infantry and six mounted men and one howitzer to relieve Mr. John Richard's train said to be coralled on the Rose Bud by a party of disbanded mountain militia."

The incredible state of isolation of Fort C. F. Smith during the winter of 1866-1867 is fully revealed in the regimental records:

> June 4. Bvt. Lieut. Col. Green, 2nd Cavalry, left [Fort Phil Kearny] for Fort C. F. Smith, M.T., escorting train. . . . 16th. Bvt Lieut. Col. Green returned from Fort C. F. Smith, having succeeded in communicating with that Post without difficulty, *being the first party through since November 30th, 1866, a period of near seven months.* Bvt. Lieut. Col. N. C. Kinney, Capt. 27th Inf. returned with the party, being the first opportunity offered since his resignation [approved January 7], he having continued in command of that Post until the arrival of Colonel Green, June 8th.[22]

The stalwart Captain Burrowes next assumed command. District Guide Bridger, who had apparently been at Fort C. F. Smith most of the winter, was instructed to report to "Commander, Mountain District, Department of the Platte" for duty.[23] In June the Regimental Adjutant also noted Captain Andrew S. Burt's transfer to the 27th pursuant to General Order No. 92, Adjutant General's Office, but "he has not yet joined the company. Supposed to be at Fort Bridger." The July returns note Burt's duty at Fort Sanders, and Colonel John E. Smith's arrival at Phil Kearny as new commander of the regiment, relieving Captain James Powell.[24]

With a new crop of grass the Sioux returned in force. Wrote Lieutenant Counselman, Officer of the Day, on June 27: "I have the honor to report the loss of 39 mules, four head halters and chains and one horse run off by Indians." The animals were grazing on the west flank of the fort, and strongly picketed, but the encamped Crows made such a demonstration during the attack that the mules ran away from instead of into the stockade. On July 3 a supply train under Captain C. F. Thompson was forty miles from Fort C. F. Smith when Sioux attacked, stampeded the stock and threatened to wipe out the detail. Corporal Driscoll made a night journey to the fort for aid, being severely wounded in the action. On July 12 Burrowes advised that the Sioux were on the Rose Bud in large force, the Arapahoes and Cheyennes at Wolf Mountain. Their avowed intention was to attack all trains en route and steal horses and mules. "The Crows also state that it is the intention of the hostile Indians to encamp in the immediate neighborhood of this post and attack before reinforcements arrive. In that report I place very little credence, having listened to the same tale last winter." This, despite the admission that "war parties and signs of war parties have lately been seen from the post, and by the regular morning scout."[25]

One day, according to Lockwood, Iron Bull led the Crows in a fight against "fifty or seventy-five hostile Sioux" which was observed by the soldiers from the stockade:

> . . . Colonel Kinney examined them attentively through a field glass, and then permitted Iron Bull to do likewise; the chief instantly pronounced them to be hostile Sioux, and requested permission from Colonel Kinney to allow him to go out and fight them, which the Colonel cordially granted. The little band of Crows hastily mounted and rode out within arrow shot, and then began a parley; a war of words and abuse followed. The soldiers lined the walls of the fort under arms, and prepared themselves for a surprise, at the same time eager to see the fight.
>
> The Indians shouted and gesticulated in an amusing manner for some little time; at length each band, in a twinkling, arranged themselves in a circle, riding furiously, one following another in an endless chain, looking like two large moving wheels with their edges together, the warriors of each band lying along their horses, on the opposite side from his enemy, which they were enabled to do by braiding the mane of their ponies so that it formed a loop, through which the rider thrust one arm in such a manner that the bow could be used to discharge arrows underneath the neck of the horse at the respective enemy, the leg being kept in place upon the back of the pony by a strong hair rope, which encircled its body. As soon as the order of battle was arranged, the arrows began to fill the air, each warrior being careful not to hit the horse of his enemy—for they understood that it would be useless to either side after the battle.

This spectacle had endured some ten or fifteen minutes when Iron Bull, arising to a bold, upright position upon his pony, rode bravely at the Sioux chieftain, and with lasso in hand skilfully threw the noose of it over the head and tightened it around the neck of his foe; then suddenly wheeling, rode for the fort, dragging the unlucky Sioux over the ground at the heels of his horse in a rapid rate. This practically ended the battle, and the Sioux retired, in a demoralized condition.

Despite the protests of the Post Commander, the Crow removed the prisoner to their camp, where he died by torture. Lockwood describes the shocking ceremony.[26]

By July 16 Captain Burrowes knew that Fort C. F. Smith was in real danger, a situation doubtless aggravated by the above gruesome incident. He declared: "The whole Sioux nation is encamped on the Little Big Horn River. They have completed their medicine lodge and are ready for war." With the 4,000 warriors reported "they can either take the garrison or starve it out and cut us off from water." Ammunition was now plentiful, but there were only about sixty effective soldiers on hand, and "should the attack be made and continue for 5 or 6 days as is the intention I may be reduced to pretty narrow straits." The tense situation was not improved by the fact that Dr. McCleery, the post surgeon, had become a raving maniac, and had to be restrained. A dispatch was sent "on the night of the 13th inst." by a civilian, H. H. Eccleston; having no confidence in his ability to run the Sioux gauntlet, Captain Burrowes sent a second appeal to Fort Phil Kearny by Boyer. "I have given him instructions to ride it through if possible without regard to horseflesh."

One week later the gloomy situation brightened somewhat. Hostile Indians were still in evidence, but on July 21 reinforcements arrived in the form of a Wells Fargo wagon train, laden with supplies and escorted by some forty recruits, three new officers and a new post surgeon, all under Bvt. Brig. Gen. Luther P. Bradley, Lt. Col. 27th Infantry, the new post commander.[27]

In a dispatch to the Mountain District, General Bradley reported that he moved his train "in double line" and had no trouble from Indians though they were in sight in small numbers every day. Attracted by the prospect of a new stock of trade goods, the Crows moved in right behind the train and "are now camped around here in large numbers." Bradley had a low opinion of the Crows: "They are a set of thieves and steal everything they can get hold of." Furthermore, he confided, "I am not satisfied that the Crows are our

FORT C. F. SMITH SITE TODAY, LOOKING SOUTH.
MOUTH OF BIG HORN CANYON, FROM SITE OF FORT C. F. SMITH.

fast friends. Iron Bull is friendly but Crazy Head and other chiefs I distrust. They have all been trading with the Sioux." To prevent any incidents involving Crows and soldiers, he brought three companies of soldiers inside the stockade. They had been encamped outside for lack of housing.

There were now five companies of the 27th Infantry at this station, all at low strength. In the new officer alignment, Lieutenant E. R. P. Shurly became Post Commissary and Quartermaster, and the other newcomers, Lieutenants Palmer and Sternberg and Captain Hartz, were assigned to companies. Acting Assistant Surgeon Geisdorf relieved McCleery who was to be sent home by the next train, "for there is no hope of his recovery here." The Colonel protested the proposed transfer of "Mr. Bridger" back to this post. "He is not needed here, one guide for this post being enough." In addition, "I have a detail of about 20 mounted men for scouting, etc., most of them armed with the Spencer carbine, which they have bought of miners." As to the Sioux threat, "I pay no heed to rumors about attacks on posts, except to put the Post in good condition as possible for a fight."[28]

After their Sun Dance, the Sioux under Red Cloud and the Cheyennes had a powwow but could not agree on which post to attack first, Fort Phil Kearny or Fort C. F. Smith. Finally several hundred warriors, mainly Cheyennes, started for the latter post, where they made their attack on August 1, while Red Cloud with about 1,00 men, set out for Fort Phil Kearny and his ill-starred collision the next day with the wood-cutting detail under Captain Powell.[29]

Cheyenne leaders of the expedition against Fort C. F. Smith may have been Old Little Wolf, Plenty Camps and Rolling Bull, all veterans of the Fetterman butchery; but even George Bird Grinnell, historian of the Cheyennes, is strangely silent about this affair, possibly because the Indians took a beating and preferred not to discuss it.[30] It is doubtful that they intended to storm the stockade, Iroquois fashion. No such direct attack on a strong fortification by Indians of the Plains is on record. They may have had a siege in mind, as Captain Burrowes feared, but it is doubtful that, lacking any disciplined organization, they had any cohesive plan. Their stock in trade was ambush or surprise, and the weight of numbers. The Indians on this murderous mission (variously estimated between 500 and 800) found just what they were looking for, a corporal's guard of civilians and soldier escort on a hay detail three miles below and out of sight of the fort. The result was the astonishing Hayfield Fight, which ranks with Captain Powell's Wagon Box Fight and the Battle of

Beecher Island (one year later, on the Arickaree Fork of the Republican River) as one of the classic victories of Plains warfare. This affair is modestly recounted in 27th Infantry regimental records:

August 1 [1867]. A party of nineteen (19) soldiers of the 27th Infantry, commanded by 2nd Lieut. Sigismund Sternberg, 27th Infantry, on duty guarding haymakers procuring hay for the Government, about 4 miles from Fort C. F. Smith, M. T., were attacked by Indians estimated to be five hundred (500) strong. The troops were partially protected by a corral made of green brush; this small party with twelve (12) citizens defended themselves against this fearful odds for eight hours until relief reached them from the Post. Bvt. Major Burrowes, Captain 27th Infantry, with Cos. G and H and one piece of artillery, was sent to their relief; upon the arrival of this reinforcement, the Indians withdrew. The Indians made frequent attempts to charge into the enclosure, but were repulsed with great loss. The new arms, handled with great coolness, saved the party from massacre. The extent of the loss of the Indians cannot be correctly stated, but was evidently severe, as they were seen to carry off large numbers of killed and wounded, while some of their dead were left on the field. Our loss in the engagement was 2nd Lieut. S. Sternberg, Private Thomas Navin of H Co., and one citizen killed. Sergeant James Norton, Co. I and Private H. C. Vincent, Co. G, severely wounded. Lieut. Sternberg joined his company only a few days previous to the engagement. Unused to Indian warfare, he is spoken of by the men, who fought under him in this engagement, as having acted with great coolness and gallantry, in the face of such overwhelming numbers. He was killed in one of the desperate charges of the enemy, by a musket ball through the head.[31]

An unofficial source of information on this engagement is participant Finn Burnett, a civilian in the employ of A. C. Leighton, the hay contractor. Young Finn was a veteran of the Powder River Expedition, and at Fort Phil Kearny he assisted in the grim job of bringing in the frozen remains of those who fell with Fetterman. He had come in with General Bradley's train to Fort C. F. Smith and, contrary to Bradley's report, claimed that there were Indian attacks on that train at Peno Creek and Tongue River, which were finally beaten off by the use of "a new type of rifled cannon." Burnett and Bradley are even further apart on their respective accounts of the Hayfield Fight. As a matter of fact, Finn claimed that through a reconnaissance of Captain Hartz the General knew of the fighting but in cowardly fashion refused to send aid until the Sioux had withdrawn. Furthermore, Finn asserted that this conduct was so disgraceful that it was a taboo subject in the army, and that no official reports of the affair were made, or at least preserved.[32]

Some credence to the idea that the subject was not discussed around the fort is given by the fact that it is not mentioned by Elizabeth Burt. This is indeed strange considering that she gave ample space in her memoirs to the fights around Fort Phil Kearny. It is not reasonable to suppose that she never heard of the Hayfield Fight, since she arrived only three months after it occurred. It is possible that she simply preferred not to discuss it, since it involved the reputation of an army officer whom she held in high esteem. Or this could have been an item in her missing diary which was pruned for family memoir purposes.

Examination of official post and regimental records, not available to or at least not searched by Finn Burnett or Dr. Hebard, clearly reveals that these authors were in error about the absence of official reports. And if General Bradley's own report is to be believed, he was not guilty of cowardice, and Finn's condemnation can only be attributed to the emotional reaction of one who was on the receiving end of a severe attack by a horde of Cheyennes. At any rate the General, crediting the hay party for a heroic defense, gave this version of his actions in a communication to Lieutenant Brown, A.A.A.G., Mt. District, Headquarters, Fort Phil Kearny, Dakota Territory, dated August 5, 1867:

> Our men fought behind a light stockade and the Indians charged it several times both mounted and on foot, gaining a position 20 paces of it in considerable numbers while others were circling around at a little distance. They showed a good deal of pluck and were determined to take the stockade. Nothing but the coolness of our men in reserving their fire for close shots saved them.

> The hay grounds are 2½ miles from the fort and entirely hidden from view by high bluffs. I did not know of the fight until it had been going on some hours [?]. Very little firing was heard and not a large body of Indians were seen, though a few rode near the fort and harrassed the timber train which was over in an opposite direction. Wishing to send out the train of hay wagons in the afternoon I directed 20 mounted men under Mr. Shurly to go in advance and reconnoiter. They intercepted a large number of Indians and were obliged to fall back. I then sent Major Burrowes with Companies G and H and a howitzer when

the Indians were driven back and the party at the stockade relieved. Maj. Burrowes put a couple of Case shots into their mounted parties and scattered them. He thinks that but for the howitzer he would have had all the fighting he wanted before he got back, and that the Indians had about 800 warriors within reach when he got to the stockade.

I enclose Maj. Burrowes' report. I am satisfied from information gleaned from Crow chiefs, when they were here, that my men were shot in the late fight with 'treaty' powder got at Phil Kearny. I might not be able to prove this to a lawyer or a judge, but I can prove it to any candid man and I ask the General Commanding to give this his consideration and to make such use of the information as he thinks proper. The Indians in this attack had but one rifle to two bows, but they used the arrow with great effect.[33]

The detailed report by Captain Burrowes to Captain Templeton, Post Adjutant, supported General Bradley's statements as to how things were after he, Burrowes, was sent to relieve Lieutenant Shurly "who was in charge of twenty mounted infantry and sharply engaged with Indians whilst reconnoitering the ground between the garrison and the hayfield." Burrowes made no mention of an earlier reconnaissance by Captain Hartz or a "refusal" of the Commander to relieve the hay party. While Finn claimed that the fighting was all over when the relief party finally did arrive, Burrowes reported that he had to contest every inch of the way.[34] In the absence of testimony by Lieutenant Shurly or Captain Hartz the full truth can never be known; but certainly the weight of available evidence is in General Bradley's favor.

Shurly was a good friend of the Burts, being with them at Fort C. F. Smith to the finish, and subsequently at Ogallala Station. What he knew about the Hayfield Fight must have been considerable, but on this matter he was silent. Without disclosing the nature of her source material, Hebard quoted "Major Shurly" on his career at Fort C. F. Smith. Among other things he stated that Fort Smith "once stood an assault against a force of Indians twenty times the strength of the garrison." This could refer only to the siege of the Hayfield corral, but that is all the information we get. He spoke further of generalities: "The Indians were bad. The government did not mean war, but the Sioux, Arapahoes and Kiowas did. They lost no opportunity to let us know it. We were then considered out of the world, and were, so far as getting news from the east was concerned. Months intervened between mails, and there was constant fighting with the large band of Indians, who took advantage of any inattention of the escort to 'jump the train.' The garrison at the fort was most of the time in a state of siege. Any man going from the stockade to the river took chances. Occasionally our friends, the Crows, to the number of three or four hundred, would camp near us. Then we had lively times. Their old enemies, the Sioux, would come in to give them a fight, and the garrison would look on."[35]

While Major Burt was heading north with his recruits, in November, 1867, cooperative Crows and a friendly band of Sioux identified as "Laramie Loafers" were assembling at Fort Laramie to meet with the Peace Commissioners. Preparations for this affair were big news at the Bozeman Trail forts. Late in August the Crows had been "invited to attend a meeting at Fort Laramie, D.T." and were issued flour, tobacco, sugar, and coffee, and other subsistence stores at Fort C. F. Smith. Early in October, Dr. Washington Matthews, "Special Agent, Peace Commission," arrived here to round up the Crows for the trek southward, and on October 13 Sergeant Pendergast, D Company, was detailed to escort him to Fort Phil Kearny.[36] According to Private Murphy about 2,000 Crows were counted there, and the war dances were held under the direction of Iron Bull, now apparently promoted as the "War Chief" of the tribe. Finn Burnett arrived at Fort Phil Kearny at this time with the A. C. Leighton train, and witnessed the proceedings, but proved to be an unreliable informant. He referred to a treaty made here to abandon and dismantle the Bozeman trail forts.[37] No treaty was concluded, either at Fort Phil Kearny or subsequently at Fort Laramie. Since the real trouble-makers, the hostile Sioux and Cheyenne, stayed away from the conference, results were negative.[38] Contrary to Burnett, there was no serious thought of abandonment at this time, for post records referred to new construction throughout the winter.

The futility of the Fort Laramie conference at this time was demonstrated by the attack on the Burt train at the Crazy Woman, and other hostile actions reported just before the Burts' arrival at the stockade. On November 2, "about 51 miles this side of Fort Phil Kearny" a Wells Fargo and Company train of sixteen wagons was attacked, with loss of mail, freight invoices and certain durable goods including window sashes, hatchet handles, grindstones, and corn. "The train was again attacked on or about the 5th inst. and five wagons containing corn were captured by the Indians. In the attack the corn was again thrown out and piled up for breastworks by order of Lieutenant McCarthy." On or about November 4 a "loss of clothing, including knapsacks" was sustained by enlisted men of a wagon train escort. "On the first volley from the Indians the mules attached to the wagons took flight and ran away in the direction of the Indians. An Indian jumped on the saddle mule and drove in safety to his party."[39]

Also on November 4, a severe fight with Indians occurred eighteen miles from Fort Phil Kearny, following an assault on another train headed for Fort C. F. Smith. The escort of forty men with one howitzer, commanded by Lieutenant E. R. P. Shurly, was surrounded and besieged by a force ten times their number. They narrowly avoided capture. Casualties were three enlisted men killed and several wounded. Lieutenant Shurly himself suffered loss of blood from an arrow wound in the foot, and a precious ammunition wagon was captured "through the carelessness of a driver employed by the Quartermaster at Fort C. F. Smith." The train was relieved by cavalry from Fort Phil Kearny, and returned to that post.[40] On November 21 a court-martial was convened to consider the case of the culprit, Joseph Bowers, accused by Shurly: "While returning from Fort Phil Kearny, at or near Peno Creek, he did wilfully absent himself from his train, permitting to be captured by Indians 6 mules, 6 sets of harness, 1 wagon complete with tent poles and pins, 3 shovels and 1,000 rounds of centre-primed cartridges." Bowers was adjudged guilty as charged but was released, presumably because his technical abandonment of the property was inspired by understandable motives!

Special Order No. 85, dated November 27, 1867, notes, "Bvt. Major A. S. Burt, Capt., 27th U. S. Infantry in command of a detachment of recruits for Companies D, E, G, H, and I, having reported at these Head Qrts in compliance with Special Order No. 195 dated Head Qtrs Post Fort Philip Kearny D.T. November 20, 1867, will relieve 1st Lieutenant R. H. Fenton of the Command of H. Company." In his report of July 27 General Bradley had branded this particular company as "the worst I ever saw in point of morale and discipline," noting the desertion therefrom of a corporal and four men. It is assumed that Major Burt, a top-notch disciplinarian, straightened up this outfit. He could not concentrate on it right away, however, for H Company was detailed as escort for the return wagon train to Fort Phil Kearny under the command of Lieutenant Fenton, while "Bvt. Major A. S. Burt will remain on duty at this post while his company is absent."[41]

Mrs. Burt was more fortunate than Mrs. Miller, also freshly arrived at the post. Lieutenant Miller was promptly assigned to I Company under Captain Hartz, and was also ordered to escort the Fort Phil Kearny train. With this train went Captain Burrowes, transferred to Omaha Headquarters, Department of the Platte. He was given custody of Hospital Steward Albert Simomns, "commended to the Government Asylum for the Insane." This, on the heels of Dr. McCleery's case, plus the frequency of desertions, emphasizes the fact that conditions around Fort C. F. Smith imposed a severe strain on personnel!

When General Bradley arrived in July he reported:

> I find this post in a very rough state, and foresee a good deal of hard work to put it in decent shape for winter. I shall commence hauling timber next week, and build up as fast as possible. I shall tear down some buildings, and alter the plan, so as to make the outer wall of the houses the defensive line. I do not think it practical to remove the Post as it cannot be got nearer a supply of timber. . . .
>
> I do not intend altering the post until about Sept. 1; meantime I shall get out timber & stone, frame buildings, etc. so that they can be put up quickly when we commence. . . . We have building stone and limestone within 2 miles of the post and good pine within 10 miles. . . . My chief want is a few good mechanics to assist in building the storehouse and quarters. . . . Every building but the storehouse has got to come down to be rebuilt; first, because they are not fit to keep officers or men in; second, because they are built without any system or order, and have got to be removed to make a permanent and safe post. In addition to this, two storehouses are ordered built and officers' quarters must be built. The quarters now occupied by the officers of the garrison are nothing but shanties, and a disgrace to the country and army. There is not a floor in the place, and the only roof is a thin layer of gunnysacks and dirt. I cannot build a good post without some skilled labor that I cannot get out of my command; and for this reason, I fear, I shall fail in what is expected of me. . . .[42]

Despite General Bradley's qualms, and the frequent interruption by Indian alarms, work apparently went forward with vigor, and alterations and additions were substantially completed by late autumn. During this period parade ground drills were suspended, and all hands not otherwise engaged pitched in to help the post engineer. Shurly recalled that a sawmill was put together with an old boiler, an engine and other parts hauled by twelve yoke of oxen from Fort Phil Kearny. "After our arrival," he wrote, "the old wooden barracks were replaced by buildings of *adobe,* the bricks being made by the men, the lumber sawed at the mill."[43]

Elizabeth Burt arrived in the midst of the new construction program. She found the quarters in her new station crude, cramped

GENERAL LUTHER P. BRADLEY.

and vulnerable to Indian attack, but still a big improvement over what they had been before Bradley:

    . . . As quarters were crowded, we could only have two rooms and a kitchen. The latter had been hurriedly built of logs for occupancy by an officer when the post was built the previous year. The floor was of dirt beaten hard and covered with gunny sacks. The new rooms were of adobe with plastered walls and planed wood-work. A good stove in each and a cooking stove in the kitchen made us feel there was now no danger from cold. Happy thought! No blizzard could harm us in these snug quarters, small as they were for three grown people, two children and Christina. At night, beds were made on the floor in the front room. Before guard mounting each morning they were piled in the back room and the table was prepared for breakfast. After this repast, we made ourselves as comfortable as possible in these two rooms.

    Our wagon train left the post as soon as unloaded, on its return journey to the railroad, taking the mail for the States. No other train was now to be expected before the roads became fit for travel in the spring. At once we settled down, prepared for the cold that invariably comes with winter in the high altitudes of Montana.

    We had no Maggie now, but a soldier as cook. The baker's wife washed our clothes but sent them home rough dry as she did the laundry work for so many officers. The requirements of social life did not demand that we should be clothed in fine linen and gay attire. To be clean and comfortable was all that was expected.

    The baker had taken a barrel of dried blackberries with him to Fort Smith which proved a lucrative investment as, with his wife's assistance, he made and sold pies to the soldiers at seventy-five cents apiece. Their three little girls were clothed in flour sacks which their industrious mother cut into all kinds of garments, making her little ones very presentable. The pie trade, together with the laundry work, proved so lucrative that a sum was accumulated sufficient to buy a home for the family upon their return to the East.

    There was nothing at the sutler's store to be sold to women but a supply of calico and beads, intended for exchange with squaws for furs. For sale to us, the price demanded was one dollar per yard. Preposterous! Though Christina needed a dress, I declined to invest in one for her at that price. A dollar a yard for common calico? Never!

The squaws traded beautiful furs, bear robes, wolf, otter, beaver and buffalo skins tanned by them, for the country was rich in fur-bearing animals, so that we accumulated many fine specimens. They made most desirable rugs for the floors in that cold climate.

The entire garrison was enclosed as a stockade. Undressed pointed timbers were set upright side by side in the vacant spaces between houses. Its two gates were closed at retreat and sentinels kept watch at its corner bastions. At each quarter-hour of the night would be heard their cry of the hour and "All's well." Sometimes it would reach us in far away tones, and at others in a very deep near-sounding bass. However, we soon became accustomed to the call, assuring us of safety, and slept undisturbed by it.

My husband always retired with his clothes and boots close at hand, ready to put on at a moment's notice.

The back part of our kitchen and dining room formed part of the stockade and, in spite of the unceasing vigilance of the sentinels, I thought how easy it would be for the Sioux to climb those logs and be upon us. The Major's chiding words, "Don't worry, the Indians will never attack us," could not entirely dispel my fears; besides there were his nightly precautions before me as an object lesson. When I called his attention to this fact, his reply was: "Of course, I must always be ready if I should be needed; possibly, fire alarm might be sounded." Small comfort that was; a fire once started among those logs would sweep through the post like a flash.

The winter proved to be very cold with the thermometer far below zero at times. The doctor gave warning to women and children not to go out of doors, as face or feet or hands might freeze before we were conscious of it.

As Christmas approached we began to ponder the possibility of making the children happy. To get a tree would be the easiest part, but to trim it would be another thing. I had brought a few ears of pop corn in my trunk. Kate and I made several kinds of candy to fill the cornucopias made of yellow paper obtained from the Quartermaster. Chains from the same material made showy trimming; cookies and doughnuts with holes through the center helped the decorations. Major Burrowes and Dr. Frantz entered into the spirit of our plans, helping us greatly, especially in decorating our rooms with evergreens, holly and red berries. Major Burt had three sleds made by the carpenter, one for our own boy, one for the baker's three little girls, and one for little Pinahawney, the daughter of Iron Bull, the Indian mail carrier. To those who had never seen a Christmas tree, the occasion proved a joy indeed and made the little ones very happy.

Several days before Christmas the civilian hunter who supplied the garrison with game—there was no beef to be had—brought in a wagon load of elk, deer, mountain sheep and bear to supply the garrison liberally, and give the men a grand feast of meat, at least, for their Christmas dinner. This man was a noted hunter who never failed to bring in what he went out too kill. Being so familiar with the country and the customs of the Indians, he was able to hunt successfully. If the Commanding Officer said, "Tewksberry, I would like a black-tailed deer," it would be forthcoming.

I might state here that upon arrival at C. F. Smith stock was taken of the commissary stores. It was found that of the canned stores there was only sufficient to allow each officer per month, one can of currant jelly, and corn and tomatoes, after the enlisted men had been provided for. For our Christmas dinner, therefore, beside a roast of venison, which replaced "turkey," we revelled in our one precious can of currant jelly, and the highly prized cans of corn and tomatoes. A delicious entree was a venison paté made and cooked by a soldier, a Frenchman by birth, who excelled in making this special dish. Raisins brought by us for this very occasion enabled me to have the pleasure of delighting, with plum pudding, the appetites of three bachelor friends who, appreciating thoroughly our efforts to bring the spirit of Christmas to that far away home, pronounced the dinner a complete success.

8

Fort C. F. Smith, 1868

To pass day after day without mail [Mrs. Burt continues] was our greatest deprivation. Chief Iron Bull of the Crow tribe went once a month with an Indian assistant to carry our letters to Fort Phil Kearny and bring the mail from that post to us. All the inmates of the garrison watched the departure of these two braves with great interest, while counting so and so many days before their return. Each Indian was mounted on a good pony and led two extra ones to carry the sacks. The fear of attacks by the Sioux necessitated their taking a secret path away from the main road. The day appointed for their return, every one listened anxiously for the signal from the sentinel which would announce the approach of the mail as it would appear in sight coming over a high hill a few miles from the post. On pleasant days we were allowed to go to the south bastion as a great privilege, to watch for the arrival.

The postal laws then forbade anything being carried through the mail except letters, papers and magazines; but of these there were always several large full sacks. As a further great privilege, the Commanding Officer, General Bradley allowed us three ladies to watch the distributions as they took place in his office. Each address was read out by a sergeant who then handed the letter or paper to a soldier to place in one of the various mail piles marked for company or for officer. How eagerly we watched the growth of our own pile and afterward devoured the month old letters and papers! To read the latter was a prolonged pleasure, shared with the officers and then passed on to the soldiers. To discuss the news with various friends helped pass many pleasant evenings; this was sometimes varied by a game of whist.

Frequent interviews during the day with Mrs. Miller, the care of baby and Andrew Gano, instructing our soldier cook, watching over and schooling Christina, together with necessary mending, filled the days for me. Kate was my able assistant, and was always busy. She continued the reading of French, but there was no time for that for me. The officers always had enough to occupy them in the care of companies and other official duties. Thus the cold days passed.

Certain orders issued by Post Commander Bradley help to illuminate aspects of garrison life during Mrs. Burt's time and amplify entries in her journal:

Special Order No. 4: Officer of the Day will see that all the water barrels in the commissary store house and the company are filled before retreat each day. The quartermaster will furnish teams to haul wood and water.... All the gates will be closed at retreat, and no gate will be opened until Reveille except the one at the Guardhouse which will be in charge of the Corporal of the Guard.... From Tattoo until Reveille each sentry will call the hour and the Post commencing with the Post at the Guard House.

General Order No. 12: The Officer of the Day will see that no slops or dirt of any kind will be emptied on the prairie south or southwest of the fort. Hereafter all refuse and slops will be thrown over the river bank.

146

General Order No. 17: The following changes are made in garrison calls: Reveille 5 a. m. Stable calls 5¼ a. m. Breakfast 6 a. m. Retreat 6 p. m. Tattoo 8½ p. m. Taps 8¾ p. m.

General Order No. 30: Troops of this command will be permitted to wear furs on the collars and cuffs of their great coats, and when the weather is severely cold the guard may wear fur caps, gloves, overshoes and such other articles as may be necessary for their comfort. . . . Hunting parties of not less than five enlisted men under a non-commissioned officer will be allowed to hunt in the vicinity of the Post.

General Order No. 1: (January 1, 1868): Hereafter until further orders Company drills will be held every day from 2 to 3 o'clock p. m.

General Order No. 2: The attention of Company Commanders is directed to the better protection of their men from frost during the extreme cold weather. A number of cases of frost bite have occurred within a few days, and severe colds are common. Hereafter no hunting parties will be sent out unless the men can be properly clad. Overcoats will be worn on drill and at roll calls.[1]

Provisioning for the garrison was something less than adequate, though not on the starvation basis suggested by some writers. There was nothing wrong with the mathematical calculations at Department Headquarters in Omaha; it was just that the Indians stole the cattle, wrecked and destroyed supply wagons, and broke up communications so often that groceries were almost always in short supply. Some losses were also attributable to shrinking, leakage, mice, rotting of meal sacks, freezing, overheating, "theft by fatigue parties" and just plain stealing from the warehouse.

Supply trains from Fort Sedgwick or Fort D. A. Russell brought in the bulk of the provisions, but there were two other sources of supply, without which the remote garrison would have really been in dire straits. One of these was the post hunter, John Tewksbury, mentioned by Mrs. Burt, who did yeoman service in bringing in carcasses of buffalo, elk, mountain sheep, venison and bear. The other was John Richard, the half-breed farmer of Gallatin Valley, mentioned but not named by Mrs. Burt, who entered into contracts with the post commissary, and made several successful deliveries of flour, beans, salt, potatoes, onions, beets and turnips.[2] Having Sioux relatives, Richard seemed to have some degree of immunity from the hostiles, a preferred status which expired in 1870 when he "'killed Yellow Bear at an Oglala Camp on Tongue River and was at once cut to pieces by the Sioux."[3]

The Monthly Return of Provisions for August, 1867 gives a fair idea of stores available to the garrison: bacon, ham, flour, corn-meal, fresh meat, beans, rice, vinegar, hard bread, coffee (roasted and java), tea (black and green), sugar (brown and white), sauerkraut, molasses, potatoes (fresh and dessicated), mixed vegetables, dried apples, dried beef, pickles, corn, oysters, tomatoes, and cranberries. Additional items listed in a Board of Survey report for September include canned peaches, condensed milk, pepper, rice, mackerel, green peas, jams and jellies.

There was nothing wrong with the variety; it was the quantity that bothered General Bradley. In a letter of January 7, 1868 he requested the Department to authorize extra rations to his troops. "The ration is barely sufficient to feed the men. One half the men here are new troops and they require more food than old soldiers. In this cold dry climate all men require more than would satisfy them farther south." In mid-March he reported that "the garrison is in good general health though within the last two weeks a number of cases of scurvy have appeared."[4] This is the only official admission that this dread disease appeared at Fort C. F. Smith. What this could mean was reported by Private Murphy, stationed at Phil Kearny: "The spring of 1867 was the time the effects of the spoiled flour and bacon showed up. All of the men that were at the fort at the time it was established got the scurvy. Some lost their teeth and some the use of their legs. In the spring when the grass was up there were lots of wild onions and the scurvy gang was ordered out to eat them."[5]

There is no evidence that the disease was as severe as this at Fort C. F. Smith. Nothing of the sort is indicated by Mrs. Burt, although it is recognized that officers and their families, with the privilege of purchasing supplies to suit their needs, would be in a better position to be assured of a balanced diet. In at least one respect Fort C. F. Smith was in the forefront among frontier posts. Bradley reported to the Department on experiments he had been ordered to conduct on the preservation of fresh beef in winter: "I have had beef slaughtered and hung where it will get the full benefit of the winter air and also packed in ice."

In February Bradley requested a leave of absence beginning April 1. About the only excitement during the ensuing month was the desertion of two more men from Major Burt's H Company. On March 15 Bradley reported that "all the troops are present with the exception of a Sergeant and ten men despatched to the Yellowstone" after the culprits. He reported further that Crazy Head and White Horse arrived with the intelligence that "the Bad Faces, Unkpapas, Two Kettles and Brules were not for peace but would take the war path this spring under Red Cloud."

Crazy Head's advice was sharply discounted by General Bradley. To the skeptical officer, only Iron Bull was "dependable."[6] Chief Iron Bull, who comes vividly alive in Mrs. Burt's pages, was indeed a remarkable Indian, who deserves better of posterity. His solid character is attested to not only by General Bradley's praise but by the fact that he was entrusted with the dangerous job of carrying mail between Fort C. F. Smith and Fort Phil Kearny. It was in his lodge that old mountain man Beckwourth died. His prowess as "War Chief" of the Crows is attested to by the battle scene described by Lockwood, but he was prominent also in the Fort Kearny and Fort Laramie peace conferences. He was a model citizen, an Indian who took baths! Visited in 1873 at Crow Agency on the Yellowstone by E. J. Stanley, he merits this tribute: "Crazy Head is smart, but said to be noisy and impulsive; Iron Bull is a wise counsellor, and shows an iron constitution and unconquerable will. When he opens his mouth, he speaks as one having authority, and they all give attention. He and Long Horse are good warriors."[7]

Another Crow warrior of note who frequented the Fort was Bearstooth. In a typescript speech which General Burt made to a patriotic society many years later is to be found his characterization of this Indian. This is his only known personal reference to affairs at Fort C. F. Smith:

> I used to have frequent visits at my office from the Crow chiefs and head soldiers of the tribe. One day Bearstooth, a noted hunter and warrior, came to my office. I liked old Bearstooth very much. He was neat and clean and never begged. Begging is quite a habit with most Indians. He was a wise old bird in many ways.
>
> On this occasion when he came into my office I saw he was very much excited about something. I nodded to him. He replied with a grunted "How," the usual Indian salutation. I did not speak. I had learned in my intercourse with the Indians that they maneuver to make you "talk" first, so when he came in I quietly walked to the window and stood looking out of it. Squatted on the floor he lighted his pipe and began smoking. After some minutes of silence, having finished his smoke he arose gathering his blanket about his hips. Thus stripped to the waist he advanced to me and said "Poomacatee (my Indian name), you are the only white

man who never lied to me. Now, I want you to tell me something. When an Absarakee delegation goes to Washington the chiefs and warriors, all of them come back here and tell big lies of what they have seen and the biggest lie is how many big villages full of warriors they have seen. They say they are plentiful as leaves on the trees. The party just back are as crazy as the others. I picked out to go with them a young man who I had known all his life. I gave him two bundles of sticks, long and short ones; great big bundles. I told him to throw away a little stick when he passed a small village and a long one when he came to a great big village. Now he comes back and tells me he threw away all the short sticks before he came to the Big Muddy, and when he had travelled on chee-chee wagon, two sleeps on the other side of the river, all the long sticks were gone. So he's a big heap liar all same as the others. Now Poomacatee you tell me the truth. You won't lie to me, Bearstooth, your brother."

It is the habit of the Indians, asked a question, to pause before answering, so I hesitated, to give me time to frame some answer to meet this very difficult situation. If I told Bearstooth how great was our population my reputation with the old chief was gone, and the cherry tree instinct was very strong in me at that time. Taking his hand and looking him straight in the eyes I said with all the earnestness I could put into my voice, "My brother, you have said that I am the only white man who never lied to you. I will not lie to you now. You cannot collect enough sticks in one moon to count the white men. Way back from the chee-chee wagon there are many, many villages your young man never saw and the white men are more numerous than the leaves on the tree."

The old warrior's head slowly sank down. He turned dejectedly and strode out of the room. He never came into my room again.[8]

Major Burt's high status with the Crows is further reflected in his wife's reminiscences:

. . . my husband . . . grew to be an intimate of the various Indian tribes in whose country we were stationed. They were many as you may know in our thirty years' service on the frontier. Of the tribes with which we came in contact, he was more closely attached to the Absarakas [Crows]. They gave him an Indian name, "The Big White Chief Little Man Who Fights the Sioux a Heap." He has often told me the translation into the Crow language but I never could master its spelling. Phonetically it sounded something like this:

150

"Ma-chee-chee ma-che-chee-poom-a-kah-tee bar-a-soops-kew a-hook-baats-aats."

Their confidence in him and his influence with them came from following strictly the rule of never failing in a promise made to them. Old Bearstooth, a distinguished chief and warrior of the Crows, came to our quarters at Fort C. F. Smith one day anxiously inquiring about some matter of importance to him, but which I now forget. He opened his remarks by saying, "Poom-a-kah-tee" (my husband's familiar name with the Crows). Then in Indian sign language which my husband interpreted for me, "you are the only white man who never lied to me." He then went on with his inquiries. I thought this a very great compliment coming from this wild Indian of the plains.

General Bradley's request for leave was granted. Accordingly, Major Burt's second post command was ushered in with his own General Order No. 7 dated April 1, 1868: "Being the senior officer present on duty at this post I hereby assume command of the same." Lieutenant Paul Harwood continued as Post Adjutant until about June 1, when he was replaced by Lieutenant McCarthy. Major Burt lost no time in sprucing up the garrison:

General Order No. 8: (April 2): Company commanders will for the time being drill their companies in the "School of the Soldier." Attention of the officers of this garrison is called to paragraphs 90 and 91 in the "School of the Soldier," *Upton's Tactics,* the strict performance of which is hereby required. Captain E. S. Hartz will conduct the Officer School of this Post.

General Order No. 9: (April 2): Until further orders, daily at the prescribed hour for drill the companies of this garrison will be drilled and instructed in target practice following instructions contained in *Heath's Tactics.* Three rounds of ammunition per day will be allowed for the use of the daily drill.

General Order No. 10: (April 16): General Order No. 9 is revoked. Companies of the garrison will be drilled in target practice twice daily at 10 a. m. and 2 p. m. In such practices Springfield Rifle musket ammunition will be used. Company commanders will exercise economy in the expenditure of ammunition at target practice.[9]

No ground plan of Fort C. F. Smith is to be found among official records, but Finn Burnett furnished information for a diagram of the fort in 1867.[10] The sketch of Fort C. F. Smith here reproduced was made by Captain Isaac D'Isay, who served under Major Burt at the fort as a late arrival, in the spring of 1868. His drawing in turn is based on a sketch by Private Anton Schonborn, who appears on the "List of Extra and Daily Duty Men" for March, 1868.[11] The original sketch and drawing are missing, but a good photocopy of the latter is preserved in the Signal Corps records of the National Archives. It clearly shows a square stockade, two sides adobe, and two of adobe and logs, with five sets of officers' quarters, three barracks, office, storehouse and quartermaster's shed surrounding the parade ground, a sentry box, two main gates, and two blockhouses at diagonal corners. Outside were the sawmill, civilian cabins, corral and sutler's store. Special Order No. 36 dated April 3, 1868, after Major Burt assumed command indicates assignment of "Building No. 3" to himself.[12] The buildings are not identified on the D'Isay sketch but the commanding officer's quarters is clearly the largest one, in the center on the west row, facing the flag pole. Mrs. Burt confirms this arrangement: "As soon as traveling was possible, General Bradley, Major Burrowes and Dr. Frantz started to leave for the states, Major Burt being left in command of the post. We then had the use of General Bradley's rooms." A map of the general fort area, with its approaches, was made by General Bradley and is preserved today in the Cartographic Section of the National Archives.

With the advent of spring Colonel Smith, the Fort Phil Kearny commander, showed up on an inspection tour. This apparently coincided with the visit of Special Indian Agent and Peace Commissioner Washington Matthews, who arrived for another parley with the Crows. On April 6, Major Burt ordered Captain Wishart, a new arrival at the post, to furnish this dignitary with stores. Matthews departed on the 12th, just in time to miss the early spring raids by the Sioux. These and other exciting events are recalled by Elizabeth Burt:

As signs of uneasiness among the Indians became apparent, the Commanding Officer issued orders for renewed vigilance and caution to be exercised by everyone.

One morning loud voices of rejoicing called us to the front window. There, out on the parade ground, was our Indian friend Good Heart, of the Crow nation, the center of a jubilant group of mounted Indians all chanting, apparently, a song of triumph. But what was that long hair fastened to a stick he was waving? Blood—yes, blood was dripping from it. "What does it mean, Good Heart?" my hus-

Courtesy, Signal Corps, National Archives and Arthur H. Clark Company

FORT C. F. SMITH, MONTANA TERRITORY, 1867.

band asked. "Sioux, Sioux! Me kill!" he said. After further conversation in the sign language the Major understood that with his little band Good Heart had just had an encounter with a party of Sioux, one of whom he had killed and scalped and now expected us to rejoice with him over his victory. A fresh bleeding scalp was too gruesome an object to awaken any feeling but horror in our hearts, and we turned away sickened at the sight, hoping never again to be brought so near an Indian victor and his reeking spoils.

A visit from the paymaster was the first event to break the monotony of our long winter. He came with an escort of cavalry from Fort Phil Kearny, bringing letters, papers and magazines from the States. To see and talk with one who had so recently come from Omaha with the latest news and telling of our friends at the posts below, gave us unbounded pleasure. To pay in one day and then leave the next morning was all the time he spent at our post; but his arrival meant so much to us as a contact with the outside world, in addition to the welcome greenbacks which he brought.

We were now to expect lovely weather enabling people to come and go though never without an escort. The temptation was great for us to roam over the grassy plain and gather wild flowers; but orders forbade our going beyond the watchful eye of the sentinels. The mountains were grand in their varied colors, since the snow and ice had disappeared. The nights were clear, making the stars seem nearer and brighter than ever. The winter nights had been too cold for more than an occasional hasty glance at Orion, more beautiful than ever, but now our view of Leo, Auriga, the Gemini and the other familiar groups was unobstructed and a great delight.

Upon answering a knock at the door one bright spring morning I was accosted by Mrs. Iron Bull, wife of a Crow chief, who was in her best attire, a buckskin dress hanging from the shoulders and elaborately adorned with elk teeth and embroidery of porcupine quills. Buckskin fringe finished the bottom. A black leather belt on which the blacksmith had embedded brass headed tacks spelling the name "Iron Bull" encircled her expansive waist and was fastened with an army buckle. No ballroom belle with a diamond dog collar could be more proud than this squaw was of her belt. Round her neck were strung rows of bright beads, that were to her also a great delight. Her glossy black hair always hung down her back. Little Pinahawney, who was her mother's constant companion, wore a similar dress without the belt. The cause of this festal costuming was to be explained by an interpreter who accompanied them, so I asked them into our living room.

It seemed there were several squaws outside who wished to see the Big White Chief's squaw and the Pale Squaw, as my sister was called, being a blonde while my hair was dark. Above all I soon found, they were most anxious to see the baby [Edith Burt] who was the first and only white baby ever at Fort C. F. Smith. I was reluctant to let them all come in the house, so carried the little dear one out of doors and showed her carefully to each squaw in turn. The interpreter told me, however, that they were very anxious to hold her in their arms. This was certainly a puzzling request as their reputation for cleanliness was not of unquestionable nature; but they were all in gala attire and looked as if their skins had been well scrubbed with soap and water. I concluded to grant their wish and told the interpreter to have them sit on the ground in a row in front of our quarters.

Mrs. Iron Bull held the little one first and with an admiring smile and comments passed her to the next squaw. What these whisperings to each other meant we could not tell, but judging from their eagerness to hold the baby and smiling conversation, their admiration appeared unbounded. The beautiful golden hair, fair skin and hazel eyes appealed as so very different from the invariable straight black hair and dark eyes of all their papooses. Kisses were of course forbidden; however, no attempt was made in that respect— indeed, I cannot say that Indians ever indulge in caresses. I never saw a mother kiss her child. Neither have I ever seen one punished.

When baby was again in my arms seemingly unharmed I was about to wish them good morning but was told by the interpreter there was something else they desired. They wished to see the interior of our house and some of the white squaw's dresses. Mrs. Iron Bull had come once before bringing Pinahawney with her and was greatly pleased to see the dresses worn by the white squaws. Evidently this visit had been discussed among the tribe and, like all women, curiosity was aroused to see the clothing and modes of living so different from their own.

One article of dress was generally worn day after day by the squaws. The garment reaching from the shoulder to the knee was sometimes made of buckskin and sometimes of calico. Moccasins on the feet and leggings of skin finished the costume. Every squaw seemed to possess a handsome suit for festive occasions of which this was one. For warmth all wore a gay blanket wrapped around them. . . .

CHIEF IRON BULL.

In regard to Chief Iron Bull himself, our interest was at first aroused by seeing him stalk past our house every morning and out through the main gate with an axe in hand. Naturally we were curious to know what was his mission and were greatly surprised when told that he was going for his daily bath in the Big Horn River. As it was frozen over he cut a hole in the ice through which to plunge into the ice cold water below. . . . He was given great credit for this unusual effort at cleanliness.

I had been more than once in the house assigned to Iron Bull inside the stockade. As he was the official mail carrier for the garrison in winter and so employed by Uncle Sam he was given this great privilege. His wife kept their two rooms in presentable condition and seemed anxious to acquire something of the ways of the white people. Of her merits as a cook I had no means of judging, and possessed no desire to test her culinary progress. That she treated Pinahawney very kindly was shown by the child's devotion to her, though there was no demonstration. Evidently, Indian children are taught at an early age to control their emotions.

In the spring when the roads about the post were in good condition the entire garrison was alarmed one day by the sound of rapid shots fired by a sentinel on a bastion, signalling the approach of some party. It was not the signal for Indians; no one was expected from Phil Kearny. What could it mean? Field glasses showed a wagon coming from the north on the Bozeman Trail. No one but Indians ever came from that direction which, whenever I thought of it, gave me the feeling of being at the very end of civilization— the jumping off place. Anxiously we watched the approach of this strange vehicle. To our astonishment it proved to be filled with potatoes, onions and a scant supply of butter, brought by two men from the Bozeman country.

What visions of delight filled our minds, of again enjoying a delicious baked potato after not only going without any for months but also being reduced to the necessity of eating the miserable dessicated potato cubes! When the prices were announced—fifteen dollars a bushel for potatoes and onions and two dollars a pound for butter, we became sorrowfully resigned to the fact that our purchases would be very scant and must be judiciously managed. In spite of high prices the wagon was soon emptied and the men returned to Bozeman with their purses well filled. It was a daring trip for them to take over the ground that so often was the scene of conflict between the Crow and Sioux tribes and was unknown country even to the occupants of our post. Looking at it in this light, the fifteen dollars per bushel was not exorbitant.

One day as I sat in my room sewing, while baby slept on the bed, without a knock or a sound the door opened and three large Indians slipped noiselessly into the room. With their invariable "How!" they seated themselves on the floor. By sign and with the few words of their language familiar to me I tried to compel them to go out but in vain. Calmly they sat and ignored me; that they were discussing baby and our surroundings was quite evident. To say I was afraid but feebly expresses my feelings. To scream was my first impulse but instead I seized baby and hurried out of the room to find a man to protect us. Very soon I returned with our soldier cook. The wily trio had quietly stolen away and I soon found they had taken my gold thimble and a jet and gold pin that I valued as a keepsake. We at once gave the alarm but not a trace of the thieves could be found. The Commanding Officer then issued the order that the sentinels must forbid any Indian entering the post without permission. One scare of this kind was as much as my nerves were capable of enduring.

A most delightful episode of our life at Fort Smith occurred upon the arrival of General Smith from Phil Kearny.[13] Escorted by a troop of the 2nd Cavalry commanded by Lieutenant Thomas Gregg, the General was making a trip of observation to the Big Horn Canyon. He kindly invited us ladies to join the party, giving it the charm of a delightful picnic. We had longed to visit the canyon but it had not been practicable as a large escort was needed to ensure safety. Really to have the pleasure of looking beyond that mountain range upon which we had been gazing so long from afar was greater delight than we had thought possible. Through the winter the post hunter had brought in game from that area and so to the sportsmen of the post it had seemed a wonderful unexplored hunting ground. Now they were to have the opportunity to realize their hopes of looking it over. Mrs. Miller, Kate and I were also charmed to avail ourselves of the great pleasure offered us. Every officer who could be spared from duty joined the party.

Now we saw the Big Horn River in all its grandeur, rushing and surging through its canyon, the high precipitous cliffs of which, beautifully clad in varied shades of green, interspersed here and there with the brilliant colors of wild flowers, confined the torrent for miles until it escaped into the plain to the north. As we ascended, the river looked like a silver thread beneath us.

Kate was on horseback. Mrs. Miller and I followed in an ambulance with the children, the nurse and the luncheon, all mercilessly jolted together as we passed over the rocky trail. But a trifle like this did not disturb our pleasure. The total absence of fear of Indians, while under the protection of the troop of cavalry, compensated for all discomfort. The most unusual sight of the day was that of bands of elk and deer grazing on the hillsides across the canyon and apparently unconscious of the longing eyes of our hunters watching them. Who knows but that they were instinctively aware that none of our party could go down the steep side of the canyon on which we were and climb the one opposite without their knowing it. In the short time we stayed there was no opportunity to try, so the graceful creatures, grazing peacefully at will, formed a picture never to be forgotten.

High up on the mountain-side we revelled in a grand display of nature's richest views. What a remarkable picnic it was indeed! What a feast we had at luncheon, what appetites to make it enjoyable! A camp kettle of good coffee, cold venison plate, a great pan of army pork and beans, were set before us. Combined with other pleasures of the trip this marked a red letter day in our memories.

Soon after our return to the garrison with General Smith's party our soldier cook announced to me that there was a beautiful spring of water quite near, just a short walk from the entrance to the fort, and he added, "Now that it is spring there are quantities of violets and ferns there. You ought to go and pick some."

"You know the Major does not think it safe for us to wander away more than a few yards from the stockade," I said, to discourage him.

"I go there every day, and so do many of the men. How can there be any danger?" he replied.

The temptation to gather those flowers and to see the spring was great. Upon consultation with Kate and Mrs. Miller we yielded to the voice of the tempter and walked out of the gate, past the sentinel, very foolishly taking four-year old Andrew Gano with us.

The picture had not been overdrawn. The clear tiny spring flowed from the foot of the hill amid a bed of violets which we at once began to gather, together with several varieties of ferns. The pleasure of the outing was such that we unconsciously lengthened our stay beside the stream until to our consternation, we heard a shot fired by the bastion sentinel and the cry of "Indians, Indians" shouted by many voices within the stockade. For a moment we stood paralyzed with horror, then sister Kate screamed, "Run, run for your lives!"

This cry broke the spell. My sister and I each grabbed a hand of the boy and gathering up our skirts ran as I believe no women ever ran before. We rushed into the stockade to see the officers and soldiers double-timing through the gates to meet the raiders who first fired on the herd, then charged toward the herd, shooting and yelling to stampede it. The herd guard, returning the fire, rounded up the herd as quickly as possible. As the troops arrived on the scene in a few minutes the Indians galloped off without doing any damage. I, of course, was waiting in fear and trembling to see my husband return. He greeted me with a reassuring smile saying, "My dear, you are pale and trembling. The affair is all over and none of us is hurt. It is possible that we got a couple of the raiders for I saw two of them curl up and grab their ponies' manes. You never can tell though, for even when mortally wounded they will clamp on to their ponies and ride to save their scalps."

This, my second experience in Indian fighting, was more harrowing than that at Crazy Woman's Creek owing to our almost personal contact with the enemy. Hidden from sight by the cliffs along the river they approached quietly unseen and passed within a short distance of the spring where we were.

We ladies created a great deal of alarm when we made known our adventures. The fearful consequences that might have followed as a result of our little expedition were so graphically impressed upon our minds that henceforth our walks were limited to within a few feet of the gate of the stockade.

After the experience that I have just recounted, the Sioux at various times made daring attempts to run off our mule herd. On each occasion an alarm given by sentinels firing and by the guard calling "Indians" was followed by the same rush of all troops to arms. During one of these small skirmishes, as the officers called them, so callous had we become that Kate and I ran to one of the bastions and mounted it to see the Indians driven off and witness the demonstration of the Crow Indian village camped near the fort and which had turned out to take part in the fray. The warriors rushed into the post to celebrate their victory and war-danced grotesquely about the parade ground brandishing their weapons.

160

It was on April 16 that the raid occurred which caught Mrs. Burt and companions on a flower-picking expedition some distance away from the stockade, compelling a foot race to avoid capture. There follows the Major's official report of the incident:

I have the honor to report the following affair for the information of the Department Commander. On the 16th inst. a band of Indians about 30 in number attempted to run off a herd of mules near this post; the herd belonging to a citizen. As soon as the Indians made their appearance D Company, 27th Infantry under command of Captain G. W. Templeton was ordered to the assistance of the citizens. After a brisk firing, Capt. Templeton succeeded in driving the Indians off, and saving the herd.

The Indians killed one mule; they however carried away one of their number, either killed or wounded. I am unable to inform the Department Commander whether said Indians were Cheyenne, Sioux or Arapahoes; they were Sioux arrows found in the mule which they killed. I make a special report of this affair that the Department Commander may be informed of the fact immediately, that there are hostile Indians in my vicinity; and that furthermore in view of the above, until further orders, I shall treat all Indians except Crows, Snakes and Nez Perces as hostile, and will not permit them to remain in my neighborhood. The Department Commander may rest assured, however, that I shall do nothing that will not reflect the evident amicable policy of the Government toward these Indians, save that which self-defense requires.

The affair led to the issuance of *General Orders No. 11* dated April 28:

I. Hereafter on Indian alarms during the daytime the Companies of this garrison will immediately fall in and form on their respective Company parade grounds and there await further orders.

II. The companies of this garrison will constitute a roster for emergencies in Indian attacks in the following order, H, I, D, E and G. Each tour of such duty will be one week's duration begining with H Company and commencing on Sunday of each week.

III. Without further orders, on Indian alarms the Commanding Officer of the Company for the week will move his company as rapidly as possible to the scene of the attack and there adopt such measures as his judgment may dictate being careful not to allow himself to be drawn too far from the support of the garrison.

IV. In case of alarm Sergeant Lysaght in charge of artillery will report for orders to Capt. E. S. Hartz. In the absence of Capt. Hartz, Sergeant Lysaght will report to the next senior officer without delay.

V. In night alarms the companies will immediately turn out and man the various loop-holes situated on the different faces of the Fort which are numbered herewith. . . .

General Order No. 12 followed a raid on May 5:

Hereafter when there is an Indian alarm at this Post, the troops are not formed into companies indiscriminately and unauthorized firing will not be permitted. Permission to fire may be given to known good marksmen by the officers and noncommissioned officers of this garrison.

The commanding officer calls attention to the fact that 600 rounds of ammunition were expended yesterday, one half of which expenditure was unauthorized and foolish.[14]

Greatly annoyed by further warlike demonstrations in his front yard, on May 18 Major Burt next came up with a rather startling proposal to Assistant Adjutant General Litchfield, Omaha Headquarters, Department of the Platte:

I have the honor to represent, since my last report of the 21st ultimo. regarding an affair with the Indians at this post, that they have visited us three times with their accustomed hostile intentions, charging on the pickets, and once on a working party some 4 or 500 yards from the post. Each of these affairs have resulted so far without injury or loss of any kind to us, although we have been assured by the Crows that the Sioux have suffered a loss of one man each time, besides having several of their ponies wounded by the fire of the troops.

In connection with this I would respectfully state, that the Crows bring to us many and various stories of the intentions of the Sioux, but their statements all agree on one point, which is the bitter and earnest hostility manifested by the Sioux toward the whites, that they are at all hazards going to continue and press their warfare. Also, that the Sioux are encamped in large numbers on the Little Horn, waiting until their Medicine Lodge is completed, before attempting in large numbers further hostile demonstrations against this post.

162

Courtesy, E. E. Ayer Collection, Newberry Library

CROW INDIANS AT FORT LARAMIE, 1868.
Dr. Mathews, Mountain Tail, Blackfoot, Pounded Meat, Winking Eye, White Fawn, White Horse, Poor Elk, Shot in the Jaw, Pretty Young Bull.

Should it meet with the approval of the Department Commander, and if he does not contemplate our immediate removal from this country, I would like his permission to make an expedition against this camp, with four companies of this battalion, leaving one to hold the post. To complete my plans, which I will not now lay before the Department Commander in detail, a Company of Cavalry would be necessary in order that, if I should take the Sioux village by surprise, as I feel confident I can, I may be enabled to follow up with telling effect the advantage I must obtain in the event of an attack. . . .[15]

However sympathetic the Department Commander may have been to Major Burt's brave proposition, it was officially ignored. The Bozeman Trail War was not an acknowledged war at all, but a police action intended to make the Trail safe for public travel. It failed miserably, for not only was the Trail closed to travel, the "police stations" themselves were subjected to constant threat and harassment. The end of all this was logical and shameful. Following the successful conference with Crows and a number of the hostiles at Fort Laramie in April, 1868, orders were issued to abandon the Bozeman Trail.[16] All the valorous sacrifice was in vain. Peace advocates on the home front were in the ascendancy, and the Indians were to regain possession of the field. Major Burt, a fighting soldier, could not have been happy about his role in this "strategic withdrawal," although he may well have been relieved to get his family away from this lonesome and sinister land.

Elizabeth Burt throws light on events which occurred during the last few weeks of Fort C. F. Smith:

> After spring was well settled, we were surprised by the arrival of a new officer and his family. It was Captain Wishart, with his wife and two children, all strangers to us, but very welcome indeed. What an unexpected pleasure to receive a lady just from the States, bringing the latest news, the new spring fashions, the most recent gossip.[17] Gossip? Yes, indeed! We all needed such a tonic to our brains, stupefied by a winter of stagnation, spent out of the world. The men were not behind the women either and the whole garrison was brightened by the new arrivals who gave us the opportunity of talking of something other than the dull routine of our small community.
>
> Such pleasant chats we four ladies had! It would have been useless, of course, to contemplate the purchase of the latest spring bonnet or a walking suit that would have been entirely out of place there, but it was a pleasure none the less to hear about such things. Fashion magazines were not the elaborate books of the present day, bringing styles so vividly before one's eyes. *Godey's Ladies Book* was the main dependence. The first Butterick pattern was originated in the early sixties and though the success of the venture was soon established, we in the Far West knew nothing about these aids to sewing. It seems difficult to realize how we mothers and housekeepers could possibly have gotten along without them. We did, nevertheless, manage to live and clothe ourselves and our little ones.
>
> As an incident of General Smith's visit to our post he ordered a mounted party of about twenty-five to be kept at Fort Smith, to be used as the Commanding Officer there might find necessary and especially in the event of trouble with the Indians. As the latter were always mounted in small

groups, mobile on fleet ponies, infantry could not pursue them effectively after the sudden dashes which was their practice to make upon us. This provided an opportunity for my sister and myself to have a horseback ride with my husband, when the horses were taken out for daily exercise. To have a canter over the plain even under armed escort was a great delight, a wonderful change from the close confinement within the stockade, which we had to undergo for so long a time.

Rumors began to reach us of the probability of Forts Smith, Kearny and Reno being abandoned and the land given back to the Indians. It scarcely seemed possible to us who realized so fully the trials and dangers through which the 18th Infantry and troops of the 2nd Cavalry had passed in leading the way for the opening of a road through this country by our Federal Government. Two years before this our officers and men had begun to build these posts under terrible trials. Many precious lives were lost. Numbers of our comrades were laid away in the little graveyard on Cemetery Hill at Fort Smith and now it seemed the country really was to be given back to the Indians.

While we waited orders which would decide our fate, beautiful days had come, making us feel life would be joyous were we but free to come and go without fear of Indians. With the approach of our son's birthday in July visions of another picnic on the banks of the Big Horn River, though not so far up the canyon, floated through my mind. In great doubt of success I broached the subject to my husband. "A picnic! On the banks of the Big Horn at this time of year!" he answered. "Impossible! The Indians might appear at any moment."

"Couldn't you post sentinels who might give warning in time for us to return safely to the post?" I timidly suggested. "We would send them a splendid luncheon and I believe it would be a treat to them as well as to us. Think of the delight of getting out of the stockade and sitting beside the beautiful rushing river; it would do us all good I am sure."

After appealing to some of the officers to add their solicitations to mine, consent was at last given to have this unique *fete champetre*. The day was perfect and everything combined to make grown people as well as children happy. The luncheon was heartily enjoyed by us all and was a great treat to the soldiers. The day passed with no Indians dashing in upon us from the canyon and we came home by the bubbling spring, bringing with us violets and other flowers, and an added delightful memory of the Big Horn River and its banks.

Soon after this orders came for the post to be abandoned and the regiment to march to Fort D. A. Russell near Cheyenne, where it would receive further orders as to its final destination. My first thought was of home and my mother from whom I had been separated for more than two years and during a time when thoughts of the dangers surrounding us worried her continuously. Now the possibility of going on to her started me packing in feverish excitement as though my small efforts might hasten the departure of the entire command.

The precise date of orders to begin the dismantling process is not available. The first definite clue is a Special Order of June 1, by which "the sale of government stores authorized by telegram from Head Qtrs Dept of the Platte, dated May 11, 1868, is hereby suspended and postponed" on the grounds of "an insufficient number of bidders." On June 5 the orders were reversed and the stores sold "at low rates." There was a plan, apparently, to transfer certain subsistence stores to new Fort Ellis, near Bozeman, Montana, but there is no record of a train from that post arriving.

Special Order No. 10 dated June 15 is illuminating: "In accordance with the suggestion made by General Smith in a communication dated June 7 and in accordance with the desire of the Department Commander for the speedy abandonment of the country by his troops, expressed in a communication dated Hd Qts Dept Platte, Omaha, Nebr., May 19, 1868 to Gen. Smith, Captain Wishart will proceed with the sale of public property at this Post." On June 16 Major Burt deplored the various reasons why the property was selling poorly. Expected bidders from Gallatin Valley had not arrived, for fear of Indians and scarcity of money. "But still it must be remembered that the most of this property is worthless to the Govt to be transported to the Railroad nor can any buyer or buyers be expected to pay large prices for articles delivered in the heart of an Indian country 300 miles from a settlement or market and that a poor one at this writing."

Counterpoint to the vivid pictures given by the wife of the post commander are a series of Special Orders by him affecting the liquidation of Fort C. F. Smith:

Special Order No. 71, June 16, 1868: Companies D and I are relieved from duty at this post, Capt. Hartz senior officer commanding. They will proceed without unnecessary delay to Phil Kearny. Captain Wishart will furnish Captain Hartz with 12 wagons to transfer the detachment. . . . Companies D and I will abandon all property that has been inspected and condemned, owing to want of transportation. . . . Captain Wishart will turn over to Burt, Wishart and Miller the horses applied for by those officers, at prices fixed by said Board. . . . Sergeant Florence S. McCarthy is relieved from charge of the mounted party. . . . The mounted party is hereby disbanded. . . .

Special Order No. 77, June 26, 1868: Mr. Reed's train now at the post . . . necessary to make a thorough scout before grazing the animals.

Special Order No. 81, July 8, 1868: Captain Shurly will take command of the detachment 2nd U. S. Cavalry now at this post, as escort to Major R. D. Clarke, Paymaster, U.S.A. . . . Wishart will take charge of the remains of the late Lieut. Albert J. Neff, 2nd U. S. Cavalry, to be delivered to the officers at Fort Laramie. . . .

Special Order No. 85, July 15, 1868: Lieutenant Matson, H Company, as escort and guard will proceed tomorrow with Mr. Reed's train now at this post to the creek west of the back-bone and camp there, for the purpose of grazing the mules of said train. . .

Special Order No. 89, July 29, 1868: Wishart hereby ordered to abandon such Commissory and Quartermaster stores for which he is responsible and which he is unable to carry owing to want of transportation. . . .[18]

Elizabeth Burt restores to history the poignant scene of Fort C. F. Smith's abandonment:

A wagon train arrived to carry away all governmental property worthy of transportation. Then each day was filled with the hurry and rush of preparation until the morning of July 29, when all was packed and the bugler sounded assembly. The soldiers fell into ranks in heavy field outfit for the 324 mile march to the railroad and civilization. The last hand baggage was loaded and the train formed.

During the few preceding days there was added to the ordinary cares of abandoning a government station the necessity of keeping a watchful eye on every Indian who filtered into the stockade. Any one of them, buck or squaw, would whisk under his or her blanket in a twinkling any small article left for the moment unguarded or which had been discarded to the trash pile. Many amusing and some serious altercations took place between various bucks, squaws and owners of property.

As a final farewell the entire Crow tribe gathered on the plain in gala attire to see the command start. One lordly looking chief seemed very proud as he walked under the protection of my discarded brown silk umbrella split in the creases. Another appeared with my stolen jet and gold cross suspended from his neck. Reluctantly he yielded to my husband's demand to restore my property.

When we were ready to enter our ambulance Kate darted after a squaw who, very portly, waddled across the parade ground. "My red shawl!" was all we heard as my sister, dashing after her, caught a red corner hanging below the blanket of the Indian. Angry protests followed while Kate and the squaw pulled in opposite directions. Gradually the shawl came safely from the latter's tight embrace. Angry mutterings of "white squaw no good, no good" came from the disappointed thief.

As my husband was now Commanding Officer, our ambulance accompanied by the hunting dogs, Jeff and Beauty, was first in the column following the men. He was entitled to ride on horseback instead of marching with his company.

Our good reliable Susie, again shod and following with the train, never wandered from the command. Again was our Brahma rooster and his family fastened in their coop and slung on the back of our baggage wagon. They never failed to go there to roost toward the night like old campaigners.

A pet elk nick-named "Monte" (for Montana), which the soldiers had captured very young and which we had had for some time as a pet, was hitched to the back of a wagon but he rebelled and refused to stir. Accordingly his lordship rode in state in the boot of our ambulance to the railroad. In camp he ran about and came regularly for his milk when he was called. We regretted afterward that we did not leave him behind, as he was old enough to graze and would soon have joined a herd. It would have been much better since eventually he died when we later took him on our long journey to my home in Ohio. He could not thrive in civilization.

To gain a parting glimpse of our last winter's home the command halted upon the crest of the hills overlooking the post from the south, while the wagons made the ascent. In spite of the trials experienced in the nine months of our sojourn there the feeling arose that if in the years to come a post might again be built upon this beautiful site we would

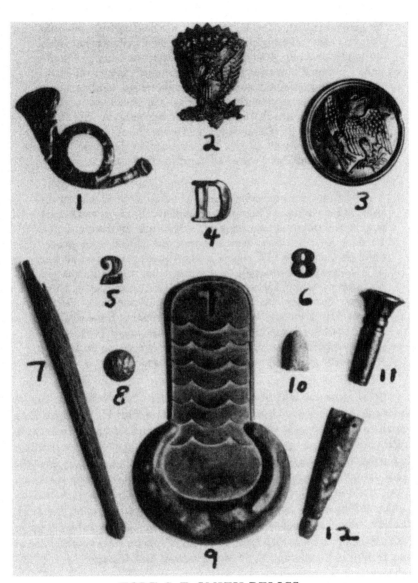

FORT C. F. SMITH RELICS.
Found by Don Rickey, 1955-1960.

1. Infantry insignia used by officers and enlisted men as a cap badge and on front of dress hat crown. (Not a bugler's insignia. Used prior to crossed-rifle insignia adopted about 1872.) Stamped brass. 2. Eagle shield arms of the U. S. worn on army dress hats to pin side of brim to crown in the 1860's. Stamped brass. 3. Eagle medallion, Infantry cartridge box shoulder sling, 1840's to about 1872. Stamped brass, lead backed. 4. Company letter worn on blouse collar and on dress hat. 5. Regimental numeral—one part of "27." Belongs in center of bugle ornament. (Used after change in regimental numbers about January 1, 1867.) 6. Regimental numeral—one part of "18." (Used until changed to the 27th.) 7. Wooden drumstick head, broken from handle. 8. Brass eagle blouse button. 9. Brass shoulder scale for enlisted man's dress uniform. 10. Minie ball, .58 calibre, for muzzle-loading Springfield rifle-musket. (Used until summer of 1867 when breech-loading model 1866, .50 calibre, rifles were issued.) 11. Brass bugle mouthpiece. 12. Brass sword (or bayonet) scabbard tip.

be glad to return, that is, provided hostile Red men be gone forever. Day and night the dread of their attacks had been hovering over us; time and again the sentinels had given the call, "Indians!", so that at the moment of departure nothing but gladness filled our hearts; still, while bidding a last farewell to this region the beauty of the scene was vividly impressed upon us. The mountains to the west, the Big Horn River sparkling in the sunlight to the north and bordered by undulating slopes of green, the post set in the grassy plain between us and the river—all combined to make a beautiful picture.

Indians innumerable taking possession of all surroundings and reveling in their untrammelled rights, gave the one touch of sadness to the moment. Although my husband had tried to impress upon them the sanctity of the little graveyard on Cemetery Hill where several graves told the sad tale of lives lost in the struggle of the past year, we could not but feel that we were leaving comrades to the hostilities of those savages. For once the Indian had won in the fight for his rights. His triumph was of short duration, however, for when the Northern Pacific Railroad was being built white men pushed into the country, killed off the game and drove the Indians gradually almost to extinction.

Soon after the withdrawal, the Bozeman Trail forts were put to the torch by the Sioux, but the adobe walls of Fort C. F. Smith long remained as its monument. In 1874 a gold prospector found these walls erect and the stone-walled cemetery intact, except that the Indians had wrenched the gate from the hinges, and hacked and defaced the headboards. "The beautiful monument in the center of the enclosure is but little defaced. Nineteen of those buried [here] were killed by Indians."[19] In April, 1876 the site was visited by Lieutenant James H. Bradley, who had escorted General Hazen on his inspection here in 1867. Another member of General Gibbon's force who paused here at that time was Lieutenant E. J. McClernand, 2nd Cavalry:

We move in the afternoon at 5:15 through the "Hayfields" of old Fort C. F. Smith, in a direction south 39° west, and after marching 3 miles, reach that place, abandoned in 1868. Most of the walls are still standing, built of adobes on stone foundations. The roofs, however, are all destroyed; the flagstaff lies across the parade ground, and from the manner in which it is cut, we supposed it was felled by Indians. The cemetery is least injured of all, and the monument erected to the late Lieutenant Sternberg and fifteen soldiers and citizens is but little defaced, the corners having been chipped away in several places with a hatchet. This monument, standing alone in the wilderness and erected by the sorrowing friends, was the last token of love for those who slept here beneath the sod, waiting long, and perhaps in vain, for the country they loved to avenge their death. . . .[20]

In 1892 after Custer Battlefield National Cemetery was established, the government transferred there the 17 identified graves and the Fort C. F. Smith memorial stone, "erected by Cos. D, E, G, H, and I, 27th U. S. Infantry, June, 1868," and with appropriate inscription to Lieutenant Sternberg, Scout Brannan, and 14 other soldiers and citizens. Scarred and chipped, it remains 100 years later a remarkable monument to that gallant garrison of which Major Burt was the last commander.[21]

The Fort C. F. Smith site itself may be reached today by following a gravel road thirty-eight miles south from Hardin, Montana. There is a simple marker erected by local citizens in 1933 on the site of the flag pole. The long-standing adobe walls have all crumbled, but the resultant rectangular mounds still clearly define the stockade. The beautiful site is today threatened by relic hunters and obliteration by the impact of construction work on the Yellowtail Dam project in nearby Big Horn Canyon. But though all physical trace may be obliterated, the embattled old fort will live on through the recorded memory of Elizabeth Burt, Finn Burnett, James Lockwood, and faded records of the United States Army.

9

Forts Russell, Sanders and Omaha, 1868-1874

Elizabeth Burt resumes her narrative of 1868:

On the march southward we found our old camps on Goose Creek and Tongue River more beautiful than ever.

Tents were pitched on emerald green grass among bushes of ripe currants, gooseberries and chokecherries. We feasted on delicious mountain trout just caught in the icy water. It was like a prolonged, delightful picnic.

One dark spot in our pleasure was the illness of Captain Wishart's little daughter. Life in camp has many attractions for strong people who feel well but it is hard for the sick. The command could not wait in the morning for the mother to be ready to start, but the Captain always had the camp fatigue party to help him and prepare his family, accompanied by an escort to follow the train. Fortunately, there was a doctor with medical supplies to care for the patient.

An excitement was caused one morning by the cry: "A bear, a bear!" Sure enough a great brown monster not far from us crashed through the thick undergrowth. We watched him eagerly from the ambulance and some horsemen followed him and fired but bruin's desire was to get away as quickly as possible. The horses could not get through the thick bushes that he easily crushed with his huge paws. Soon he disappeared from sight. That was the only glimpse I ever had of a bear in the wilds.

Upon reaching Phil Kearny we found General Smith and his command ready to start and we then became subject to his orders. My husband now marched with his company but the daily eighteen miles or more were no trial to him and his men who were accustomed to long marches. The band from which we had been separated so long gave us a delightful concert upon our arrival at Kearny. A great pleasure it was, after we had been without music for so many months. Happiness beamed on every face at the idea of going home and to the states.

The tents were now pitched according to regulations which necessitated those of the officers being placed too near to each other and to the enlisted men to insure the privacy that we ladies desired, but we knew the trip would not last long, so why be dismayed by events over which we had no control?

In our further progress southward we soon bade farewell to the land of grass and trees, trout streams and glorious mountain views. Camps were pitched on sand, among sage brush and prickly pear plants. Again we reached Crazy Woman where the Indians had attacked us last November; no fear of them disturbed us now, though the Sioux, still showing signs of discontent, were in an ugly mood and not to be trusted. They drove off stock when possible and molested trains, making it necessary to keep the camp closely guarded.

At Fort Reno there were no ladies to call on us and we did not go to the post, already prepared for abandonment. On to the railroad as quickly as possible was the cry. At Fort Fetterman we found comfortable quarters. General Wessell's dugout had been supplanted by a house that seemed quite palatial compared to those we had just left.

Here an officer was eager to buy our good Susie and the chickens—dear Susie, who had been so reliable for two years and a half and become part of our family! After having added to our health, comfort and pleasure through these many months of travel and hardship, how could we leave her? Never was there another cow so really loved. The appeals of our little son to take Susie with us were a strong inducement to refuse the officer's request but we did not know where the company would eventually be stationed and the verdict therefore was to part with her. Almost in tears the whole family visited Susie to say "Goodbye" while we steeled our hearts against the separation. She, however, ruminated all unconscious of the affection lavished upon her!

As for the chickens, our attachment was almost as fond. Not one had died nor had we raised any young as we had always been moving or anticipating a change. Each hen had her name and her own little characteristics that were remembered by us with fondness. Now we were to enter a land where an occasional ranchman was starting a home; where it was possible to purchase occasionally butter and milk.

Again we wound around the base of Laramie Peak and camped on the Chugwater where the country was green and attractive; where currants, wild grapes and buffalo berries were scattered about the camping ground.

A particularly sad feature of this, the latter part of our journey to the railroad, was that our dear friend Captain Templeton was visibly failing in health as the result of his life of exposure in the two years spent at Fort Smith. From a strong man of robust appearance, day by day his strength failed until the hollow cheeks and sunken eyes told too clearly his days were drawing to a close. Every care that was possible was given by the surgeon and many friends. Finally upon our arrival at Fort Russell, after our twenty-one days trip, he started East with a nurse but only lived to reach home.[1] So passed away another fine soldier lost in his effort to do his duty for our country.

We were welcomed at Russell by many officers and ladies of our regiment who were unknown to us. However, among those we did know, General Bradley and his bride greeted us warmly. Major Burrowes and his wife, whom we had learned to love before meeting her, were already near and dear to us. It was a great pleasure to join so many old friends.

Where we had slept in a tent a year ago a comfortable house stood. Frame quarters for a regiment had sprung up as it were, into a small village but the surroundings were destitute of any green to relieve the eye and the wind, constantly sweeping the parade ground bare, drove the garrison almost to despair with its monotony. They longed for the quiet of some sheltered eastern post.

In spite of the disadvantages of tent life which we had to put up with, and our appearance among ladies from the East dressed up in the latest fashion, we would have spent a few happy days there had not Mrs. Wishart's sweet little Jennie been lying at the point of death. The doctor's care and the help we all tried to give the little one failed and she died soon after reaching Russell. The only comfort was that the parents did not lose their baby while on the march, and could feel that everything possible had been done to save the young life.

During our nine months spent in Montana, Cheyenne had grown into quite a town with many houses, stores and churches. All things really necessary could be purchased there, but at exceedingly high prices. Corn on the cob was a great treat, especially as it was the first we had eaten for three years. Peaches and pears from California were enjoyed sparingly as eating them was like consuming gold. Luscious red watermelon too, cold and tempting, how delicious! A very great object of interest was the Union Pacific Railroad with a passenger train going east and another west every day. What a never failing delight to hear the engine's whistle and watch the train fly by! Really flying it seemed to us; but very slow time compared to that now made by the "Limited." The friendly telegraph poles made us feel we were again in "God's Country."

We were here joined by Lieutenant and Brevet Captain Shurly and his wife. He had been badly wounded at Fort Smith in an Indian fight. Covering himself with glory he won a brevet but the wound cost him his health and he was soon retired for disability.[2]

The regiment was now to be divided and scattered along the railroad. Our company was assigned to Ogallala Station.[3] What this would turn out to be I had not the most remote idea, but had the satisfaction of knowing that it was east of Cheyenne and that much nearer home.

While the railroad was being constructed, small towns, among them Ogallala, sprang up. They consisted in general of a few houses hurriedly built for the convenience of the great number of men employed. Sometimes these were used as stores where exhorbitant prices were asked; too often also, they were used for barrooms and their accompaniments. The greater number of these hamlets were abandoned as the rough element followed the advancing railroad. We had no idea therefore that Ogallala was any beautiful village and were not disappointed!

On the day of our departure for that town we drove to the station to take the evening train and for the first time in years saw a dazzling head-light, our first pilot toward civilization. The cars were new and seemed very handsome to us who had lived the very simple life for three years. Our Ex-Mormon nurse, Christina, was lost in admiration of such grandeur. We rested very little for the run to Ogallala was only a few hours. Arriving there that same night we were hurried from the train to the loneliness of the prairie with nothing in sight but the stars overhead. At length the station was discovered, the only building within reach, a tiny frame house used by the telegraph operator who kindly placed it at the disposal of the ladies.

Mrs. Shurly, my sister and I, my two children and the nurse were to be the occupants of the one sleeping room. The soldiers brought hay and laid it on the floor. Upon this we placed our wraps and on this bed tried to finish the night in sleep.

Early in the morning our fitful slumbers were disturbed by loud cries and talking. Upon peeping out of the window, what appeared to our astonished eyes but two soldiers carrying a tent pole from which was hanging a line of horrible rattlesnakes—yes, veritable rattlers that had been killed on the site where our tents were to be placed. This was on the banks of the Platte River where the high grass had to be cut before camp could be made. In doing so this terrible array of snakes had been killed. A pleasant prospect, indeed, to be camped among such poisonous reptiles!

When we were at Leavenworth the older officers who had been stationed on the frontier before the war had told us such thrilling stories of the probability of our finding snakes in our beds, or on the ridgepole of the tent, or creeping under the edge of it, that our fears were roused lest all kinds of terrible creatures would disturb our peace of mind. My husband took the precaution at that time to purchase two buffalo hair ropes long enough to lay on the ground around our tents. Snakes would not cross the hairy surface, we were told. Through several years this proved to be true in our case and we now rejoiced in their protection.

Mrs. Shurly was here introduced to camp life and it naturally gave her a very disagreeable impression of the frontier. I believe that she needed nothing further to convince her that Chicago was a more desirable home than

177

Ogallala Station, especially as her husband was soon to retire. During the days spent at Ogallala we met many officers travelling up and down the railroad—old friends and strangers. This helped to make the days pass more pleasantly and quickly but our hearts were longing to go home to our mother in Ohio. A very delightful French gentleman now appeared upon the scene, preparing for a hunt, Monsieur Pichot of Paris, who spoke English perfectly, and after my sister and I started east with the children, proved a worthwhile acquaintance for my husband. For years they kept up an interesting correspondence.[4]

When we left Ogallala, Major Burt could not go with us farther than Omaha, so there we had to say goodbye for the time being, and Kate and I and the babies took the train east. At Chicago we were detained several hours and concluded to go sightseeing. When we came to the river near the depot we waited while the bridge turned to permit a vessel to pass. A number of young girls evidently coming from school soon directed their glances toward us. From their whisperings and smiles, Kate and I soon appreciated the fact that our appearance was causing comment and we speedily retreated to the sheltering walls of the depot. At Cheyenne we had no time to replenish our wardrobes so were now wearing the same hats we had on our heads when we left Leavenworth, while our dresses and wraps were just as we appeared in them three years before.

At Fort Smith we had been in a great dilemma as to shoes. Andrew Gano and Christina were almost barefoot; moccasins would do for Fort Smith but not for the trip home. How about buckskin? Yes, a soldier shoemaker said he could use buckskin for tops and he had soles on hand. By these means he made comfortable foot-coverings; but as yellow shoes were not then worn our feet became very conspicuous. As for myself, I had to have something serviceable for the trip home. Our good friend Major Burrowes kindly came to the rescue by offering the tops of an old pair of boots. Blessed thought! The leather was soft and good. Behold the shoe-maker's successful work! A pair of comfortable shoes for me to travel in. Not with French heels! Oh no! But they did have heels.

Now you can imagine the appearance of the party in Chicago. No wonder the ladies from school stared at us. When we reached Springfield, Ohio, the next morning and had a joyous meeting, no comment was made on our appearance, but after our faces had lost some of the weather-beaten look of mountaineers and our wardrobe had been replenished, our dear mother remarked, "It was not strange that you were stared at in Chicago for you were indeed an old fashioned looking group, showing unmistakable proofs of roughing it on the frontier."

Seven happy months were spent at home in Cincinnati, Ohio. How lovely it was to be again in the land of civilization among churches, theatres, schools, fine music; meeting charming people, hearing talented men lecture, listening to the grand pipe organs, and last but not least, having access to well supplied markets. None of these privileges had been enjoyed for three years. How appreciative we were, only those can know who have been deprived of these accompaniments of civilization for a length of time. Surrounded by loved ones, amid these pleasures, time soon glided by.

Major Burt had come East on four months leave, parting from his company at Omaha Barracks, where it was quartered for the winter in new barracks, not then completed. The four months among old friends and familiar scenes, were as great a delight to him as to the rest of us.

In the early spring, he tore himself away from parents, brother, sisters and other relatives and the charms of city life, to take command of his company and return with it to Fort D. A. Russell in Wyoming. Later in the spring, the children and I bade farewell to my dear mother and all who had helped to make our visit so happy and joined my husband at Fort Russell where we found portable frame houses, that had been made in Chicago and brought west ready to put up. The west wind, coming from the mountain peaks still covered with snow, blew through our battened walls and whistled in the crevices.

Unfortunately our children fell ill with measles contracted before leaving Cincinnati. Blankets were tacked round the beds to keep off the icy blasts and the patients escaped without serious results. Fortunately we had left Christina at Omaha with her parents or we might have had another patient upon our hands. I had become convinced that the responsibility of training so young a girl to be a capable servant was not compensated by her services. She was really only another child on my hands.

In time the Quartermaster had our walls covered with tar paper and this, with wall paper, added greatly to our comfort and the homelike appearance of the house. However, after a hard snowstorm in the following winter, water began to drip from the ceilings upstairs and upon investigation it was found that snow had been blown in under the eaves and shingles of the roof. A party of soldiers dug out a large wagon load of snow before the trouble was remedied.

"Coal bills must have been heavy?" you ask. Yes indeed, making a large charge against a captain's pay. Here allow me to correct an impression too generally prevalent among civilians that an army officer's uniform even, is provided by the Government; that the food we eat is all given us. No indeed; an officer pays for all he and his family eat and wear. Our son came home from school one day in deep distress, because a boy had insulted him by saying his father helped pay taxes to buy clothes for our family. Our indignation can readily be imagined.

The two years spent at Fort Russell proved to be socially most pleasant. Our regiment had been consolidated with the 9th Infantry, with Colonel John H. King of Lookout Mountain memory, for our Colonel.[5] The admiration felt for him at that time increased into warm affection during the thirteen years succeeding our meeting at Russell.

Five companies of the 9th Infantry and five troops of the 5th Cavalry under Lieutenant Colonel Duncan formed a delightful garrison. Among others whom I remember with pleasure were General L. P. Bradley, Lieutenant Colonel 9th Infantry; Colonel Royall, Major of the 5th Cavalry;[6] Major Sam Sumner, Captain 5th Cavalry; Major Thomas Burrowes, Captain 9th Infantry; Lieutenant Colonel Devin, Captain 9th Infantry; Major Mears, Captain 9th Infantry. Among the lieutenants was Walter Schuyler, just arriving from West Point.[7] Major General Greeley, then a lieutenant, has been retired with a distinguished record not only as an arctic explorer, but as Chief Signal Officer of the Army.[8] We met for the first time at Fort Russell, Lieutenant and Mrs. Jesse M. Lee who are now among the few survivors of our old 9th Infantry.[9]

The ladies appear in memory fitted to grace the most cultured society and drawing rooms of any sphere of life. The present Senator Warren was then one of the promising young citizens of Cheyenne; a brilliant [example] of the wisdom of the advice to young men to go west and grow up with the country.

Cheyenne had grown rapidly into quite a flourishing town, supplying some of the luxuries in addition to the actual necessities of life but at prices calculated to impoverish an officer. An increase during this year in the list of supplies to be kept in the commissary, giving us a comparative abundance over that of one can of currant jelly, corn and tomatoes per month, enabled us housekeepers to supply our tables with a more appetizing variety.

Among the officers and ladies enough theatrical talent appeared to make it possible to place on the stage many very entertaining plays such as "Caste" in which my husband won laurels in the despicable character of Pop Eccles, and again as Golightly in "Lend Me Five Schillings," and others. Colonel Bartlett, Major Burt and Lieutenant Stembel were among the stars. Major Mears shone prominently as stage manager. Mrs. Royall as the Duchess, with her young daughter as the Prince, assisted by Major Burt as Ruy Gomez, made "Faint Heart Never Won Fair Lady" a brilliant success.

There was musical talent, too, among the ladies, who kindly contributed their share to the social entertainment. To hear Mrs. Bradley's rich soprano voice sing "Robin Adair" is recalled by me now as a rare delight. These diversions, in addition to the weekly hops, combined to make the long winter evenings pass in a happy social way, which without these aids, would have been drearily monotonous. Sleighing was a pastime when the cold wind would permit. The rough snow-covered ice spoiled all efforts to skate but horseback riding and driving were delightful recreations in the milder weather.

Sometimes distinguished guests would visit friends. One party of tourists to be remembered, especially, was composed of Secretary W. H. Seward and party traveling across the Continent, to sail from San Francisco for the noted trip around the world. He, with Miss Olive Risley and her father were the guests of General and Mrs. Bradley and left a most pleasing impression upon us all.

On pleasant days to drive to the station in Cheyenne, about three miles from the post, was one of our pleasures. Often in this way we had a passing glimpse of friends. A walk to hunt mushrooms was a pastime for those who were fond of them. One rare species, largest I ever saw, was gathered there; some of these were of the size of a dinner plate and possessed all the qualities and unmistakable mushroom aroma of the better known meadow mushroom. One of this large specimen sufficed to make a delicious stew.

With so many agreeable companions about us, two years passed pleasantly, when an order came in April [1871] for Major Burt's company to take station at Fort Sanders, over the divide of the mountain range. With the surprise occasioned by this unexpected order, to which was added the excitement of going back to an old home, was mingled a feeling of regret at leaving the good friends of our present post. As was our custom after years filled with an endless series of packings and unpackings, not a moment was wasted in contemplation or hesitation. The men brought the well-worn boxes from the store house and in two days all was ready to go into the wagons and start with the command across the mountains. On the third day the Major left with his company, again to march over the same road we had traveled in going to Bridger in '66. Our seven year old son, accompanying him, was driven by the cold to seek the warm folds of a buffalo robe in one of the wagon beds, and was particularly glad to reach Fort Sanders where our old friends Major and Mrs. Noyes welcomed and housed him and his father. We, the rest of the family, followed by rail. Crossing at Sherman, the highest point of the divide—even in that month, April, covered with snow and ice—we reached Fort Sanders the afternoon of the day of starting.

Early in the year 1873 a rumor reached us that our company would be ordered north to join General Stanley's expedition, escort to Chief Engineer Rosser and his assistants, who were about to survey and establish the line for the Northern Pacific Railroad.[10] The order soon came and filled me with dire forebodings. I knew it meant another summer of daily anxiety with my husband far away in the wilds where hostile Indians waited to do all possible harm. They were bitterly opposed to the building of another railroad across their hunting grounds and were determined to fight its construction. But what mattered the Indian's rights or wishes as long as the white man wanted the road!

As soon as navigation was open on the Missouri River my husband was ordered to take his company east over the Union Pacific to the river at Omaha, Nebraska and there board a steamer which was in readiness to transport several companies of different regiments north to the expedition's rendezvous. No mails would reach me with regularity. Occasionally a telegram would be received by the Commanding Officer telling of the slow progress of the boat up the treacherous and winding Missouri. A copy of this wire would be brought by an orderly to be read by the wives of the officers on the expedition. When the steamboat reached its destination at Bismarck, the troops disembarked and proceeded on their march westward, progressing from day to day as the engineers made their surveys through what was then called the "Bad Lands" of Dakota, and the desolate country of eastern Montana. This unknown land was far from a telegraph line or mail facilities.

The ever watchful Indians annoyed the command in every way possible, killing and wounding a number. No husband, whenever a mail was sent out, wrote harrowing details of these encounters. Not till the command came home did we hear of fights and hair-breadth escapes. Should a hunting party try its skill on the game of the country, I always felt my husband would be with it. His love for hunting was always enticing him into various kinds of danger with thrilling escapes. His excuse to my remonstrances was that he was always very careful, took good and trusty men with him, and that "his party could stand off any ordinary lot of stray Indians." As to the truth of his words, he now [1912] points to the fact that he is alive.

In September [1873] rumors of a return of the company reached me. Later a telegram came to the Commanding Officer in effect that we would change station to Fort Omaha and that the Captain would come back to Fort Sanders with a sufficient party of men to pack the company property. At once the work of preparation began, so as to be ready and have our household goods in condition to be handled for final packing by my husband. On his joyous arrival, bronzed and weather beaten, we made short work of the crating. Then the house had to be scrupulously cleaned to leave it in good order for the incoming family.

To be again at Headquarters with General King was a great pleasure. Omaha was a large city at that time, compared with the western towns near which our lot had lately been cast. The people were hospitable and added greatly to the sociability and gaiety of our garrison, composed of 2nd Cavalry and 9th Infantry. Most pleasantly the winter passed under favorable circumstances. Spring of 1874 came and April had ended without orders to move, as so often had been the case. All preparations were made for a pleasant summer, when one day in June, as the ambulance came from town with a number of ladies and officers aboard, a voice called to me: "Mrs. Burt, the regiment is ordered to Fort Laramie!"

10

Fort Laramie,
June, 1874 to June, 1876

Andrew and Elizabeth Burt were actors in the stirring pageant of America. They saw "the glory of the coming of the Lord," with Andrew marching in the exalted ranks of those who dedicated their lives to save the "last best hope on earth," the Federal Union. They were stationed at historic Fort Bridger on the old Mormon Trail and the overland stage route, just before the coming of the thunderous iron horse. They braved the rigors of the frontier to occupy lonely Fort C. F. Smith, establishing a Christian home amid scenes of primitive savagery. They saw the birth of Laramie City at Fort Sanders, the lusty infancy of Cheyenne near Fort D. A. Russell, and the flexing of civic muscles in the new metropolis of Omaha, Headquarters of the Department of the Platte. Major Burt helped to guard the clanking new Union Pacific Railroad and he defended surveyors for the Northern Pacific against hostile Sioux. In the decades to come he and Elizabeth would travel around the earth, witness many great events, and achieve high rank. But the historical zenith of their lives was their residence at famous old Fort Laramie during 1874-1876, when the ancient struggle with the American Indian for possession of the land reached its dramatic climax.

As time passed on the Great Plains, Fort Laramie was of venerable antiquity, ten years older than Jim Bridger's first rickety post on Black Fork, twenty years older than Omaha, already forty years old when Elizabeth Burt arrived there. It was in 1834 that William Sublette and Robert Campbell, St. Louis fur traders, erected the first fort at the junction of the Laramie and North Platte Rivers, an imposing bastioned log stockade called Fort William, and ran up the first American flag to fly over the Wyoming plains. Past here filed fur traders' caravans bound for rendezvous points in the Rocky Mountains, manned by such notables as Kit Carson and Joe Meek. In 1841 the rotting structure was replaced by an adobe-walled quadrangle, named Fort John by the American Fur Company, but known as Fort Laramie to covered wagon emigrants who then began to roll by toward Oregon. In 1847 this was a haven for the Mormon Pioneers led by Brigham Young. In 1849, the first year of the California gold rush, 25,000 emigrants swept by Fort Laramie, many of them taking time to note in their journals that the United States Army had just then purchased the old adobe fort from the fur company. None of the Forty-Niners dreamed this was the beginning of a military occupation which would endure to 1890, spanning the "pageant of the west."[1]

During the 1850's the California boom reached its crest and by 1856 an estimated 200,000 hopeful gold-seekers had passed Fort Laramie enroute to South Pass. In 1851 a great treaty council of Plains Indians was held near here, sponsored by Indian Agent Thomas Fitzpatrick and the famed missionary Father De Smet; the peace then declared was shattered in 1854 by the Grattan massacre eight miles east of the fort.[2] In 1857-1858 Fort Laramie was a supply base for an Army sent westward toward Fort Bridger to do battle with the Mormon rebels, and thereafter the old Oregon-California Trail was traversed by thousands of lumbering ox-drawn freighters. In 1859 Fort Laramie was a jumping-off place for Denver, focal point of the Colorado Gold Rush. In 1860-1862 it was a prominent station on the Pony Express, the first transcontinental telegraph, and the swift overland stage line.

DRESS PARADE AT FORT LARAMIE, 1868.
A portion of the Commanding Officer's Quarters (Old Bedlam) at right.
The Burts probably lived in one of the adjoining adobe quarters, 1874-1876.

From 1863 to 1865, when it was occupied by the energetic 11th Ohio Cavalry, Fort Laramie and its chain of sub-stations were frequently under siege by Sioux and Cheyenne Indians, and several campaigns and skirmishes were fought along the North Platte.[3] Hostilities reached a climax in 1866 with the Bozeman Trail War. In 1867-1868 when the Burts traveled to and from Fort C. F. Smith, they drove on a direct line from Cheyenne to Fort Fetterman via Laramie Peak, thus passing about forty miles to the west of Fort Laramie.

If they had visited there in 1868 they would have found a large open fort completely transformed since that June day in 1849 when Captain Sanderson's Mounted Riflemen occupied the old trading post. The adobe pile at the Laramie River bend, at the south end of the plateau, had long since vanished. Now there was a large parade ground surrounded by frame and adobe officers' quarters and enlisted men's barracks; an imposing two-story frame and brick building occupied by the commanding officer and bachelor officers, the famous "Old Bedlam"; a stone magazine and a stone guardhouse. To the north was a squat stone and adobe structure occupied by the post trader and the trader's grandiose residence. In this area also were the post office, bakery, and hospital structures, cavalry stables and quartermaster's shops and storehouses, of frame and adobe.[4]

The mountain howitzers lined up on the parade ground were for decoration, but to the north on the edge of the Laramie River stood a brand new business-like structure with ten-foot adobe walls in the shape of a rough parallelogram, and diagonally placed bastions. This was a fortified corral, designed to protect the horse herd from Indian attack. For many years Fort Laramie residents as well as travelers would be confused and conjecture that this structure was of ancient origin.[5] Cynthia Capron, a contemporary of Elizabeth Burt, c. 1876, mistakenly states that the adobe "corrall" was "built by a fur company before the post was established."[6] Even an official report of September 13, 1874, mentions "mules and horses kept at a place called the old Fort."[7] The widespread misconception about this fortification that prevailed only a few years after its construction is truly astonishing.

In June, 1874, just before Reynolds Burt was born, Major Burt and the 9th Infantry were summoned from Fort Omaha to Fort Laramie. They arrived in time to witness the advent of new lime-concrete or "grout" construction. During the summer of 1874 three imposing new concrete structures were taking form—the two-story hospital high on the old cemetery hill; a long two-story cavalry barracks, with veranda; and a post bakery. In 1875 the hospital was completed, and a new double set of concrete quarters constructed. In 1876 a new concrete guardhouse was constructed which appeared to be at an odd angle, though it was actually the only building at the fort which was properly oriented in a north-south direction. At the same time the old stone guardhouse was converted to a magazine, and the old magazine became part of a new officers quarters.[8]

Two other notable structures arose during Major Burt's time. In 1875-1876 appeared the wonder of Wyoming Territory, a United States Government-constructed iron truss bridge across the North Platte River. The girders were hauled by ox-team from Cheyenne, whose citizens rejoiced upon the completion of this glorious improvement on the Black Hills Trail. It replaced a crude and unreliable ferry-boat which had capsized frequently with fatal results.[9] Also in 1876, west of the fort proper, John S. Collins, the post trader, erected the Rustic Hotel, the fanciest establishment between Cheyenne and the roaring new gold camp at Deadwood.[10]

But Major Burt did not come to Fort Laramie to observe its architecture. The 9th Infantry came on urgent government business, just in time to participate in momentous Western events which rushed to a climax in the National Centennial Year of 1876. Elizabeth Burt was alone during much of her residence here, for her husband was long absent on three famous expeditions. In 1874, shortly after arrival, he defied Red Cloud once more and escorted the Marsh paleontological expedition to the Nebraska badlands. In 1875 he

188

Courtesy, Fort Laramie Collection

FORT LARAMIE, 1876.

escorted Professor Jenney on a scientific invasion of the Black Hills which led to the official and spine-tingling confirmation of the discovery of gold. And in 1876 he played a conspicuous role in the historic Big Horn and Yellowstone Expedition under General Crook against massed forces of hostile tribes led by Crazy Horse.

The Fort Laramie Treaty of 1868 which ended the Bozeman Trail War had merely postponed the showdown with the Sioux and Cheyenne.[11] For a few years these tribes were again able to enjoy the spacious hunting grounds between the North Platte and the Yellowstone without white encroachment. In the early 1870's their only complaints were about the Northern Pacific Railroad surveys west from Bismarck and up the Yellowstone River Valley, and the annoying insistence of the government that they keep away from their beloved North Platte. Ever since the Treaty of 1851 Fort Laramie had been a kind of tribal headquarters; and now Red Cloud resisted the scheme to set up an agency far removed from this place. In order to keep the peace, therefore, in 1871 the Indian Office set up the first Red Cloud Agency on the North Platte, near the present Nebraska-Wyoming line, only twenty-five miles east of the fort. By late 1873, however, the warriors had tamed down enough to be persuaded to move their agency to White River in the Pine Ridge country south of the Black Hills, about eighty miles northeast of Fort Laramie, near present Crawford, Nebraska. The Spotted Tail Agency was located at the same time further down the White River.[12]

The Sioux disdained the suggestion that they cultivate the land. They much preferred their ancestral custom of hunting buffalo and stealing horses, visiting the Agency only to receive generous government handouts. They also persisted in their quaint habit of collecting an occasional scalp, finding the Fort Laramie vicinity well suited to this type of operation. Here, in a region otherwise devoid of settlement, were to be found stray soldiers and a few pioneer ranchers.

In a report of February 5, 1874, to the Department of the Platte, Colonel John E. Smith, Post Commander, complained bitterly of raids on the beef herds of the outlying ranches, when the Indians were already lavishly supplied with agency beef. He deplored the wasteful practice of supplying them with flour which they scattered over the countryside, keeping only the sacks for their wardrobes. He proposed to attack all Indian parties found henceforward south of the North Platte. One week later he was obliged to report the death of Lieutenant Levi H. Robinson and Corporal Coleman of the 14th Infantry, killed near Laramie Peak by a war party suspected to be from Red Cloud Agency. As the uneasy year progressed ranch buildings were burned, and isolated cowboys and teamsters were murdered.[13]

Finally the Indians made the mistake of biting the hand that fed them. Reckless young braves wantonly killed clerk Frank Appleton in the doorway of the Red Cloud Agency office, and the terrorized agent sent a courier to Fort Laramie. Wiring the Department of the Platte for reinforcements and leaving Major Blunt in charge, General Smith marched with a strong cavalry and infantry force to White River and, much to the consternation of the Indians, proceeded to set up a permanent fortified post a short distance from the Agency. He named it Camp Robinson in honor of the recently martyred officer.[14]

In response to Smith's call for help, Colonel John King, 9th Infantry, arrived at Fort Laramie from Fort Omaha on August 18 with staff, band and Companies B, E and H. This force was later supplemented by units of the 4th Infantry and 2nd Cavalry. King assumed command at Fort Laramie, which then became headquarters for a new Black Hills District. The new district included Camp Robinson and new Camp Sheridan at Spotted Tail Agency.[15]

When marching orders reached Fort Omaha, Elizabeth Burt remembers:

> I was sitting on our front porch sheltered by a luxuriant prairie queen, then a climbing mass of beautiful pink roses. If a thunder clap from a clear sky had burst upon my ears the surprise could not have been greater. Not the faintest rumor of an intended move had been heard. We had settled down for the summer feeling secure. Then to go back west where we had just spent eight years was most astounding. I had never expected to return to that part of the world and could scarcely believe this was to be our fate; but true it was. In a few days some of the companies started. Ours was left until August, when headquarters moved.

> August 2 [1874] the stork came to our house and left me a splendid boy [Reynolds Johnston Burt]. This was before the day of trained nurses, with their strict rules as to mother and babe, but we progressed beautifully. However, it was impossible to be ready to start with Headquarters when it marched out of the post on the morning of August 12—husband, company, everybody but Captain Pease with his wife and little ones who were also left behind. Hard fate, indeed, I thought, but with Kate and a black mammy we improved and were ready in a month to take the railroad trip back to Cheyenne. There Major Burt met us with camping outfit to take us to Fort Laramie.

REYNOLDS JOHNSTON BURT.

To sleep again in a tent for three nights and travel in an ambulance seemed so natural that the journey proved an easy one. The month had been well spent by my husband in changing a forlorn set of quarters into a clean comfortable house. A frame building of one story and six rooms, with white washed walls and a stove in each room awaited us.[16]

Again we had a pleasant garrison composed of 9th Infantry and parts of 2nd Cavalry and 4th Infantry. To meet old friends helped greatly to reconcile us to the change. The ninety miles to the railroad seemed a short distance to a connecting link with the outside world, compared with those of the remote places in which we had hitherto often been stationed.

On September 16, shortly after Mrs. Burt's delayed arrival with her three children, Company H left Fort Laramie to escort a supply train going to the agencies, returning in ten days after a journey of 250 miles. On September 18 Colonel King departed on recruiting detail and command was assumed by General Luther P. Bradley, Burt's old commander at Fort C. F. Smith. As of September 30, the garrison numbered 17 officers and 455 enlisted men.[17]

With the new evidence of military strength in the Fort Laramie region, the Indians saw fit to behave for a while—around Fort Laramie. Their indignation now turned northward when they learned that their precious Black Hills were being reconnoitered by General Custer and his 7th Cavalry out of Fort Abraham Lincoln on the Missouri River. This expedition of 1200 men, 110 wagons, 60 scouts and assorted artillery, plus miners, photographers and newspapermen, did not look like an innocent outing, and it was not.[18] With irresponsible enthusiasm Custer announced the presence of gold on French Creek, the nation was electrified, and the Sioux angrily branded him a robber and a thief. In October the Sioux appeared at the Agency in a foul mood, hauled down the American flag, chopped up the flagpole, and insolently defied the small garrison that had been left at Camp Robinson.[19]

Running head on into this explosive situation, the Marsh expedition from Fort Laramie to the Nebraska badlands in the autumn of 1874 probably achieved more publicity than any fossil hunt in history. The Yale professor was no stranger to the West, having gained a great reputation as a pioneer paleontologist in a remarkable series of explorations through Wyoming, Colorado and Nebraska beginning in 1868. Armed with a letter from General Sherman, he was liberally furnished with military escort by various post commanders, and became known to puzzled Indians as "The Big Bone Chief." Army officers proved eager amateurs, so it was not surprising that in June, 1874, he received word from Colonel T. H. Stanton at Cheyenne that the area south of the Black Hills was teeming with fossils, and would he like to join a little military trip in that direction? He then declined, being busy building a new museum, but in October when the invitation was repeated he caught the next train out of New Haven.

Arriving at Fort Laramie in early November, he found a distinguished bodyguard awaiting his pleasure. This included General Bradley and Colonel Stanton, and infantry and cavalry units under Major Burt and Captain John Mix. This was an odd time, indeed, for another "scientific" expedition into this country; the idea of "bone-hunting" seemed to the Sioux like a flimsy pretext to prospect for the hated yellow gold. At Red Cloud Agency the Marsh party found over 10,000 excited savages who were practically besieging the agent and the small garrison at nearby Camp Robinson. In a touchy conference, Red Cloud and his chiefs blew hot and cold over Marsh's proposition that a Sioux delegation accompany him. They threatened the whites with a frenzied show of armed might and insulting gestures. They were feasted royally at the Professor's expense, agreed to permit the expedition to proceed, then changed their minds. Marsh gave up on diplomacy and connived with Major Burt to slip past the Indian villages after midnight while the braves were slumbering.

This was a foolhardy venture. In the White River badlands precious fossils were found in abundance, but even as the excavation work proceeded, Indian sentinels were seen on nearby buttes. There were less than 100 in the Marsh party, including soldiers, workmen and dignitaries, and they were threatened with extinction. The paleontologist was determined to gather and properly pack his rare Oligocene specimens, however, and Major Burt supposed that Red Cloud could be handled one way or another, as he had been seven years earlier on the Bozeman Trail. The gamble paid off, and the party returned to the Agency with specimens and scalps intact.

Immensely pleased with his treasures, Marsh now condescended to listen to Red Cloud's complaints of maltreatment and took with him moldy samples of the kind of provisions that were being issued. This eventually resulted in a full-dress Congressional investigation of affairs at the Agency; meanwhile, the precious remains of camels and rhinoceroses which flourished some sixty million years ago were escorted triumphantly to Fort Laramie by Major Burt's infantry.[20]

One year later Burt revisited the fossil beds while returning with Dr. Jenney from the Black Hills to Fort Laramie. The famous geol-

PROFESSOR O. C. MARSH OF YALE COLLEGE.

ogist paid tribute to the "distinguished paleontological discoveries" of Professor Marsh in this district which his labors "have rendered as famous as the Sivilik Hills of India."[21] Two years later Burt again visited the scene in company with General Crook and Lieutenant John G. Bourke, pointing out "the bones of countless thousands of fossilized monsters—tortoises, lizards and others—which will yet be made to pay heavy tribute to the museums of the world."[22]

Mrs. Burt remembers the Marsh affair:

Before the troubles with the Indians again broke out, Professor O. C. Marsh arrived at Fort Laramie from Yale College with a party of scientists to search for fossils in the "Bad Lands" several days' march north of the post. Major Burt with a detail from his company was selected by the Post Commander to go out with these scientists. Again this meant a separation for my husband and me. He, however, enjoyed being intimately associated with this noted scientist and his party of eminent men. After some weeks they returned jubilant over their success in the discovery of many fossils in a region hitherto unexplored by paleontologists.

We at the post were shown some of the specimens they had collected on the trip. One particularly interesting, was that of a camel which when living was not larger than a sheep of today. The greater part of their find had been packed in the field and shipped to the scientific school of Yale College.

Major Burt found and has kept to this day as a memento, part of the jawbone of some monstrous creature. This we have in our collection of Indian relics and other curiosities gathered in our frontier and Filipino station days.

Receiving instructions from an ornithologist of the party, Major Burt became interested in taxidermy and collecting bird skins. Afterwards on the General Stanley expedition, he was fortunate enough to collect a specimen of the Missouri skylark, at that time very rare and much sought after by collectors.

Professor Marsh was in his time one of the foremost, if not the greatest paleontologist in the world. On this expedition he unearthed several fossil remains heretofore undescribed. At that time he was having an exciting controversy with a rival scientist about a prehistoric animal which both claimed to have discovered and named. Professor Marsh called it the Brontotherium and the other named it the Gigantotherium, I believe. As my husband understood the debate, Professor Marsh's claim depended on finding a third

196

trochanter (whatever that means), on the fossil relic. Let the Major tell the story: "One morning Marsh and I went from camp on our usual exploring trip for fossils. We hadn't gone far when passing by a high cut bank, I happened to glimpse a fossil bone sticking out of that bank. I pointed it out to Marsh. The instant his eye caught the object he wheeled his horse, dismounted and rushed to what afterwards looked to me like the leg-bone of an ox. Marsh dug around the specimen awhile, then suddenly seemed to have gone crazy. He danced, swung his hat in the air and yelled, 'I've got him, I've got him.' It seemed that the Professor had found the third trochanter."

On the party's return to Fort Laramie, Professor Marsh gave us an interesting talk on his great success in this latest search for fossils in those "Bad Lands" and the vast difference between that part of the world then and what it was in the Tertiary Period.

A daily mail and telegraphic communication with Cheyenne and the world beyond were blessings. Also my husband's rank gave him better quarters than many of the other officers had, even if they consisted of only six rooms poorly constructed. With good stoves and plenty of wood we could keep comfortable in our living room at least. At night it was impossible to make the dining room and kitchen warm. Milk was found frozen solid in the pans in the morning. Jack Frost played havoc with everything. The precious sack of potatoes was covered with a buffalo robe and placed near the stove in the living room each night.

Amateur theatrical and weekly hops often occupied us. Committing parts, preparing costumes and rehearsals kept us busy and quite happy in the post. But an escort was necessary for anyone going to Fort Robinson, Nebraska, and to the agency beyond. The Indians received rations and accepted everything to be obtained from the Government but lost no opportunity to take a life or drive off a herd of cattle or stampede horses or mules when within their power, and then creep back to the agency and call themselves good Indians on ration day.

The black mammy whom we brought from Omaha, Nebraska, to be my great assistant with baby, was too slow to accomplish much more than work in the laundry, where she dragged out the washing and ironing and smoked her beloved pipe. To supplant her was impossible. If a white girl were ever brought into the post, no matter how old or ugly, she soon began to yield to the blandishments of the captivating soldiers and in a wonderfully short time entered into the bonds of matrimony.

Happily for us there were men in the company glad to exchange company work for that of cook in an officer's family, the salary added by us to his government pay per month being quite an inducement. I was fortunate enough in finding two men in our company who became apt pupils of mine in the kitchen. When needed, one or the other would come to my assistance and both proved treasures.

The winter of 1874-1875 was the coldest on record at Fort Laramie. With the mercury disappearing in the bulb at forty below zero, it is small wonder that Elizabeth Burt had her hands full keeping her children and the family potato supply from freezing solid. The post surgeon had to cope with numerous cases of pneumonia and frostbite, and Private Luby of the 4th Infantry was found dead on nearby Deer Creek, a bullet in his skull, and stiff as marble. A company of cavalry sent from Camp Robinson to chase white men out of the Black Hills was caught in an arctic blizzard and there was wholesale amputation of frozen ears, fingers and toes. During this inclement season Major Burt was kept busy in a temporary assignment as Post Quartermaster. It does not appear, however, that he was excused thereby from commanding his company on a frigid escort trip to the agencies in mid-February.[23] Meanwhile, backwoods politics were brewing.

On January 2 Bradley had reported to his superiors that Red Cloud and Spotted Tail had sent word "by a white man married to a relative of the former" that they desired to visit Washington to negotiate a sale of the Black Hills country. Washington was glad to comply and in late March, as soon as the countryside had thawed out a bit, the noted chiefs and a colorful entourage passed through Fort Laramie enroute to Cheyenne where they boarded the Union Pacific Railroad for the big village on the Potomac.

Spring saw the arrival of the new Argonauts. A few gaunt and hungry "sooners" arrived from the Black Hills with leather sacks of genuine gold dust. And hundreds of assorted citizens from out of Cheyenne began to congregate on the Laramie River, impatient for the government to make a settlement with the Indians so they could get on with their gold rush. Many chose to defy both the government and the Indians, slipped across the North Platte River by swimming or bribing the ferryman and began to infiltrate the Hills. Now conscientious about its treaty obligations, as it had not been in 1874, the government ordered the War Department to hold the miners at bay, and to arrest those found in forbidden Sioux territory. On March 23, Company M, 2nd Cavalry, was ordered to the Hills "to eject a party of miners reported encamped near Harney's Peak since December 24."

CHIEF RED CLOUD.

199

This was the Gordon party from Sioux City, which had erected a stockade on French Creek and defied the whole world. Thenceforward Fort Laramie, Fort Russell and Fort Randall post records bristle with orders to cavalry units to intercept and arrest overanxious miners.[24] Although most of them evaded the military net, civilian prisoners soon jammed the Fort Laramie guardhouse. This was the status of affairs in May, 1875 when Professor Jenney's scholarly figure appeared on the horizon.

Rumors of Black Hills gold had circulated for years. The report of the treaty-breaking Custer expedition of 1874, lacking scientific confirmation, was still only a high-class rumor. The Fort Laramie Treaty of 1868 held the Black Hills to be the exclusive hunting grounds of the Sioux and Northern Cheyenne; but if the gold was real, nothing would keep the citizens away. The Hills had to be purchased or there would be war; but before the government paid good money for this rock outcrop, it would be wise to see what it was buying. President Grant ordered the Secretary of Interior to investigate.

Upon advice of Major J. W. Powell of the Geological Survey, Walter P. Jenney of the New York School of Mines was appointed geologist in charge. Arriving at Cheyenne on April 25, 1875 he assembled an imposing staff of geologists, topographers, astronomers and seasoned prospectors. The party reached Fort Laramie on May 20 and there all arrangements were consummated for transportation and military escort. The impressive cavalcade of 400 men and 75 wagons, big enough to give the Indians fresh cause for alarm, was commanded by Lieutenant Colonel Richard I. Dodge and included eight companies of troops: C and H, 9th Infantry (Munson and Burt); C and F, 2nd Cavalry; A, H, I and K, 3rd Cavalry. The start was delayed while Captain Horace P. Tuttle of Cambridge Observatory made celestial observations for the latitude and longitude of the Fort Laramie flagstaff. On May 25 the expedition, which had been congregating on the far bank of the North Platte, struck northeast to Rawhide Creek, up that creek to Rawhide Butte, thence north across the headwaters of the Niobrara to Old Woman Fork and Cheyenne River, and entered the Hills by the east fork of the Beaver on June 3.

A permanent camp was established on French Creek near the Gordon party stockade. While Jenney concentrated on an examination of mineral resources, his assistant, Mr. Newton, aided by Captain Tuttle, and the topographer, Dr. Valentine T. McGillicuddy, undertook to make a geographic map of the region.[25] The official Newton-Jenney report summarizes the project.

As the work of the survey progressed northward, the main body of the escort of troops was transferred from one

PROFESSOR WALTER P. JENNEY.

base of supplies to another so as to keep up with the course of the explorations. In this manner, with scarcely a day's remission from work, the survey continued until the entire area of the Black Hills between the forks of the Cheyenne had been mapped and its geology and mineral resources determined as fully as the rapid progress would permit. Having passed over the entire country and accomplished the object of the expedition, the various parties assembled on the Cheyenne at the mouth of Rapid Creek, and began the march homeward, reaching Fort Laramie, via White River and the agencies of Spotted Tail and Red Cloud, on the 14th of October, after an absence of four months and twenty days.[26]

Elizabeth Burt's commentary on the Jenney expedition is limited to the unfortunate accident which befell her eleven year old son Andrew, struck by lightning:

When my husband was ready to leave, our eleven year old son, Andrew, begged so hard to accompany his father that I at last consented that he should have this novel experience. I was assured that he would be perfectly safe. From Indians, yes, but alas! We did not consider the thunder storms that are so violent in the Black Hills. When a terrific rain came one day, accompanied by violent thunder and lightning, our son left his horse and sought shelter with some of the soldiers under a large tree. A gun was resting against its trunk, a lightning bolt struck the tree and running down the trunk was deflected when it met the rifle barrel. The deflected bolt killed the horse standing near. A portion of the electricity hit our boy, making a mark on his cheek, and evidently passed through his body and out through the side of his shoe, leaving a hole as large as a dime in the latter. His father was soon beside him with the Doctor. They worked with our son over an hour before restoring consciousness. It was a struggle for the child's life. God was good to us and spared our dear boy but with one eye paralyzed beyond redemption. Oh, that Andrew had stayed at home with me, has been my life long cry.

Although all of the soldiers were stunned, the great force of the current was spent on the horse and gun (which latter was shattered to bits), otherwise the results would have been much more fearful.

There is no mention of this, of course, in official records, but the records do disclose that the weather that spring was of unprecedented violence with rain on sixty-seven consecutive days, severe thunderstorms, and hailstones so vicious that "a gold pan was stove full of holes." On June 2 it snowed for several hours at Fort Laramie.[27] It was as if the elements conspired with the Sioux to defy the invading white man.

Professor Jenney reports that, on the outward journey, in the bluffs adjoining Rawhide Butte, a complete jaw and numerous other fragments of *Oreodon,* a pig-like animal, were found by "Captain Burt," who had been well coached in this department by Professor Marsh.[28]

The Burt and Munson companies of the 9th Infantry played a stalwart role in Jenney's momentous first discovery of "gold in paying quantities" in the valley of Spring Creek, "near where the immense quartz formation known as Mammoth ledge crosses the gulch," about twenty-five miles northeast of Harney Peak. On June 29 prospector Thomas Mallory discovered a line of large "boulders" forming a dam or riffle in the stream; these were embedded in blue gravelly clay and a compact gravel, full of small garnet crystals, "rich in coarse gold." After prospecting this area for several days, Jenney realized that his small force of miners unassisted could not properly examine the gravel deposits along this section. Accordingly, on July 14 he summoned to this locality the 9th Infantry, all hands being drafted. The pay-off discovery, in which Major Andrew S. Burt figured as "acting foreman," is given in the official report:

> In order to test the richness of the gold deposits in the bed of the creek, it was necessary to turn the water out of its present channel. With the assistance of the soldiers a dam was built across the stream above the point of discovery and the water of the creek conveyed by a ditch 1,000 feet in length across a bend and returned to the channel below the place we wished to test, leaving comparatively free from water about 400 yards of the former bed of the stream. Before reporting definitely on the richness of the new discovery I wished to test on a practical scale the gravel from the different bars, and for this purpose constructed from rough boards, whip-sawed from the native pine, a small box sluice, 10 to 12 inches in width, formed of two boxes 14 feet in length. This work had consumed more than a week. In the meantime the soldiers who were not employed in assisting me had been hard at work in the bed of the creek above the riffle washing the clay-gravel in pans and rockers with quite remunerative results. Several ragged and irregular pieces of gold with oxide of iron adhering in the cavities had been found, weighing from ¾ pennyweight to 1½ pennyweight and worth from 75 cents to a dollar and a half. From 5 to15 cents to the pan

was usually obtained from the pay streak, and the soldiers sometimes washed out nearly a dollar's worth of gold in three or four hours' work with a pan.[2b]

News of the discovery spread like wildfire among the prospectors then illegally in the Hills, causing the first of many stampedes. Nearly 200 miners came over from French Creek, staked out claims, established a mining district, and "rendered great assistance" in prospecting the region. On July 17 Jenney sent a telegram announcing his find of "the richest deposits yet found in the Hills." The gold rush was now official.

In addition to his mineralogical research, Dr. Jenney found time to explore the furthest reaches of the Black Hills, including the great geological oddity Bear Lodge, now called Devils Tower. It is not known if Major Burt and the infantry units saw this phenomenon, but probably not, for there were other things to be done besides exploring and panning gold. The Fort Laramie records disclose that Captains Burt and Munson twice, in June and July, escorted the supply train from the Hills to the fort, in each case having a layover at the fort of a week or more. The injured Andrew Burt was probably brought back to the fort in June. It is a fair guess that the doctor who aided in his resuscitation was the expedition's chief medical officer, Surgeon George P. Jagnette, subsequently stationed at Fort Sanders.[30]

The colorful Dr. McGillicuddy offers sidelights on the Jenney interlude. He claims to have been the first white man to climb Harney Peak, which would be an impossible thing to prove. What is more plausible, he explains how Jose Merrivale, the official Fort Laramie guide, managed to lose the trail into the Hills. The real hero, it seems, was the guide Jenney put on the Interior Department payroll, a mountaineer named California Joe, who is credited with keeping the expedition out of trouble with the Indians. And he tells us that one Jane Dalton, alias Calamity Jane, a dubious Fort Laramie character, went along on this trip disguised as a cavalry trooper. Being discovered and brought before Colonel Dodge, she was ordered to drop out of the column, which she did—until the wagons rolled by. Hiding herself in the cargo, she later turned up in the Hills and made herself so useful as a hunter and forager that no further action was taken against her.[31] Major Burt would run into Calamity Jane again, one fateful year later.

While the Jenney expedition was confirming that gold in the Black Hills was in plentiful supply, and after Red Cloud and Spotted Tail returned with the good will assurances of Great White Father

Grant, preparations got under way for the treaty council which, it was hoped, would peacefully settle the Black Hills problem. In August, a sub-committee, including J. S. Collins, the Fort Laramie post trader, visited the Jenney party to get the gold picture first-hand, finding hundreds of happy prospectors turning up the yellow metal in exhilarating quantities. On September 4 the full commission reached Red Cloud Agency, led by Senator W. B. Allison and General Alfred Terry. They were greeted by a raging, quarreling horde of Indians in war regalia, and the futility of reaching any kind of a reasonable agreement soon became apparent. Before the noisy conference was over, on September 23, it seemed a distinct possibility that the august commissioners, protectected only by Captain Egan's small troop of cavalry, would be slaughtered en masse by the 7,000 milling, shouting savages.[32]

At this time Andrew Burt obtained the permission of Colonel Dodge to take leave and visit Red Cloud Agency to witness the conference proceedings. The story of his adventurous journey is told in elaborate literary detail by a companion, an anonymous journalist, "The Casual Observer," writing serially in *The New Haven Morning News*, June 13 and 20, 1891. This was but a few months after the Wounded Knee massacre at Pine Ridge, when public attention had been focused again upon the South Dakota Badlands.

It was in 1875 that I crossed this region under peculiar circumstances, in close proximity to the scene of the late conflicts between the hostile Sioux and the troops under Generals Miles and Brooke.

I was then but little more than of legal age and in the language of a military friend of mine, "as green a specimen of the tenderfoot as ever ventured beyond the outposts of civilized settlements." I am free to confess that the description is accurate and that it took six good months of rough life and hobnobbing with danger in various forms to take at least a part of that greenness out of me. . . .

Lieutenant-Colonel Burt (then captain and brevet-major) and myself were companions on one of the most risky rides, perhaps ever undertaken in the Indian country, one that neither of us will ever forget, though we have since been in other tight places, he in a hundred times as many as I . . . Everybody who has ever campaigned with Andy Burt has but one word to say of him. He is as true as steel, a fast friend, and "clear grit." Burt commanded a model infantry company in the Ninth Regiment, was indefatigable as an explorer and knew more Indian languages and dialects than any other man whom I have ever met.

205

Four months of gold hunting in the Black Hills, with the license of Uncle Sam, with its attendant incidents of adventure, camping in the veriest natural paradise on earth, fishing in the clearest and most prolific streams and hunting the fattest deer and antelope and the most pugnacious cinnamon and brown bear, tracing our way at times through a trackless wilderness never before trodden by the foot of white man, climbing dizzy heights and threading our way along the edge of awful canyons, all this had lost something in its novel zest towards the latter part of August. . . . Vast preparations were on foot for the Grand Council to be held at Red Cloud Agency in September. . . . Naturally burning with curiosity to be present at so great an event I was both surprised and delighted on August 31st when a courier, who had ridden 180 miles in four days from Fort Laramie to Camp Terry, handed me a dispatch from Mr. Bennett of the *Herald* ordering me to proceed to Red Cloud Agency and report the doings of the Great Council. . . . We were fully 200 miles from Red Cloud Agency by the route I would have to follow. There was no detachment that I knew of going in that direction. But there was a troop of soldiers at French's Creek near the Miner's stockade, under Captain Pollock. This was about 90 miles distant from Camp Terry. I resolved to make that distance, alone if necessary but to make it somehow, and to trust to fortune to enable me to go further. . . .

To say that I was warmly welcomed at Captain Pollock's camp and that my arrival and lonely ride created some wonder is to put it mildly. The Captain treated us with knightly hospitality. Upon making known my intention of proceeding at once to Red Cloud Agency, I very gladly learned that Major Andrew S. Burt of the 9th Infantry proposed to do the same, having obtained a seven days' leave of absence. Captain Pollock gave us all the assistance in his power. Sergeant Bolling, Corporal Fisher and Private Robinson had been detailed to go to Fort Robinson, accompanied by a dispatch bearer named Williams, and they were ordered to start immediately. Our party was thus composed of six persons. Williams, who knew the country, was to act as guide.

Reports from the Red Cloud and Spotted Tail Agencies indicated that the Great Council might last only four or five days. If this proved true it might already have ended before we reached our destination, and in that case, if the disposition of the Indians turned out to be as ugly as rumor had represented it to be, there was every probability that we would meet with some difficulty in completing our journey in safety. We knew that the country was already crossed and checkered in every direction by fresh Indian trails leading towards the agencies and that many semi-hostile Indians had gathered in their vicinity, even though they had no intention of participating in the deliberations of the council, hoping, undoubtedly, that the outcome of it would be a general defiance of the white authority. Sitting Bull and Crazy Horse, then more vaguely known than they afterwards came to be, had sent emissaries down from the North to do what they could by their disturbing influence to prevent the cession to the Great Father of the favorite hunting ground of the Plains tribes, the Black Hills. The feeling of the Sioux and Cheyennes at that time was such that it would have taken but a little incitement to cause the whole of both nations to go on the war path.

We counted the risk somewhat soberly therefore as we set out from Captain Pollock's camp. Two sturdy pack mules carried all our baggage. We moved in the direction of Buffalo Gap, the natural gateway to the Hills, by the trail which General Crook had made in August, with his large escort, when returning to Omaha. . . . [there follows a detailed account of travel through the tortuous badlands]. . . . We saw traces enough of tepee poles to account for the movement of at least 300 lodges to the southward. . . . We noticed also that there were some cross trails, and this fact made us apprehensive that the council had already broken up, that the Indians were dispersing and that our long ride was bootless except, perhaps, for the signal pleasure of being scalped. For if the council was broken up there was every possibility that the Indians were not in the best of humor, and that if we chanced to meet any stray party of them they would proceed to annihilate us with a peculiar zest.

Just at dusk we sighted an enormous Indian village on the right bank of White River and heard discordant barking of its hundreds of irresponsible curs which had sensed our approach. Our coming was the signal for the hasty herding of all the Indian ponies which had dotted the neighboring hills, a movement which in itself struck us as suspicious. However, we did not betray any fear. We bivouacked in a convenient spot about a mile away from the village. We built our fire and ate our supper, just as if there was nothing in our surroundings which suggested apprehension. One of the party—our dispatch bearer—became moon-blind because of the white glare of the Bad Lands. We had to wait on him as if he were a child. We lay down to sleep on the grass without undressing ourselves, with our arms beside us. We had no canvas over us—nothing to cover us save our blankets and buffalo robes.

It was before I had got fairly asleep the first time that Burt in his characteristic vein thought to play a practical joke upon me by getting up a false alarm. He sent one of the men over to a clump of bushes which was close at hand and bade him move stealthily about. A few minutes later he laid his hand on my shoulder and assured me that he thought there were Indians lurking near us. He said it would be a good idea to be ready and made a show of loading his rifle. The admonition was not needed. I had lain down with a cartridge in my gun. I was at first deceived by his manner and I remember that I advanced my gun with some eagerness at full cock in the direction of the luring figure. It did not occur to me that a single shot at such a time with an Indian village so near at hand would be sure to create a devilish disturbance and might cause our destruction. But it did occur to Burt, and now that I look back at it, it seems to me decidedly ludicrous to think of the Major's sudden anxiety that I should remove the cartridge from my rifle at the same time that he was endeavoring to ascertain whether I would scare or not at his bidding. That was the only hoax that was attempted, but two or three times in the night the whole party suddenly found themselves on the alert on hearing some unusual sounds in the direction of the village. The dogs howled vociferously in the spectral hours before the dawn.

In the morning Burt was able to identify the village by certain marks on the tepees which we could distinguish through a fieldglass. It was the village of the Brule band and Spotted Tail's own lodge, of lordly dimensions, was in the midst of it. An hour afterwards I was seated beneath its buckskin folds, talking to the youngest of Zintigaliska's four wives, while her hand-maiden was helping to complete her toilet. Spotted Tail himself had ridden away that morning to Shadron Creek, where many lodges of the Sioux had congregated, as I was informed by Crazy-in-the-Lodge, the great chief's confidential man, in readiness for the council. There was, therefore, no immediate danger of the outbreak, and we resumed our journey toward Red Cloud Agency with hearts a good deal lightened.[33]

With the failure of the treaty council, miners flocked to the Hills in uncontrollable numbers, and the hard-pressed Army officers, whose civilian prisoners were all promptly released by civil authority anyhow, gave up any pretense of enforcing exclusion. In November the President and his cabinet agreed that it would now be necessary to compel the Indians to agree to a sale of the Black Hills, and that a drastic step would be necessary to prevent a massacre of the adventurous citizens. Citing instances of their misdeeds, the President issued a proclamation ordering all Indians to be at the various Sioux agencies by January 31, 1876, or face military action. The Indian office dutifully sent messages to all known bands, but these were received in winter camp too late to make compliance with the deadline possible. In any event, discounting the threat, Crazy Horse, Sitting Bull and other proud Sioux had no intention of meekly turning themselves in. On the other hand the Army, which had fretfully played second fiddle to the peace advocates of the Indian Office since the Bozeman Trail fiasco, was now given its long-awaited chance to settle old scores. Two things would soon conspire, however, to sour the sweet smell of victory—the surprising strength of the Sioux and Cheyenne horde, operating on interior lines, and the treachery of the Northern Plains. Instead of a frolic the Army found it had its toughest assignment since the Civil War.

General George S. Crook of the Department of the Platte, conqueror of the Southwestern tribes, led the initial assault. He decided to deliver a swift "one-two punch," and quickly organized a winter campaign. Late in February he met Colonel J. J. Reynolds at Fort Laramie, then both proceeded to Fort Fetterman, leaving that point March 1 with ten companies of cavalry and two of infantry. Crook parked his wagons and his infantry at the old Fort Reno site, then pushed on through extreme cold and snow on a circuitous route to Powder River. Colonel Reynolds led six companies of cavalry to attack a Sioux-Cheyenne village of over 100 lodges, capturing the pony herd and blowing up the tepees. Making a spirited comeback, the Indians recovered most of their ponies. Lacking provisions, Crook had to abandon further efforts and withdraw. He and Reynolds paused on March 31 at Fort Laramie, en route to Cheyenne.

Mrs. Burt's version of the Reynolds campaign is illuminating:

It was not surprising that the harmony of our pleasant garrison life received a dreadful shock when a winter campaign was announced. Fortunately for us "Infantry" wives, the expedition was to be composed of cavalry with only two companies of Infantry. General J. J. Reynolds was to be in command under General George Crook. Fort Laramie, Wyoming, was designated as the place of rendezvous for the various arms of the service ordered to take part in this campaign. The morning the column started it was bitter cold with snow on the ground and my heart ached for General Reynolds braving the winter elements on this march planned to surprise the Indians. His gray hairs proclaimed that such hardships were better suited to a younger man. The appeal to my sympathy would have been vastly greater had I the

GENERAL GEORGE CROOK.

remotest idea of the bitter trials awaiting each member of that expedition. To say the ground was covered with frozen snow, conveys an imperfect idea of what was endured by those officers and men. The snow had thawed and then frozen, making it slippery, dangerous and very fatiguing for marching soldiers and animals. Reaching Fort Fetterman they traveled north from there towards the Yellowstone River. The thermometer was always below zero and sometimes went thirty or forty degrees farther down. Many hands and feet were frozen.

Part of the time the command was ordered by General Crook to leave all tentage behind and push on with only one buffalo robe and the clothing worn for covering. Picture night after night of such intense cold when each man rolled in one robe tried to sleep on the ground with no tent over him! It is but justice to say that General Crook allowed himself or officers no comfort denied the enlisted men, so he and General Reynolds bore their full share of the hardships of that terrible expedition.

The capture and destruction of one large Cheyenne village ended this remarkable campaign, typical of the varied and strenuous life and exposure to which our army was subject in Indian warfare.

The absence from the post of the Infantry and Cavalry officers on the expedition made a great vacancy in our social life. However, there were enough left to keep the gaieties and amusements going in the post to a certain extent. As was the practice in those old days on the distant frontier, many miles from towns or cities, theatricals were very much resorted to and with considerable dramatic success. I recall particularly Captain Butler Price (now retired Brigadier General), and his wife as brilliant stars in the play of "Cricket on the Hearth." Of course I recall Major Burt's successes on the stage for he was a star, at least I thought so. His persistent study at home of parts for which he was cast, to be "word perfect," as he called it, and I hearing him rehearse, made me also letter perfect in the characters which he played. Among a number of his pronounced successes were "Major DeBoots" in "Everybody's Friend," and "DeVarville" in "Camille."

Of course it was very quiet for those wives left in the Post whose husbands were absent, but most of them were kept busy with children and household duties.

In late March Major Burt was given the unenviable assignment of conducting a soldier to the Government Insane Asylum in Washington. In April there was further excitement when Corporal McKinzie of the 9th Infantry drowned in a premature swim in Laramie River,[34] the Metz family was massacred by Indians at Red Canyon, and the body of H. E. "Stuttering" Brown, official of the new Black Hills stage line, was returned from Hat Creek to the fort. It was generally believed that the fatal gunshot wound in his abdomen was the handiwork of an outlaw named Persimmon Bill.[35]

By this time there was a booming traffic on the Cheyenne-Deadwood road composed of miners, gamblers, gunmen, dancehall girls and just plain honest citizens, all readed for the new Eldorado. White renegades or "road agents" as well as Indians preyed upon travelers and stage coaches often carrying gold shipments. The commanding officer at the fort received frequent calls for help to pursue the culprits or to send an ambulance for victims. In May, upon the request of the stage company, Company F, 9th Infantry and Captain Egan's Company K, 2nd Cavalry were ordered to patrol the road between Fort Laramie and Custer City.[36]

11

The Big Horn and Yellowstone Expedition, 1876

In the spring of 1876 [Elizabeth Burt writes] a startling order was received directing that every available man
be prepared for field service; the post was to be stripped of
every soldier not absolutely necessary for its protection.
Other commands were to combine with this one, all under
General Crook, to make a summer campaign against Chief
Sitting Bull, one of the head chiefs of the Sioux. This gave
us wives ample cause for sorrow as the Indians were in a very
angry mood and were determined to make a combined effort
to drive the whites from their lands. We wives who were left
behind knew the inevitable danger to all in the field. With
aching hearts we watched the soldiers march away while the

band played, "The Girl I Left Behind Me." So many times have I listened to that mournful tune played when a command marches out of garrison to take the field. This time we knew so well there was to be fighting to the death.[1]

The indecisive Reynolds campaign gave impetus to a grand military scheme to have Crook, Gibbon and Terry converge upon the Sioux stronghold on Powder River. Crook bided his time, so that grass would grow long enough to support his animals on a long field campaign. The point of concentration was to be Fort Fetterman, and the date set as early as practicable after the first of May. It would be closer to June 1 before all of the scattered companies would be assembled and the famous march of the Big Horn and Yellowstone Expedition would get under way.

Troops from Fort Russell and Laramie reached Fetterman by the Platte River route. Those from Fort Bridger and other posts along the Union Pacific Railroad went north from Medicine Bow by a road which had been blazed in part by Major Burt in 1867.

General Crook, with Colonel Stanton and Lieutenant Bourke, paused briefly at Fort Laramie enroute to Red Cloud Agency in an effort to induce peaceful Sioux to join his ranks and thus divide the enemy. He failed in this, being bitterly opposed by both Red Cloud and the Indian agent. Not only this, but in returning to Fort Laramie on May 17 he and his escort narrowly escaped ambush and destruction by a war party, which then wreaked its vengeance on a lone mail-carrier. On the 18th he proceeded to Fetterman. On the 22nd three companies of the 9th Infantry marched for Fetterman: "C" under Captain Sam Munson and Lieutenant T. H. Capron; "H" under Captain (Brevet-Major) A. S. Burt and Lieutenant E. B. Robertson, and "G" under Captain T. B. Burrowes (another Fort C. F. Smith veteran) and Lieutenant W. L. Carpenter. The following day there arrived at Fort Laramie the main cavalry column from Fort Russell under Colonel William B. Royall. They crossed the new bridge and camped on the prairie opposite the fort to dry out after a soaking on the Chugwater. On the 24th they marched up the north bank of the Platte to a point opposite Fort Fetterman, thus saving themselves the nightmare of a river crossing at that point. Here Crook had rigged up a crude cable ferry, but the river was full and the current had the velocity of a mill-race. In moving the large mass of his other men and equipment to the north bank, there were several accidental spills and drownings as the boat swamped, the cable snapped and the ferrymen gave out under the severe strain.[2]

CAMP OF GENERAL CROOK'S COMMAND NEAR
FORT FETTERMAN, 1876.

By the 27th the last trooper and teamster arrived in camp, and
on the 28th General Crook formally assumed command. Colonel
Royall was given the fifteen companies of cavalry. In the absence of
General Bradley, who was now back in Philadelphia on recruiting
service, the three companies of the 9th Infantry were commanded by
Major Burt. These, along with two companies of the 4th Infantry,
were organized as a battalion under Colonel Alexander Chambers. On
May 29 the column pointed north, a cavalcade of over 1200 men, 120
six-mule wagons, pack mules, stretching out over four miles. Crook
and his staff led the way. A puff of dust marked the line of march of
the infantry battalion. Then followed the serpentine white-topped
wagon train, and finally the cavalry, stirring up great clouds of dust,
the sun glinting from carbines and bridles. "We used to joke about
the infantry," wrote war correspondent Finerty, "but, before the campaign was over, we recognized that man is a hardier animal than the
horse, and that 'shank's mare' is the very best kind of a charger."[3]

Major Burt was now traversing the same Bozeman Trail over
which he escorted his little family in 1867 and it was still infested
with Indians. On June 1, writes Capron, "Burt, who was out hunting,
stated that he found a fresh trail of a small party of Indians, about
fifteen in number."[4] On June 2, after a miserable snowstorm and
freezing winds, the column arrived at the ruins of Fort Reno. From
here scouts Grouard, Louis Richaud and Baptiste Pourier were sent

ahead to see what had become of promised Crow allies. At Clear Creek reinforcements appeared in the form of sixty-five miners who were en-route from the Black Hills to Montana. On June 5 the column reached the ruins of Fort Phil Kearny, killed six stray buffalo, and wondered at the glory of the Bighorn Mountains. On June 7 Private Tierney of the 3rd Cavalry, killed by the accidental discharge of his own revolver, was buried, and Crook, a nature lover, rejoiced in finding the nest and eggs of "the Missouri skylark." On June 9 the column, comfortably encamped on Tongue River, received the first Sioux and Cheyenne "calling cards." A rain of bullets ripped through tents, stove-pipes and tailboards, and inflicted a few minor casualties. Major Anson Mills, Burt's old commander at Fort Bridger, was sent with cavalry to charge and clear the bluffs of the enemy, while Burt, Munson and Burrowes were ordered out with rifles to hold the bluffs until after sundown. Writes Capron, "Companies C, G and H were soon formed and counted off by fours, as if for drill or dress parade, and marched to the support of the pickets on the hills. As they marched along in good style and until they took a position in the hills, the Indians kept up a strong fire upon them, but for some reason no one was hit."[5] One reason, doubtless, was the notably poor quality of the Indian marksmanship.

Major Burt, it may be assumed, performed his assignment with grim determination in view of the fact that his white horse, which had a fine reputation as the swiftest racer in the outfit, was among the animals killed by the Sioux fusillade.[6]

After this affair the command moved to Goose Creek, on the flats now occupied by Sheridan, Wyoming, and settled down to await the Crow allies. Bear-hunting, trout-fishing, card games, foot-races and prospecting for gold helped to while away the time of most, but Burt and Carpenter had a special hobby which they were able to indulge freely in this virgin land, that is, "their search for rare birds and butterflies." General Crook frequently joined the captains in this innocent pursuit. Some excitement resulted from the occasional discovery of an immense rattlesnake coiled up in a bed-roll. And once more Calamity Jane, "as rough and burly as any of her mess-mates," was detected among the mule-skinning fraternity, placed under arrest and sent packing back to Fort Laramie with the next wagon train. It is doubtful that her sex would have been discovered had not the wagon master noted that the language she used in addressing the animals was not up to the usual standards of vituperative eloquence![7]

On June 14 the scouts returned with one of the Crow chiefs and news that they had found a Crow village way up at the Fort C. F.

Smith ruins, but that these Indians were reluctant to become embroiled in the Sioux war. However, their main camp was now not far distant and they might yet be induced to come in. Crook thereupon sent the old chief back with Louis Richaud and Major Burt, who was known to enjoy the friendship and confidence of the Crows from his service among them eight years before. This mission was an entire success. That very evening, writes Bourke, Burt " was with us again, this time riding at the head of a long retinue of savage retainers, whose grotesque headdresses, variegated garments, wild little ponies, and war-like accoutrements made a quaint and curious spectacle."[8] The new-comers, numbering about 175 including old friends Medicine Crow and Good Heart, proceeded to bivouac in the middle of the camp and bask in the admiration of the soldiers. They were well supplied with ponies, breech-loaders, lances, medicine poles and murderous bladed war clubs.

No sooner were the Crows settled than a contingent of Shoshones, resplendent in fantastic adornment, arrived with three white men to swell the ranks of the allies. A grand council of Indians and soldiers was followed by a night-long orgy of Indian dancing, wild yells and the beating of tom-toms. The hideous noise kept the troopers awake and the beef cattle herd broke madly for the hills.

Crook now ordered each man to prepare for invasion of the Sioux stronghold on the Rosebud by stripping down to four days rations of hard bread, coffee and bacon, 100 rounds of ammunition and one blanket. The wagons would be left behind in a defensible position in the care of Captain Furey. June 15 the furious preparations were high-lighted by one of the strangest spectacles in the whole history of Indian warfare, the conversion of the infantry to a cavalry unit— mounted on mules. Upon Crook's order, Colonel Chambers, Major Burt and Captain Luhn, who were all expert horsemen as well as crack infantrymen, went through the ordeal of acquainting some 200 obstinate animals and a like number of unhappy foot soldiers with the saddle. Bourke chuckled that "the first hour's experience with the reluctant Rosinantes equalled the best exhibition ever given by Barnum."[9] Frank Grouard related that he never had so much fun in his life, to behold the "walk-a-heaps," as the Indians called them, getting their riding lesson. "The valley for a mile in every direction was filled with balky mules, frightened infantrymen, broken saddles and applauding spectators."[10] Burt himself reports soberly: "On the 15th I was ordered to receive from Capt. Fleury Q. M. necessary number of mules and saddles to mount my company which after much vexatious delay was accomplished."[11] When the cavalcade of troops, barbaric Indians, miners and pack-train moved out on June 16,

THE WESTERN UNION TELEGRAPH COMPANY.

Dated *Camp on Tongue Fork Tongue R* 187*6*

Received at *Via Fort Fetterman 23d*

To *Mrs. A. S. Burt*

Fort Laramie

None of Company wounded

All well. Letter by mail.

A. S. Burt

Courtesy, Burt Collection

TELEGRAM RECEIVED BY MRS. BURT
AFTER THE ROSEBUD BATTLE.

wrote Finerty, " in the rear, galled but gallant, rode on muleback the hardy infantry, under Col. Alex. Chambers and the brave Major Andy Burt."[12]

The 1300 men who had enjoyed the "circus" on Goose Creek had need of this relaxation to steady their nerves for the contest with Crazy Horse. On June 17 they had the fight of their lives with perhaps 1500 maddened Sioux and Cheyenne in the spirited Battle of the Rosebud, prelude to the disaster eight days later at the Little Big Horn. The details of this encounter have been covered in exhaustive detail elsewhere.[13] It is sufficient to note here that Crook narrowly escaped a clever trap planned by Crazy Horse. The many-pronged see-saw fight over rugged terrain lasted six hours, and Bourke notes fourteen killed and forty-three wounded. Historians agree that the number of losses is surprisingly small considering the length and ferocity of the conflict. There is also wide agreement that Crazy Horse displayed superior fighting tactics and that, despite the valor of Crook's forces, the result was something less than a white man's victory, since Crook's campaign was brought to a standstill, and the Indians were now free to deal with Custer.

Throughout this affair, Major Burt added luster to his already excellent reputation. In the early morning, before the Sioux attack, his cheerful encouragement of the tense soldiers was a conspicuous morale-builder. Early in the battle his company successfully held a hill and ravine in the face of determined enemy attack. He planned an ambush, using Shoshone and Crows to pretend retreat, but this failed when he was detected by the Sioux. Still under enemy fire, he gathered the wounded in his sector and brought them to the field hospital. Later, at the climax of the battle, when Colonel Royall's battalion was in danger of being surrounded, Burt and Burrowes were sent to the rescue "to stop those Indians and occupy that ridge." To quote Burt's official report, "We dismounted and moved forward at double time and on reaching the ridge stopped the Indians quickly and decisively without loss on our part. My company disabled two Indians and three ponies. I make this statement carefully, believing greater damage was done to the enemy." It was while observing this maneuver that Captain Guy V. Henry received a severe face wound, the hostiles rushed forward to "count coup" on the prostrate officer, and the most fierce hand-to-hand fighting of the day occurred. A special correspondent for the New York Herald reported the incident: "As soon as the junction of the line was effected the Sioux began to yield, and the infantry, under Major Burrowes and Burt, drove them at last from the high cone which they had held so long. The Snakes caused their final flight and pursued a party of four Sioux two miles, killed them all and took their scalps."

But the correspondent for the New York Graphic goes much further, crediting Burt and Burrowes with the salvation of the 3rd Cavalry. Coming down from their hill, he reports that each fired a volley into the mass of savages that threatened to overwhelm Royall. "This aid, though late in coming, checked the main body who were rushing over the crest."[14] J. W. "Captain Jack" Crawford, onetime Chief of Scouts, U. S. Army, in a letter of February 17, 1898 to President McKinley, commended then Colonel Burt as "one of the bravest and best soldiers in the Army," and cited "one particular service of his that has never been rewarded by those in authority." He bluntly stated that "Burt's battalion of Infantry rescued from massacre" Colonel Royall's cavalry. "This was notorious in the command to my knowledge. In later years Colonel Royall stated this to others."[15]

Vaughn, historian of the Rosebud, pays this tribute: "The five infantry companies formed the backbone of Crook's defense; and had it not been for the companies of Burt and Burrowes, it is doubtful whether Royall's men would have escaped. It was true, then as now, that when the more glamorous branches of the service got into difficulty, it was the Walk-a-Heaps with their little rifles who were called to the rescue. Who was there who could laugh at the 'Mule Brigade' now?"[16]

Crook now withdrew to his wagon train corral on Goose Creek, bringing in the dead and wounded in travois. Most of the Crows, having their fill of battle and nursing many wounds, quit and went home. They reported to their confidant, Major Burt, that they were displeased with the way the battle was conducted, although the real reason may have been their fear of early reprisal against their villages on the Big Horn.

A wagon train was made up to return the wounded to Fort Fetterman, and bring back supplies, the escort being commanded by Colonel Chambers. Crazy Horse must be pursued, but not until there were fresh provisions and reinforcements. Thus began a long period of waiting and killing time. Crook has been often criticized for enjoying an idyllic interlude while Crazy Horse advanced to meet Custer and annihilate him; true, telephones and radio were not yet invented, but no one knows why Crook failed to send a courier northward at once, even if he had to make a wide detour to avoid the hostiles, to make the earliest possible contact with Terry and Gibbon on the Yellowstone.

Trout fishing on the Goose and the Tongue was so rewarding that it soon palled and on July 1, unaware of Custer's demise, Crook made up a party to explore and hunt in the Big Horn Mountains. This included Colonel Royall, Major Burt, Lieutenant Bourke and Correspondent Finerty. Bourke claims that this was the first party of white men to ascend these mountains. Trappers and gold-hunters probably made the ascent earlier, but this is certainly the first recorded in detail. They were charmed by the alpine scenery and abundant wildlife, and returned to the main camp in time to celebrate the Fourth of July.

General Crook sent out a force of twenty men under Lieutenant Sibley to escort Grouard on a reconnaissance to determine the whereabouts of the Sioux. Finerty went along and got his fill of Indians when the party was jumped by a band of hostiles and narrowly escaped with their lives. Meanwhile, various rumors of a bad fight drifted in causing uneasiness. Finally, on July 10, Louis Richard and Ben Arnold arrived with dispatches from Sheridan bringing the first

COLONEL ALEXANDER CHAMBERS.
Major Burt's Commander in 1876.

official account of the Little Big Horn fight of June 25-26. Everyone was shaken by the terrible news; that same day the hostiles reappeared on Goose Creek and set fire to the grasslands. On July 11 Chief Washakie appeared with over 200 Shoshones, and the following day three messengers appeared with word from General Terry. On the 13th Colonel Chambers reappeared with the supply train, and advice for Crook that General Merritt with two companies of the Fifth Cavalry would soon arrive to join him. Arriving also with the train was the versatile Dr. McGillicuddy (Professor Jenney's topographer, now in the role of Army physician), a whiskey peddler and "two abandoned females, disguised as mule drivers." The whiskey was seized, but not before it caused considerable havoc in camp, and on Crook's order the women were arrested and returned to Fort Fetterman.[17]

Merritt and the 5th Cavalry were ordered to intercept Cheyennes leaving Red Cloud Agency in force; this bit of business delayed things so that it was not until August 3 that Crook and Merritt were united on Goose Creek, with a combined force of 2,000 men. Among notables in the new brigade were Captain Charles King, author of *Campaigning with Crook*, and the famed scout, William F. Cody. The 5th had paused at Fort Laramie on July 21 to 23. The wife of Lieutenant Capron was impressed. "I remember [Cody's] fine figure," she writes, "as he stood by the sutler store, straight and slender, with his scarlet shirt belted in and his long hair."[18]

For the grand invasion of hostile territory, baggage was reduced to a minimum. As before, all wagons were left behind, transportation consisting of a train of about 400 stolid pack mules. Every man carried only the clothes he was wearing, plus one overcoat, one blanket, and one poncho or "one half of a shelter tent," rations for fifteen days and 250 rounds of ammunition. The backbone of this second phase of the expedition was composed of no less than twenty-five troops of cavalry, commanded by Merritt, Carr and Royall; but the Achilles heel in the situation was the fact that the horses started out on their marathon in poor condition, and the grass was ruined by the scorched earth policy of the Sioux. In contrast, says Finerty, "the infantry under Col. Chambers appeared stout and soldierly, and moved off at a swinging step three hours ahead of us."[19] Captain Charles King also pays tribute to the performance of the foot-soldiers on this cavalry expedition: "The infantry was a command to be proud of, and Lieutenant-Colonel Alexander Chambers was the man to appreciate it. Detachments from three fine regiments gave him a full battalion of tough, wiry fellows, who had footed it a thousand miles that summer, and were all the better prepared to march two thousand more."[20]

On the Rosebud a junction was effected with Terry, making a combined force of 4,000 men. A crossing was made to the Tongue and the Powder. Now the strain of the march began to tell on horses and men. The heat was oppressive, the country was hard, repulsive and sterile, "like the surface of a non-atmospheric planet," lice were abundant, and food was in such short supply that the men experimented with fried cactus. Then the rain came, as if it would never stop, making here "the most adhesive mud on the American continent." Cases of rheumatic and neuralgic fever were commonplace, boots shrank, teeth chattered and noses turned purple and indigo. The horses began to die off like flies and Terry's "green infantry," with feet bleeding and legs swollen, had to be mounted on Indian ponies. But the Burt and Munson infantry columns astonished everyone by their ruggedness, making the full march without a man dropping out of rank.[21]

The remaining Indian allies, Crows and Shoshones, abandoned the enterprise as hopeless. General Crook again drafted Major Burt to proceed upriver to try to persuade the Crows to join forces, fearing that without native guides the expedition might soon become lost. But in this project he was unsuccessful.[22]

At Yellowstone River, at the mouth of the Powder, they met the steamer Far West, gained a few meager supplies, and placed on board the most severe cases, the first of many whose health would be wrecked by continued exposure to heat, chills and violent storms. Terry's force recrossed the Yellowstone, while Crook elected to pursue an Indian trail to the Little Missouri Badlands, where he arrived September 4. The advance column caught up with the Sioux rear-guard and there was sporadic firing. At the head of Heart River, near present Medora, North Dakota, the expedition was yet seven days away from the Black Hills, and had but two days rations. The men were soaked with rain and mud, and dispirited. Four days would take them to Fort Abraham Lincoln on the Missouri River; but General Crook elected to go to the Black Hills, announcing that they would survive on horsemeat.[23]

Southward they marched in a pelting rain, a weak and scarecrow army, many horses and a few men going to their doom. Already the horse population was down, and now 300 dismounted cavalrymen were glumly straggling behind what Finerty describes as "the wonderful infantry battalion." An occasional rifle shot announced the death knell of another horse and the availability of a few more stringy flank steaks. In later years General Burt vividly recalled the ordeal:

It is an established fact that once settled down to marching the infantryman can outlast the horse. Some cavalrymen will take issue with this assertion. As an instance. In Crook's campaign of 1876, against Sitting Bull, I recall a spirited dialogue between two soldiers. We of the infantry, Chambers's command, were plodding along, literally puddling in mud, for our trail lay over an alkali country which means no vegetation whatever and a light soil, and the going was awful. Every step a man would pick up several pounds of mud. The infantry were in the lead, with a small cavalry detail in advance. It was well into the day when the main body of cavalry caught up with us and there was the usual good-natured exchange of chaff between the soldiers. One of the cavalrymen swung around in his saddle and addressed one of my men:

"Casey, old man, how are your corns? Is it fine walking? Don't you want to ride a horse?"

Casey, in the richest brogue you ever heard, replied: "To hell wid your harse. Gwan now, we'll walk your harse off his legs and thin we'll eat him."

This was a veritable prophecy. . . .[24]

On September 7 a select crew of 200 men under Mills was ordered forward on the strongest surviving horses, to obtain all possible supplies from the nearest Black Hills settlement. On the 8th, couriers from Mills brought word that at Slim Buttes he had surprised an Indian village of forty lodges, was holding his own, but needed help. All hands were ordered forward; hunger, cold, wet and fatigue were forgotten as the dismounted battalion tramped through the mud with a new tempo. Major Burt arived in time to assist in the process of besieging a small band of hostiles in a ravine, finally flushing out Chief American Horses, fatally wounded in the abdomen, and a few pitiful survivors. Crazy Horse now appeared with a large number of savage reinforcements and attempted an assault. They were repulsed by a volley from cavalry carbines. Then, reports Bourke, "the Sioux were not left in doubt long as to what they were to do, because the infantry battalion commanded by Burt and Daniel W. Burke got after them and raced them off the field, out of range." They retreated into a very rough country, "only appearing on high cliffs." The fight continued about three hours, writes Capron. "Burt's company did splendid service," having but one man wounded.[25]

Again Crook sent forward an advance party under Mills and Grouard to contact the nearest mining hamlet. On the 12th the main body made a heroic march of thirty-five miles through gumbo, which attached itself in great balls to their feet. The next day, when they reached the Belle Fourche, they were succored by a wagon train from patriotic Crook City, laden with "crackers and vegetables," and accompanied by fifty head of beef cattle. Thus on a joyous note ended the dismal rain-soaked march through the wilderness; but many soldiers would pay the rest of their lives with wounds and ailments resulting from the rigors of this journey.

On the 15th General Crook received orders to turn the command over to Merritt, and proceed to Fort Laramie. Major Burt, Lieutenant Bourke and Correspondent Finerty were in his entourage which made a rapid and triumphal progress through the Black Hills. A delegation of Deadwood dignitaries led by the mayor advanced to meet the officers, bringing welcome gifts of precious butter and eggs. Upon entering the city on September 16 they were greeted by an artillery salute of thirteen guns, and the wild acclaim of the citizens. General Crook and his officers, wearing badly tattered uniforms but cheerful in the knowledge that a square meal awaited them, were quartered in a two-story slab structure known as the Grand Central Hotel. After supper and a visit to the public bathhouse the General appeared on the hotel balcony, where he addressed the crowd, assuring them of the Army's solicitude for their safety.[26]

Accounts vary as to just what happened after this balcony scene, the lack of unanimity among eye-witnesses perhaps due to the fact, attested to by Finerty, that some of them were prevailed upon to consume quantities of a potent local brew called "forty-rod." The least credible story is that of Dr. McGillicuddy who reports that "General Crook and Calamity Jane led the grand march at the dance given at McDaniel's theatre."[27] Nobody else mentions such an incident or a theatre by this name, and it is scarcely possible to believe that the austere General would thus comport himself with a woman who had been declared *persona non grata* and ejected by him and others from at least three recent military expeditions. Finerty and Bourke both describe a reception in "the Deadwood theatre" where the General was formally addressed and given the "freedom of the city."

Probably referring to the same occasion, Richard B. Hughes calls it the "Langrishe Theatre," and states that the speeches made by prominent citizens were replied to by Major Burt on Crook's behalf. According to this account, the Major told the lurid story of the march, and extolled the General under whom he had "enjoyed the satisfaction of standing in a Sioux village and seeing it burn." A man in the crowd shouted, "You had better turn over those Sioux prisoners to us. If you take them to the agency, Uncle Sam will feed them up until they

225

want to take the war path again." To this Burt is alleged to have replied: "No, we can't do that; we won't give you those Indians to kill, and we won't kill them ourselves—provided they show us where there are more to kill."[28]

Spurred on by further dispatches from Sheridan, Crook left Deadwood the next day, arriving in Custer, sixty miles away, on the 18th. Here the exhausted men found a hotel and gratefully crawled into bed, only to be kept awake through the night by a "bawling infant." The next morning Captain Egan of the 2nd Cavalry greeted the party with fresh horses, and on the 19th they began a forced two-day ride of 106 miles via Buffalo Gap and the Badlands to Camp Robinson. As they galloped up on foaming horses, the bleary-eyed, ragged, bewhiskered officers, says Bourke, were almost mistaken for a squad of highwaymen. After a brief stop here to harangue the unrepentant Red Cloud, Crook resumed his journey to Fort Laramie, finally arriving there September 21.[29]

Major Andrew S. Burt had been an eager companion on Crook's whirlwind ride. He had been absent four months on one of the most harrowing campaigns in American military history. Elizabeth Burt's rejoicing on this occasion may well be imagined.

How had it been with Elizabeth and her three children during these four months at Fort Laramie? Her journal is not too revealing, nor is the heavily edited journal of Cynthia Capron, her friend and neighbor. The fears and apprehensions which must have racked them at this trying time are muffled in drab domestic routine and only occasional historical flashbacks.

June to October, 1876, at Fort Laramie, while General Crook's army was campaigning, was probably one of the most tense periods in its tempestuous history, rivaling the gold rush summer of 1849, the time of the Grattan massacre in 1854, the Utah War of 1858-1859, and the Sioux wars of the frantic 1860's. Military comings and goings at Fort Laramie reached a climax, numerically, in 1876, with several regimental units and high-ranking commanders pausing here before advancing to combat. But while the armies of Crook, Reynolds and Merritt were out on the Plains, Indians and white bandits and renegades raised havoc around the fort, keeping it in an almost perpetual state of alarm.

After General Bradley's departure for Philadelphia and Major Burt's assignment with Crook, Major Edwin F. Townsend became the ranking officer at the fort, and assumed command.[30] The bulk of the Fort Laramie post records for 1876 are mysteriously missing from the National Archives, but there is enough evidence left to piece together a very melodramatic picture, extending the "reign of terror" along the stage road which began with the springtime demise of "Stuttering" Brown.

In June a mule train was besieged for nearly three hours at Rawhide Buttes, with several casualties, and the Fort Laramie mail carrier was killed near Red Cloud Agency. In swift succession ranches and stage stations were burned and horse herds stolen. In July James Hunton, a prominent rancher on the Chugwater, was killed and scalped, and early in August a stagecoach was assaulted near Hat Creek station and the passengers had to take to the brush. Meanwhile, efforts to construct a telegraph line from Cheyenne through Fort Laramie to the Hills were hampered by Indian raiders. It was not until December that a message was received in Deadwood.[31]

A final spasm of Indian hostility in the Fort Laramie area occurred in early October, when the Indian-mutilated remains of two civilians and a cavalryman were brought in to the hospital "deadhouse" for burial.[32] Then, for good measure, "Harris, a civilian engaged in hauling hay and wood for the Quartermaster Department, was killed in an altercation with his brother."[33] The small three company garrison left at the fort during these parlous times was sorely beset to dash out after each frantic report in futile efforts to overtake and apprehend the culprits. Mrs. Capron reports that "Captain Egan's company was always going on these disappointing trips. There was no use saying nothing could be done even when everyone knew it." At times the fort was virtually destitute of soldiers. When news of the Custer disaster was received, there were only thirteen men at the fort to answer roll-call.[34]

Post trader Collins had a word to say about the enlisted men of 1876, and some of their civilian colleagues:

> The soldiers during my stay were a rough, devil-may-care assortment from all states. Many of them were refugees from justice, some had been former penitentiary convicts, and nearly all were as tough a lot of men as could be sifted through the mesh. To them no service was a hardship, no order too strict to obey; scouting for Indians, sleeping without tents in the coldest weather, wading through mud knee deep, and frozen streams and snow. When the march was over for the day many of them were employed by officers to pitch tents, cook, make beds, carry wood and water and prepare meals, for an additional compensation of $2.00 to $5.00 per month over the regular pay of an enlisted man, of $13.00 per month. These were designated by others of the company as "dog robbers."

Some of the "bad" men of the country found employment at the ranches nearby. It seemed beyond the ability of that stripe of off-scourings to lead a fairly respectable life and keep their own council, and when payday came around it was the rule to come to the post and get gloriously drunk. With a Colt's revolver in one bootleg, hunting knife in the other, and carrying a reputation as a "bad" man, respectable people were on their guard. If the clerks in the trader's store did not come in contact with them at the height of their rage it was considered a quiet day. To the credit of these clerk employes of mine, with good judgment and plenty of "sand," the very toughest of the "bad" men could be wallowed in the mud in front of the store for any great breach of conduct. The calling of the sergeant of the guard or officer of the day sometimes landed the toughest in the guard house, and when they sobered up they were usually quietly led off the reservation in front of a bayonet point never to return.[35]

Collins himself was the local grandee. He secured the coveted tradership by virtue of his father's former association with U. S. Grant in the tanning business back at Galena, Illinois, but he had achieved prosperity in his own right with a thriving harness and saddlery store in booming Cheyenne. His Rustic Hotel was crowded with distinguished wayfarers, while his "Sutler's Store" was the social and economic center of Fort Laramie's transient population. The store was well-stocked with every imaginable article, including flour, bacon, tobacco, whiskey, wolf poison, beauty aids, beaver traps, shotguns and carpet bags, and it was generally crowded with customers and loafers. Some of the latter overflowed outdoors on benches provided for their benefit. Leathery troopers and roughly garbed civilian employees lounged about, idly watching the parade of hopeful Black Hills pilgrims, officers' wives with parasols, and an occasional friendly Indian in outlandish garb.

Among the latter was Red Cloud's rival, Spotted Tail, who moved serenely about in green pantaloons and a large, dark blue blanket. Mrs. Capron describes him as "the best representative of his nation, as to sagacity, dignity and good manners." She reports that "one of the ladies invited him into her house," and that "several ladies went in to see him, and made a good deal of him, giving him some polite compliments which pleased him."[36] Spotted Tail had a strong sentimental attachment to Fort Laramie. In 1866 his comely daughter, Wheat Flour, died, and her remains were buried at the fort with military pomp. But this was a "burial" of a different sort. In the Sioux custom the coffin was raised and placed on a scaffold, covered with a buffalo robe tied down with thongs. This sepulchre was located on the hospital hill overlooking the fort and was a prime conversation piece. In 1874 the Post Quartermaster undertook to repair the collapsed structure and replace the bones; in the summer of 1876, however, Spotted Tail sent the remains of his daughter back to his agency on White River, "which some consider a sign of future hostility."[37]

Another Indian landmark was the "papoose tree" on the bank of the Laramie River. This was a big box elder that stood 300 yards from and opposite the quarters called "Dobie Row" where Mrs. Burt lived, its branches covering a space of at least seventy-five feet in diameter. At one time, according to Collins, it contained no less than forty bodies of Indian children wrapped in skins and robes, and lashed with buffalo thongs. As the thongs rotted away the bundles would fall to the ground, thus proving quite an attraction to coyotes and souvenir hunters.[38]

The Caprons had arrived at the fort in April "of the centennial year" via ambulance from Cheyenne. The road was muddy and cold, but "hospitable doors were opened for the reception of the Lieutenant and family." In a few days they were domiciled in Old Bedlam, "the best set of available quarters," and the officers and ladies of the garrison called. Old Bedlam was normally the habitat of unmarried or unaccompanied officers; in a few weeks after Capron and fellow officers had marched off to Fort Fetterman, his wife was shifted to other more suitable quarters. She briefly recounts the routine of post life:

> For a little time things go on as usual in time of peace. The band comes out to guard mounting in the morning and the children play around, enjoying the maneuvers and the music; and again the band plays for an hour before sundown. Then the cannon boom announces the hour of "retreat" and simultaneously the flag is hauled down, and the sun disappears from the western horizon.
>
> If there is no school the children recite their lessons to their parents. In mild weather people almost live on their porches, and generally, the houses were in those days built around a square—the parade ground—each house being in full view of the others.
>
> There was a sense of nearness and a feeling of sociability which must be missed by the veterans now stationed in the large posts of the present day.[39]

Officers' wives were not left entirely uninformed about military developments. Explains Mrs. Burt: "As there was no telegraph line to the north into the Indian country, news came only by an occasional courier, generally a friendly Indian. It was surprising how quickly news was brought by these fearless riders." When dispatches came through, and after required action was taken by the Officer of the Day, "an orderly carried it to all the officers' quarters so that the families of those in the field might read it. Meanwhile occasional letters passed back and forth between husbands and wives by courtesy of official couriers, wagonmasters and fellow officers who were on various missions." In June when "the cavalry left Fort Laramie after the infantry, the officers called on the families of those gone before and offered to take letters." First news of the Crook expedition was received in early June from unidentified officers who were sent down to Cheyenne to attend a court-martial.

Mrs. Burt remembers the dreadful moment:

> In late June came the heart rending news of the massacre of General Custer and his men. It was all so horrible! It filled us with increased dread of what might follow, if a part of our command were detached as Custer's was, and meet with an overwhelming force of Indians as he did. History has impressed the facts of that terrible slaughter upon the minds of the nation, making it unnecessary for me to enter into the details of that awful day. The people all over the country mourned with Mrs. Custer and the other wives and families who were so terribly bereaved.

> Naturally we at Fort Laramie were a profoundly depressed collection of women. Letters were seldom received and those of the most meager details. Just brief and hurriedly written notes. You can well imagine how hard and sorrow-breeding it was to sit and think and think and imagine all kinds of disasters. Truly, wives of soldiers and sailors have mixed with their happiness, very many anxieties unknown to other wives.

On June 27, while escorting the wagon train with those wounded at the Rosebud, Lieutenant Capron received news of the death of his two-year old son through the telegrapher at Fort Fetterman. "That night at 8 o'clock, with three men of his company who volunteered to go, he left, riding on horseback until morning when they hid themselves and rested three hours. They arrived at Fort Laramie at half past 2 in the afternoon, having ridden eighty-one miles in eighteen and a half hours without a change of horses."[40]

The boy probably died of typhoid fever, or other disease related to the deplorable state of sanitation at Fort Laramie in 1876. Considering the conditions revealed by available post records, it seems a miracle that the Burt family and other post residents were not wiped out by an epidemic. In the light of modern medical knowledge, their salvation might be attributed to a gradual immunity acquired by two year's residence, beginning with the severe microbe-killing winter of 1874-1875. It is significant that the young victim was a new arrival at the fort, at the outset of a cold wet spring.

The danger was present from the beginning. On August 24, 1874, the post surgeon noted "a considerable epidemic of diarrhoea among the children," and called attention of the commanding officer to the fact that the company sinks are in an exceedingly bad state of police. "The foul odors which arise cannot help but effect a bad influence on the health of the garrison." In September of that year General Bradley reported that the sinks in the rear of the men's quarters were "a nuisance that should at once be abated." The policing of the Laramie River was bad "and the peaks of manure from the cavalry stables and the filth and rubbish from the post, all of which has been deposited for many years on the north side and immediately contiguous to the post, is offensive in every particular."

A medical report of November, 1874 admitted to no complaints of enlisted men about the food, but went on to deplore the lack of a post garden, the dismal state of hygiene in the post guardhouse where there was indiscriminate crowding and "felons are in contact with the innocent." Bathing in the Laramie River was "abundantly performed during the warm weather," but not at all during the winter, "and the men suffer in consequence thereof." Furthermore, complained Post Surgeon Hartsuff, "I cannot learn that the men's blankets are ever washed." In January, 1875 General Bradley requested authority to purchase out of post funds a quantity of carbolic acid "for the extermination of bed bugs in the men's quarters."

The lack of a post garden, with consequent vitamin lack, is understandable, considering the hot windy summer, the absence of effective irrigation, and the prevalence of voracious wildlife. In July, 1876, too, clouds of grasshoppers filled the air and crawled on the ground, consuming every leaf and green blade of grass in the countryside. The Fort Laramie parade ground, normally quite barren, presented a particularly drab appearance that summer, and the sun shone brassily through the resultant pall of dust. But Mrs. Burt did not complain of these trying conditions.

In December, 1876 Surgeon Hartsuff reported that the "sanitary condition of this post remains in status quo." In May, 1877, six months after Elizabeth Burt's departure, he was still crusading:

The hygienic condition of the post is objectionable. Water closets in the rear of the commanding officers' quarters, for four or five years reported as a nuisance, still stand, and continue to saturate the atmosphere with noxious odors. . . . Putting of manure, offal, debris, dirt and filth into the pond above and immediately contiguous to the post is productive of the usual results. . . . The stench is at times almost unendurable, especially to the officers who live in nearest proximity to this generative apparatus; besides, a considerable portion of the garrison and all of the stock drink the water of the Laramie that is contaminated from this source. . . .

And the prospects for improvement were still dim. To this tirade A. W. Evans, Major, 3rd Cavalry, Post Commander, made an indignant rebuttal, explaining to the Adjutant General in Omaha that things weren't really as bad as they seemed.[41] His philosophy seemed to be that if it's good enough for the cavalry, it's good enough for everyone; and in time one can get used to anything!

Returning to a more pleasant theme, Elizabeth Burt vividly recalls the warriors' homecoming:

Upon the return home of these haggard weather beaten men [in September], General Crook accepted Major Burt's invitation to be our guest at Fort Laramie.

The General's long experience on the extreme frontier prepared him for the home life of a Captain living with his family in six rooms of a primitive kind. He became a most agreeable guest, adapting himself readily to any inconvenience that arose. He was not a great talker but while speaking of his early experience, he said: "There was never a greener boy than I went to West Point. I lived on a farm near Dayton, Ohio, and knew nothing of West Point when I arrived there."

Perhaps some homesick discouraged plebe beginning his life of trials at the U. S. Military Academy at West Point may take courage when he thinks, "Major General George Crook who began his career with no brighter prospect than I, became a famed General of the Civil War and later noted Indian campaigner." The General's visit was prolonged only long enough to finish the military business connected with his campaign.

During this time Crook conferred with Lieutenant General Sheridan and Colonel McKenzie on grand strategy for a winter campaign against the Sioux. As Commander of the Military Department of the Platte during this hectic summer, Sheridan had appeared at Fort Laramie on June 14 en route to Red Cloud Agency and had then directed Colonel Merritt's movement northward. On September 16 he appeared again, sending off his impatient telegram to Crook via Deadwood and settling down to await Crook's arrival. "Fishing was his principal pastime. General Sheridan proved himself a No. 1 sportsman in addition to his other accomplishments." He was also "a modest unassuming man. He made the acquaintance of all the officers and ladies at the post, calling soon after his arrival, and again before his departure."

Colonel McKenzie appeared on September 18, and as soon as Crook showed up on the 21st there was a council of war regarding another Powder River expedition, with its target a November campaign against Dull Knife's Cheyennes on the Crazy Woman Fork. On the 22nd Colonel McKenzie departed for Fort Fetterman, and the following day Sheridan left by stage for Cheyenne, in company with Major Powell and "the commander-in-chief of the royal army of Japan and two of his best generals." These oriental emissaries had been making the rounds, "inspecting the workings of our military system."

Early in October General Crook departed for Laramie Peak on a grand hunt with the indefatigable Captain Egan's company as escort, "returning October 10 with over sixty deer and antelope, besides other game." On or about October 15 he left for Cheyenne with Lieutenants Bourke and Schuyler. But on the 26th he was back again with fresh troops for the Powder River campaign. On the 28th, units of the 9th Infantry and 3rd Cavalry which had been left to patrol the Black Hills after the Yellowstone Expedition finally returned to Fort Laramie, "virtually in rags" and blackened by sunburn and the smoke of campfires. Lieutenant Capron was with this outfit, and it was now Mrs. Capron's turn for a tearful reunion.[42]

It was on his mid-October trip to Cheyenne, apparently, that General Crook did Elizabeth Burt a favor. She reported the incident as follows:

> . . . taking with him in his ambulance my sister and our thirteen-year old son on the way to Cincinnati, Andrew there to attend school. Our parting with the boy was heart-rending but to educate him was our first duty. Few and simple were the schools that he had been able to attend.
>
> Little time was given us to weep at home over this separation as an order hurried us for station with the Company to Sidney Barracks, Nebraska, not far east of Cheyenne on

the Union Pacific Railroad. The trip was overland, requiring us to again sleep in tents though for a few nights only as the distance was not great.

According to the Regimental Returns, "pursuant to orders dated Headquarters, Department of the Platte in the field, October 27, 1876," the Headquarters, Field Staff and Band and Major Burt's Company H left Fort Laramie, W. T., November 3 and marched to Cheyenne, arriving there November 7. The following day they proceeded to Sidney Barracks, Nebraska.[43] Company H was more fortunate than most of the 9th Infantry which that autumn marched north again under Crook and McKenzie, on another Powder River expedition against the Sioux.[44] Thus ended Elizabeth Burt's first residence at Fort Laramie, at the apex of its military glory.

In 1887-1888 Lieutenant Colonel A. S. Burt, 7th Infantry, was again stationed with his wife at Fort Laramie.[45] Those were the sunset years, the historically uneventful years, pleasantly filled with picnics, buggy rides, charades, and lemonade on Colonel Merriam's veranda.

In April, 1890 the post was abandoned, and various buildings sold at aution. Homesteaders promptly moved some buildings in their entirety, others they dismantled for the salvage lumber. Unsympathetic owners used other buildings for ranch houses, cow barns and chicken sheds. The storms beat down, roofs collapsed, walls tumbled. John Hunton, post trader from 1888 to 1890 and brother of the James Hunton killed on the Chugwater, had bought most of officers' row, but he alone seemed anxious to preserve it for posterity. In 1904 John S. Collins proclaimed that if Fort Laramie should "be set aside as a government reserve park, commemorative of one of the oldest and most important military posts in the United States, not a taxpayer in this broad land would begrudge his small contribution to the fund. But there is too much politics, both in the house and senate of the United States, to take an interest in such a trifling thing."[46]

By some miracle, which included a large measure of John Hunton's sentimentality, much of the old fort, however decrepit, was still in evidence in 1937 when the State of Wyoming, encouraged by a few patriots, finally bought some 200 acres embracing the historic remains for $25,000. In 1938 the site was donated to the Federal Government, becoming Fort Laramie National Monument. The collapsing structures were shored up and, after twenty years of cautious stabilization measures, preservation of the historic remains is assured. In April, 1960 Congress authorized an extension of the area boundaries and changed its name to Fort Laramie National Historic Site.

What the visitor can see today is but a fraction of the fort which existed in 1888 when Elizabeth Burt last lived there, but it is no longer a scene of neglect and decay. The American flag once more flies over the parade ground, where the ghosts of Indian-fighting armies march in review. Along Officers' Row to the west stands the old Sutler's Store and Old Bedlam, both century-old witnesses of the California gold rush; the double concrete quarters built in 1876; the restored old magazine of 1852; the ruins of three concrete quarters which in 1881 replaced "Dobie Row," and an imposing single quarters of 1886 with mansard roof occupied by Colonel Burt and his family in 1887. To the south stands double board and brick quarters of 1870 vintage, and to the east is the Old Guardhouse of 1866 and ruins of the large Administration Building of 1886. At the northeast corner stands the restored New Guardhouse.

North of the parade ground lie the concrete Cavalry barracks of 1875, the restored Old Bakery of 1876, the Post Commissary Warehouse of 1884, and ruins of the concrete hospital of 1876, the New Bakery and the Non-Commissioned Officers Quarters of the 1880's. All trace is gone of the adobe fort of 1849, the fortified adobe corral of 1868 and the scaffold grave of Spotted Tail's daughter. But the iron truss bridge across Laramie River, which echoed to the sounds of General Crook's cavalry and the Black Hills stage coaches of 1876, still survives, a creaking monument to ancient glories.

Fort Laramie is now a living memorial to men and women like Andrew and Elizabeth Burt, who helped to carve the destiny of America.

12

The Golden Years

In January, 1877, after two months at Sidney Barracks in Western Nebraska, on the Union Pacific mainline, Major Burt's company was again ordered to Fort Omaha. Established in 1868 in proximity to the Omaha Headquarters, Department of the Platte, it actively survives nearly 100 years later, a fenced rectangle of eighty acres with its axis north and south, paralleling 30th Street, Omaha's main north-south traffic artery. The "Fort" today is an island of grass and tree-shaded brick buildings (erected mainly in the 1880's and 1890's after the Burts' departure) surrounded by the homes, pavement and noisy traffic of a metropolis of 300,000 citizens. But when the Burts arrived in January, 1877 it sat quietly on the treeless prairie a good three miles northwest of young Omaha city, then claiming a population of 25,000, and about one mile south of the sleepy village of Florence, the old Mormon Winter Quarters of 1847.

Company barracks and officers' quarters were one-story frame, lined with brick, plain batten finish and painted a dull yellow. Coal oil lamps and wood-burning stoves were standard equipment. Except for the two-story residence occupied by the commanding officer, all the "plumbing" was outdoors, "ten feet to the rear of each kitchen." Before 1874 leaky water-barrels were supplied by wagons brought from the Missouri River one mile distant. In that year a cistern was built for each set of quarters. "Drains discharge into a small stream that flows in front of the post and empties into the river. Slops and excreta are hauled away and deposited on the commons northeast of the post." Bathing facilities were available in mild weather to those who cared to take their chances on drowning in the wide, muddy and treacherous Missouri.[1] But no such recreational delights intrigued Elizabeth Burt:

> When we reached the new post we were at once greatly chagrined to find the weather so cold that all the water for the garrison's use was frozen in the supply barrels and that scrubbing had to be done with melted snow. Despite difficulties, it was not long before we were comfortably settled in our seven room frame house. . . . During the summer the Quartermaster gave us the luxury of hydrants in our yards but brought no water into the house. . . .
>
> Post improvements were made from time to time. A handsome brick house was built for General George Crook who occupied it upon completion. This also brought his staff out from Omaha and a large brick building for their offices was erected on the parade ground still leaving what was then considered sufficient ground for regimental drills. . . .[2]
>
> Private theatricals again proved so successful that "Lend Me Five Shillings" was given for charity at the theatre in the city, reaping a harvest for the poor. Mrs. George Ruggles, the wife of the Adjutant General, Doctor Charles Page and Major Burt covered themselves with glory as stars.
>
> The winter passed pleasantly among so many agreeable people, including General and Mrs. Crook, General and Mrs. John H. King, General and Mrs. Luther P. Bradley, Major and Mrs. Edwin Townsend, General and Mrs. Robert Williams, Lieutenant and Mrs. Jesse Lee, Major and Mrs. Alfred Norton and many others. Mrs Williams had been a reigning belle in Washington as Miss Cutts and later as Mrs. Stephen A. Douglas. She was our near neighbor and a

most charming woman who, though now the busy mother of six children, still possessed the same characteristics that marked her brilliant career in the capital.[3]

Two remarkable events were the reception given to President Hayes and his wife, and that given by General and Mrs. Crook when they had for their guests General and Mrs. Grant following the famous general's return from his triumphal tour round the world.

Our two years stay at this post passed quickly, leaving none but pleasant recollections of the kindness and hospitality extended to us by many prominent citizens of Omaha, among whom General Charles Manderson and his wife are remembered especially. The General, a veteran of the Civil War, at that time had just begun his practice of law and was making himself so felt in the councils of his political party that ultimately he was placed in the Senate Chamber.[4]

On July 25, 1877, pursuant to Special Order No. 61, Headquarters, Military Division of the Missouri, General King led six companies of the 9th Regiment, including Major Burt's Company H, by rail to Chicago. They remained there one month, "guarding the public property endangered by the mob subsequent upon the strike of the railroad employees." In May, 1878 Companies B, H and I, under Major Townsend, proceeded by rail to Cheyenne, thence by marches via Fort Laramie to establish a "summer camp on the Little Missouri River, Wyoming Territory." The apparent purpose was to patrol the Sioux country and erect telegraph lines. In August Major Burt returned to Fort Omaha, on detached duty to serve as a member of a General Court-martial.[5]

The most memorable incident of the Fort Omaha years was the celebrated murder trial of Ira P. Olive, in which Major Burt and the 9th Infantry played a surprise role. In the winter of 1878-1879 one of the most atrocious crimes that ever stained the pages of Nebraska history was committed in Custer County in the central part of the state. The crime grew out of the clash between cattlemen who had occupied the open range land without valid title, and the new breed of lawful homesteaders. As the dominant rancher in Custer County, the ruthless Olive, in an adroit maneuver which set the pattern for countless later Hollywood dramas, got himself elected sheriff and then proceeded to abuse the law by trumping up false charges against certain homesteaders, compelling them to leave the country. Two stalwart citizens named Mitchell and Ketchum defied Sheriff Olive and his deputies, refused to accept a warrant, and in an exchange of gunplay wounded Olive's brother. In retaliation Olive rounded up a posse, "arrested" the two homesteaders, took them to a wild and desolate region north of Lexington, and then brutally murdered them, attempting to destroy the evidence by incinerating the bodies. So great was the clamor over this outrage that the Nebraska legislature in 1879 passed a law appropriating special funds for the prosecutions. In April the case was removed to Hastings for trial, under Judge Gaslin.

While John M. Thurston, special prosecutor and later United States Senator, argued the case with the expensive array of legal talent assembled by Olive, it was observed by him and the judge that the town and the courtroom were rapidly being overrun by desperadoes and tough-looking cowboys, all packing six-shooters. It was understood from grapevine sources that if there was any danger of Olive's conviction this army of thugs would shoot up the courtroom; and it so happened that Olive's conviction was virtually assured by the planned surprise testimony of one of the gang, Bion Brown, who had secretly sworn to turn state's witness. The judge and his associates wired Governor Nance in Lincoln urging military intervention to ensure that justice would take its majestic course; and the Governor in turn burned up the wires between Lincoln and Washington. On April 11, the critical morning of the scheduled unveiling of the surprise witness, word was received at dawn that two companies of regular infantry had left Fort Omaha at 5 A. M. by rail and would reach Hastings about 10 A. M. Court was to open at nine o'clock. Senator Thurston recalls "the thrilling crisis":

> Well, court opened and the crisis was at hand. I stood up and made some motion, the nature of which I do not now recall, but it was only made to give me a chance to talk against time and I commenced an argument. At ten o'clock I was still speaking and nothing was heard from the troops, so it continued on until eleven and we were getting quite desperate, but I kept on talking and at about fifteen minutes after eleven we heard Uncle Sam's bugle blowing down the street. I think that was the sweetest music I ever listened to. The court did not stop to order a recess, but everybody in the building rushed out the front doors and here, coming up the street, was the finest sight my eyes ever fell upon. Ninety-two regulars marching with steady swinging steps with a gatling-gun and squad, and at their head was the man we used to call Little Andy Burt, a captain in the regular army, and over all the old flag.

> Andrew S. Burt was one of the best soldiers I ever knew. He served through the war of the rebellion as a boy winning his way to a captaincy. At the close of the war, he was appointed as a lieutenant in the regular army, and was almost

immediately ordered into this western country where he remained all of his military life until the breaking out of the Spanish-American war. General Ord, General Crook, General Gibbon, General Miles and others considered him as being the best officer on the frontier for Indian warfare.

On came the ninety-two regulars and deployed upon a vacant block diagonally across from the courthouse, ammunition was passed out and the gatling-gun squad stood ready for action. The other soldiers commenced making camp.

I never saw so surprised and so quiet a crowd of men in all my life as those cowboys were. They would cheerfully have attacked five hundred untrained militia men, but ninety-two regular soldiers with a gatling-gun and the flag, and Little Andy Burt in command, put the fear of God in them in two seconds. Trouble was all over. We went back into the court room and the trial was resumed.

The upshot of this dramatic appearance of United States Infantry was the conviction of Olive and a companion named Fisher, both of whom should have been hanged promptly, but through the stubbornness of one juror were merely sentenced to life imprisonment. The Nebraska Supreme Court upset the decision on an absurd technicality, Olive and Fisher were freed and the case against the other defendants dismissed. Although the fiendish crime was therefore unrequited, there was no further organized lawlessness on the part of the cattle interests in that area, and the Senator gave his military friend much of the credit: "So, I say God bless Andrew S. Burt, one of the bravest, best soldiers the country ever produced."[6]

Recruiting service in Chicago, 1880-1882, was a pleasant interlude for the Burt family. The children were able to go to an actual public school for two years, the only formal education they ever enjoyed during their early youth in the knockabout military service. Mrs. Burt, after fourteen years of a life of inconveniences on the raw frontier, was able to have a luxurious fling at shopping, entertainments, and a home with a fully-appointed bathroom! The gregarious Major, with headquarters on Clark Street north of Randolph, joined the nearby Chicago Press Club, on Clark Street, over Dale's Drug Store, there finding congenial company. This included Elwyn A. Barron, dramatic critic of the *Chicago Inter-Ocean*, who urged him to capitalize on his western adventures and write for the theatre, where live audiences were eagerly gobbling up raw red melodrama.[7]

Ned Buntline was the leading dramatist of the palpitating "western" school, and Buffalo Bill was his prime hero. The flamboyant

William F. Cody, alias Buffalo Bill, had been among Major Burt's acquaintances in the Big Horn and Yellowstone campaign of 1876. When news of the Custer "massacre" hit the headlines, Cody had closed down a show he was playing in the East, and hastened out to Fort D. A. Russell in time to join General Merritt's cavalry as a well-publicized scout. Hat Creek, west of Fort Robinson, was the scene of the apocryphal duel between Cody and the Cheyenne Chief Yellow Hand, and when Cody appeared with Merritt's column at Crook's camp on Tongue River he carried the chief's odoriferous scalp as a trophy. When the expedition reached Yellowstone River he decamped on the steamboat that appeared there, hastening back to the footlights to cash in on the lurid Custer debacle and the Yellow Hand incident, inflated by a maudlin press to the proportions of a Greek epic. At all events, by just being himself in a hairbreadth drama billed as "The Scouts on the Prairie," Cody resumed his role as a gate-crushing matinee idol.[8]

Major Burt was no stranger to the footlights, as his wife makes abundantly clear. His enthusiasm for this literary form, his own histrionic talents, and his apparent admiration for Cody's fashionable brand of heroics, conspired to bring him and the celebrity once more together. In 1882 Major Burt, U.S.A., received accolades as the author of *May Cody; or Lost and Won*, a drama in four acts starring "the Hon. William F. Cody," the incomparable Buffalo Bill. In New York it was reported that:

> A tremendously large and enthusiastic housefull welcomed Buffalo Bill and his associates to the classic boards at the Bowery Theatre on Monday night, and similar ovations have greeted the party every evening since. The drama is by Maj. Burt, U. S. A. and is replete with adventurous incident, in every scene of which Mr. Cody (Buffalo Bill) has ample room for the portrayal of his own indomitable heroism and in which he is ably assisted by a bear, several horses, one mule, and a troupe of genuine red men, headed by two Sioux chiefs.

The Academy of Music in Scranton, Pennsylvania, was also densely crowded during *May Cody*, which the local critics proclaimed as,

> ... something wholly different from anything ever before presented by Buffalo Bill, and possesses a finish, and indeed an elegance, which proves that the dramatic taste of Mr. Cody has undergone a decided change for the better. It was written expressly for him, and exhibits him in a far higher type of

manhood than any of the pieces in which he has heretofore appeared. For those who like these intensely thrilling plays, surely this is the peer of any. The playing is fearfully realistic at times, and Mr. Cody has a superior company for this business. The most thrilling scene of the piece, however, is the marvellous shooting displayed by Buffalo Bill who, at a distance bounded by the entire length of the stage, cuts into pieces with his rifle a potato placed upon May Cody's hand, then upon her head, then repeats these operations standing with his back to the mark and shooting between his knees, then with his back upon a stool and his hanging down so as to bring his head into an inverted position. He snuffs a candle at the same distance, and finally knocks the fire from the end of a cigar in the mouth of the Indian Cha-sha-cha-o-pogso. He then caps the climax by shivering a potato from the head of the lady, standing with his back to her, and using a mirror to effect his aim. It is fearfully straining to the spectator's nerves to witness these exhibitions of marksmanship.

One is puzzled whether the Scranton production was a play or a shooting match. No copy of the script survives, but a better conception of the plot that figured in this dramatic triumph may be gleaned from a piece in the *New York Sun*:

"May Cody; or, Lost and Won," a new drama, in four acts, by Major Burt, U. S. A., was produced last night before a vast and eager assemblage. The leading character is "the Hon. Wm. F. Cody" himself, who takes the part of Buffalo Bill, which is the name he goes by out of the play as well as in it, and the name he is best known by to the boys of the east side. May Cody, the heroine, is his lost sister, and he comes to New York to find her. She has just been turned into the streets by Mrs. Stoughton, in whose house she has been living, and whose son falls in love with her. At the same time John D. Lee, the Mormon, who was recently executed, is looking for her, having formed a passion for her, and wishing to take her forcibly to Utah. Lee is one of the villains of the play, and the tableau in which Buffalo Bill hurls him to the ground, and stands over him with a revolver, called forth wild applause from the sympathetic multitude.

Buffalo Bill, his sister and Mrs. Stoughton's son cross the plains with the intention of going to California. On the way John D. Lee waylays them, and the Mountain Meadow massacre ensues. Brigham Young appears at this point to incite the massacre in unvarnished terms. May Cody is carried off by Lee, who wishes her for himself, but Brigham appropriates her, and is about to make a Mormon of her and marry her, notwithstanding her resistance and entreaties, when Buffalo Bill, in the guise of a Ute warrior, dashes into the "endowment house," and at the foot of the altar rescues and escapes with her.

Lee pursues the fugitives and has a hand-to-hand conflict with Buffalo Bill, in which he succumbs after two repeating rifles and a pair of revolvers are emptied. He comes to life again later, and gets Buffalo Bill into trouble, having him arrested and condemned as a spy; and Bill comes near his death, sitting on his coffin and having a file of soldiers fire at him. In the end of course he gets the best of his enemy and sees May happily married.

The fun of the play is contributed by an Irish footman, who was in Mrs. Stoughton's employ and accompanied May when she was thrust into the streets. The most popular of the performers with the boys was naturally Buffalo Bill, for whose first appearance they were extremely impatient, and whom they greeted with prolonged yells and cheers. Bill marks his progress through the drama with powder and ball. An effective scene was secured by the introduction of a bear, with which he has a terrible conflict, emptying his rifle and revolver, and finally coming to a close fight. Several horses, a real, though diminutive and very funny, mule, and a camp fire, were among the novelties brought upon the stage. An amusing scene was presented by Brigham Young's family sitting room, where his wives were assembled, and the favorite Amelia swayed an arbitrary sceptre.

It is needless to say again what has been said before in these columns, that although Buffalo Bill is not as great an actor as Salvani, and lacks the elocution of Edwin Booth, he has the soul of a hero and the action of the fiery, untamed steed of the Plains, and he never appears upon the scene but he thrills his spectators, for he is sure to kill or rescue somebody, and to do it with a certain wildcat grace that no art can teach.[9]

In June, 1882, the Major launched his second and final dramatic production, with further hope of royalties to aid him in educating his young family. This was an entirely different show, a "comedy-opera" with classic overtones entitled *Robin Hood and Rosalind*. A copy of this play survives, bearing notice that it is a collaboration between Elwyn Barron and Sheridan Burt, "Andrew" having disappeared momentarily, we can only suppose on the theory that the abbreviated name seemed more elegant for a playwright. Where *May Cody* took literary license with the American frontier West, the later product was pure romantic medieval fancy, with shades of Sir Launcelot, Don Quixote and Sancho Panza. Evidence is lacking as to how this work was received by the public or whether royalties were forthcoming; however, there is preserved a quite extravagant preview of the coming attraction in the *Louisville Courier-Journal* for June 5, 1882, dateline Chicago:

> A New Comedy-Opera. A soldier and a Journalist Produce a Work that is to Paralyze the Public. *Robin Hood and Rosalind* to make a New Standard of Perfection in the Blending. . . .
>
> It is with deep interest and real satisfaction that the amusement world will learn of another most worthy achievement, an accomplishment which carries with it not only the certainty of coming pleasure of the intensest nature, but also an absolute assurance that we possess in this country, indeed in this very city, the genius for creation which will make a new standard of perfection in the blending of dramatic and musical unities into rounded and harmonious symmetry. This has surely been achieved in the new comedy-opera. . . .
>
> It will not lessen the interest which this announcement will cause to know that the work has been the result of three years' most arduous and conscientious labor on the part of those well able to labor speedily and effectively. In it has been concentrated not only the best of dramatic and musical culture of a lifetime, but the work has the additional advantage in its fruition of the fine flavor and savor of keen dramatic and musical intelligence, blended with that refined sympathy which everywhere pervades that art which is self-expressive. The author of *Robin Hood and Rosalind* is Maj. Andrew Sheridan Burt, of the United States Army, a gentleman of middle age, who has had the advantage of unusual study and culture. He is a soldier with a record of gallantry on the field; has been for 20 years in the regular army; was for 17 years continuously in command of a company in active service on the frontier; and is now on vacation here in charge of the recruiting service at this point. Not only has he achieved distinction as a painstaking journalist, but he has been known among his brother army officers for years as an enthusiast in dramatic and musical matters. He has had wide experience; is a close observer; possesses most scholarly attainments; has real genius in constructive ability; is possessed of large and glowing ideality; and tingles to his finger-tips with sympathy in and mastery of human emotions. As to the ground-work of this comedy-opera, he has constructed an acting play so bright, so warm, so mellow, so rich in the fruitage of pictures

of a time and its folk long gone, and withal so simple and clean and loveable, that him who told *A Winter's Tale* might not blush at its parentage.[10]

The laurels of Ned Buntline and Will Shakespeare were not long threatened. Leisurely recruiting duty in Chicago was bound to come to an end, and Major Burt was doomed to return to the cultural Sahara of the frontier. In the summer of 1882 he made the biggest geographical jump of his career thus far, from Chicago to California, and now became a full-fledged Major in the 8th U. S. Regiment of Infantry. Oldest son Andrew Gano, the Civil War baby now age twenty, was left behind to make his own way in the business world. After a brief and uneventful stay on Angel Island in San Francisco Bay, the Major was assigned to Fort Bidwell as post commander. Edith Burt, the "blockhouse baby" of Fort Sanders, was then left behind at Snell's Seminary in Oakland.

Named for John Bidwell, one of a group which blazed a new trail to California in 1841, eight years before the gold rush, Fort Bidwell was established in August, 1865, in the northeast corner of California. It quartered one company of infantry and one troop of cavalry. Its civilian counterpart, also named Bidwell, is described as "a very small town" but it was the metropolis of Surprise Valley, nearly a mile above sea level. Though the valley floor was destitute of timber, pine logs for the construction of the post were in plentiful supply in the Warner Mountains to the west. Outside communication from the post was by "semi-weekly mail to Reno on the Central Pacific Railroad, interruptible by snow."[11] Reynolds Burt, then eight years old, shares with his mother vivid recollections of the bumpy 200-mile stage ride over this route, and aspects of the domesticated life at this somewhat obsolete outpost.[12]

The Burts were assigned "a pleasant frame house consisting of four large rooms with a hall between, a dining room and kitchen back of them." Water reached a kitchen spigot, but bathing facilities were by immersion in Willow Creek or "Saturday night tin tub" until Major Burt rigged up a bathhouse supplied by a miraculous hot spring nearby. The only available servants were Chinese with mining camp experience, and after a dismal period of indigestion, the Burts were happy to relinquish domestic cookery and join the officers' mess. Other members included Post Surgeon George Kober, who would rise to medical fame, Lieutenant and Mrs. Wainwright (parents of Jonathan Wainwright of World War II Philippines fame), and Major Wilhelm, whose hobby was photography.

THE BURTS AT FORT BIDWELL.

Top: Lieutenant Lynch, Edith Burt, Lieutenant Colonel Andrew S. Burt,
Dr. Kober, Contract Surgeon.
Bottom: Mrs. Lynch, Mrs. Elizabeth Burt, Reynolds J. Burt, Nettie Lynch.

The only visible threat to the tranquility of the region which might justify the existence of Fort Bidwell was the Pah-Ute tribe near Pyramid Lake, but these Indians were so subdued by earlier fighting and so impoverished that the garrison could pursue its pleasures without hindrance. Progressive euchre, minstrel shows, picknicking in the mountains, ice-fishing on Lake Annie and bob-sleighing down Sawmill Canyon provided a relaxed atmosphere in marked contrast to that which had prevailed at Fort C. F. Smith. Reynolds' fondest recollection is that of "Jack Rabbit," an Indian pony purchased from the Pah-Utes; but he also recalls efforts along spiritual and educational lines:

> There were no regular church services as there was no chaplain at the fort, and no minister at the town of Bidwell. This deeply concerned my mother. She arranged Sunday School classes for six or eight children on the post but they were not regularly attended. A great event centered in a yearly visit by the Bishop of the Episcopal Diocese. A plain pine pulpit was set up in the small recreational hall. My mother's best embroidered cloths were used for covering, and her two small brass candle sticks flanked the pulpit and provided the only religious atmosphere available. A foot pedal organ with an amateur organist provided music for Moody and Sankey hymns. . . .

> A school, approved by War Department Regulations, which provided small sums for payment to an enlisted man to serve as teacher, was set up in the recreation hall. Few qualified at Fort Bidwell, but an Irishman, Delany, of stolid mien but with twinkling eyes, possessed the necessary abilities, and he conducted classes for about ten students, including children from the town. . . .

One of the best antidotes to the monotony of peace time frontier duty was target practice, and Major Burt constantly drilled his men in the art of marksmanship. He was himself a crack rifleman, reporting, "I am published in War Department Orders as standing at the head of Army sharpshooters in 1885."[18] A post correspondent, sending to San Francisco papers "Items from Fort Bidwell," reports an incident of August, 1884:

> On Sunday last we had a rifle contest on the post range between Major A. S. Burt, 8th Inf'y and Mr. Brown, book-keeper in A. C. Lowells and Cos.' store, who is an expert shot; the match consisted of a string of fifteen shots fired by each contestant at each of the following ranges, viz: 200, 300 and 600 yards, for a purse of $50, which was won easily

by the Major, although he fired several of his shots at 600 yards standing. . . .

The Major's prowess, and that of his infantry unit, is also reflected in the report of a rifle tournament held at Fort Bidwell on Christmas day, 1884, appearing in the *Army and Navy Journal*. On this occasion five teams participated in the affair with these scores: Co. F, 8th Infantry, 224; Troop C, 2nd Cavalry, 215; Citizens, Fort Bidwell, 223; Independents, 221, and Pah-Ute Indians, 180:

> . . . The shooting was pretty close between the two leading teams, so much so that the winning of the prize depended on our commanding officer, Major Burt, who shot last in the infantry team. The excitement was quite tense between the time he fired his last shot and when the result became known; had it been a "magpie" the citizens of Bidwell would have carried off the coveted prize, but when the four disk loomed up close to the bull's-eye, quite a relief was experienced by the boys of the 8th Foot.[14]

In their "tour" of western posts the Burts were not to be denied the opportunity of being stationed in the Southwest, and in the good old blistering desert summer time, besides. In 1886 they accompanied the 8th Infantry to Camp McDowell, Arizona Territory, which vied with Fort Yuma for the dubious reputation of being the hottest place in the United States. This post, which was esablished in 1865 by California Volunteers to guard the Butterfield stage line, was situated on the west bank of the Rio Verde, eight miles above its junction with the Salt River and "45 miles north of the Maricopa and Pimo villages." It connected with the outside world by mail stage to Yuma and Maricopa Wells, no longer threatened by Indian uprising, but frequently interrupted by flooding of the Colorado and Gila Rivers. The structures were of adobe, since the building timber in the surrounding mountains was largely in inaccessible situations. The flats were covered with mesquite, ironwood, palo-verde, willow, alder and artemisia.[15] Elizabeth Burt recalls the ordeal:

> To leave Fort Bidwell when the country was beautiful in its summer foliage, when the garden was beginning to supply delicious fresh vegetables, and arrive in the sands of Arizona at the miserable station of Maricopa, on the Southern Pacific Railway, we thought hard fate indeed. An ambulance met us to carry us to Fort McDowell, while the company went to Tucson. The heat was so intense that the ride could only be taken in the evening. Never can we forget that horrible day spent in that wretched Maricopa. The only

palatable water obtainable was given us by the engineer of a passing train and it was so warm one hardly cared to drink it.

A drive of seven hours brought us to the town of Phoenix towards midnight where we found the inmates of the hotel sleeping under the stars in the patio among tropical trees. We insisted upon taking our night's rest in bedrooms but the heat prevented sleep. The next day was too hot for the mules to travel so we started late in the evening for Fort McDowell where our old friends Major and Mrs. Henry Noyes, 2nd Cavalry, welcomed us most cordially. The first night after our arrival we spent with them and were most surprised to find a ghostly row of seven beds prepared for our host's family in the back yard, unprotected under the stars. We were not prepared at once to adopt this custom of the natives but were compelled to become reconciled later to sleeping on the large porch of our house, where an occasional night breeze made the temperature less oppressive than indoors. Early in the morning we would go inside and close the windows and doors to keep out the hot air. . . .

At the time of our arrival at the post, the soldiers had but lately returned from a campaign against Indians in the Apache War that was then drawing to a close, so no garden had been prepared to furnish vegetables for the table. Luxuries were few and among them most appreciated was a small quantity of ice which, once a week, the Quartermaster hauled from Phoenix, about 25 miles away. Each officer purchased his 150 pounds in a block. One of these blocks lasted four days and during that period made our meals somewhat tempting; but in the other three, as far as the table was concerned, the butter was oil, the cheese already melted for a rarebit. . . .

But few pleasant memories remain of that isolated spot. Its desolation was relieved only by the green of the cottonwoods that grew luxuriously along the acequia which carried a stream around the parade ground, and by the trees on the banks of the Verde River which flowed by the post.

Of the unpleasant memories there are unfortunately many, among them the break in the floor of the veranda and the rattlesnake that, 'crawling from the darkness below, was killed after quite an exciting battle; the numerous scorpions and centipedes that overran the old adobe walls of the kitchen; the monstrous tarantulas that were killed every now and then in the vicinity; and how our shoes each night were carefully filed with paper or other material to prevent an invasion from these repugnant and venomous creatures.

Just as the summer declined, and living conditions at Fort McDowell began to wear a more cheerful aspect, the 8th Infantry again received marching orders, this time to western Nebraska. While most of the regiment was destined for Fort Niobrara, in the sand hills near Valentine, the Burts were to report to Fort Robinson on White River. Elizabeth Burt recalls, "Happily the [Pullman] cars carried us to Fort Robinson where we were soon comfortably settled in our house built of logs and clapboarding and whose six rooms were lathed and plastered. Not long did we wait before the cold blasts came roaring from the north."

The dramatic period of this post had been in 1874-1878 when it had first been visited by Captain Burt as a focal point in the Sioux Wars. It was here that United States Indian Commissioners were once in danger of their lives, Red Cloud sulked, Crazy Horse was bayoneted to death, and Cheyennes under Dull Knife made a Thermopylae-like stand against their white tormentors. Now things were quiescent on the frontier. In 1890, after the Burts had departed, there was a great flare-up of military activity here, resulting from the Ghost Dance War on the Dakota Reservation. Through World War I it served as a cavalry post and remount station; during World War II it was a training center for dogs used in "commando" operations. Today the old fort precariously survives, and in some respects it still resembles the fort known to Elizabeth Burt, with the old original small parade ground area, and the oversize parade ground of later years, with surrounding structures of frame, adobe and red brick.[16]

Our garrison was composed of parts of the 8th Infantry and 9th Cavalry of which General Edward Hatch was colonel. Although not at Robinson at that time, he came in the spring with his headquarters, adding greatly to the pleasures of the station. Social gatherings of various kinds made the months pass pleasantly.

Dr. Walter Reed, the famous discoverer of the yellow fever-bearing mosquito, *Stegomia,* was there at Fort Robinson, beginning his medical career. He and his wife added much to the social side of post life. . . .[17]

During the winter the weather was too cold to make either sleighing or skating agreeable pastimes. Early in the spring driving and horseback riding became great sources of enjoyment. General Hatch was seen almost daily driving his spirited four-in-hand team drawing a handsome drag filled with ladies and officers of the post. To accompany him, though, was a nervous strain on account of his spirited driving. Many thought some accident would befall him on one of these drives. Though the particulars of his death were never known positively to us, yet rumor reported it as having happened in some way in connection with that fiery team.[18]

Reynolds Burt, twelve years old upon arrival at Robinson, found the place a rather complete bore, with haphazard schooling and church arrangements, no fishing or hunting in the neighborhood, a few listless dances, and much monotonous card-playing—euchre for the families, gambling on a modest scale for the soldiers. Just two things relieved the tedium. First, there was plenty of baseball, a sport which always commanded Major Burt's enthusiasm, and there was one memorable day when the visiting team from Fort Laramie protested an umpire's decision, precipitating a near riot. Secondly, there were the Indians.

The Sioux no longer lived near Fort Robinson, since their Red Cloud Agency had long since been moved northward near the Dakota Badlands, but the appearance of an occasional stray Indian, just ten years after the butchery of the Little Big Horn and the starvation march to the Black Hills, still caused a tremor of excitement around the garrison. Most of the Sioux were concentrated on the Pine Ridge and Rosebud Reservations, where they received periodic handouts. Major Burt was ordered there one summer to inspect the supplies issued, and Reynolds went along for the ride, via railroad and buckboard. At the Pine Ridge Agency, consisting of a few one-story buildings and a warehouse, they were kindly offered bed and board by the agent and his wife. Reynolds remembers:

> Procedure for issuing was as follows: The Indians were grouped by the agent, ten families to each group. These gathered at the warehouse. Items were called out in English. One item remains with me yet, viz: "Two skirts, Balmoral!" Even as a youngster I wondered how these would be divided among ten families! For the beef issue a steer would be let loose from the corral and a young Indian buck, bareback on a pony, would chase the steer, finally killing it with bow and arrows. A cruel, cruel sight! The squaws then gathered around and divided the carcass.

Elizabeth Burt mentions the fact that in his Fort Robinson days Major Burt became acquainted with Red Cloud, the old war chief, and had opportunity to discuss with him the "old fighting days." The meeting may have occurred on the occasion Reynolds mentions, but the details are given by Andrew Burt himself in a speech given in later years to a patriotic body, one of his rare first hand accounts:

AT FORT LARAMIE, 1887.
Reynolds J. Burt on horse, third from left.

7TH INFANTRY OFFICERS IN CAMP NEAR FORT LARAMIE, 1887.
Colonel Andrew S. Burt, front row, right.

Years afterwards I met Red Cloud at Pine Ridge Agency on which occasion he arranged for me to meet a lot of Sioux Indians and Cheyenne Chiefs and head soldiers of these tribes. We had a council smoke, one pipe being passed from one to another round the circle. This important ceremony concluded, there was a pause, then Red Cloud arose and delivered an address of welcome, giving my Indian name in full, "The-Big-White-Chief-Little-Man-Who-Fights-The-Sioux-A-Heap," and lauding my achievements against his warriors. . . .

On this occasion Red Cloud, the famous militant savage, was one of the most picturesque red men I ever saw, a model of physical excellence standing over six feet in height, straight as an arrow, with the impress of command stamped on every line of his powerful face and revealed in his every movement, so full of dignity that he appeared like a Chesterfield of the Plains. Untutored in the ways of civilization, he was a splendid creation of the earth and air and sunshine— free from the conventionalities of polite society but full of decorum in the extension of his primitive hospitality as any diplomatic representative at our Capitol City. . . .

Andrew Burt, whose wife and family as well as himself were the target of Indian attacks, harbored no ill feelings. Unlike most frontiersmen he displayed a romantic sentimentality more characteristic of an Indian Bureau "peace advocate" than of an Army Officer. In the preface to a published newspaper story of his about the Cheyenne flight from Oklahoma to Fort Robinson in 1877, he makes his position clear:

> . . . Right here I want to say that since the landing of the Pilgrim Fathers, the United States Government has never kept faithfully and honorably any treaty made with the Indians, and further, that there never was a grosser libel than the words of Sheridan, who said that, "The only good Indian is a dead one," for I myself have personal recollection of many good Indians, who were upright and honorable, and who grieved over the wrongs done their people.[19]

It is understandable that Crow, Sioux and Shoshone, who had no love for the U. S. Army as an institution, had a warm regard for this man, who defended their right to live honorably, and was one of the few Army officers of record who took pains to learn and communicate with them in their native tongues. Reverend Tuttle, in a learned discourse entitled, "Why Do Indians Scalp Their Enemies?", cites Major Burt as a recognized authority on Indian customs.[20]

AT FORT LARAMIE, 1888.

From left to right: Captain Louis Brechemin, Miss Lonnie Hall, Mrs. D. A. Frederick, Miss Kitty Graves, Miss Bowness Briggs, Helen Worden, Carrie Merriam, Edward Frederick, Kitty Johnson, Captain Constant Williams (7th Infantry), Mrs. John London, Edith Burt, Mrs. Louis Brechemin, Sr., 1st Lieutenant Van Orsdale (7th Infantry), Mrs. Andrew S. Burt, 1st Lieutenant D. A. Frederick (7th Infantry), Mrs. Charles A. Booth, Mrs. Daniel L. Howell, Lieutenant Colonel Andrew S. Burt (7th Infantry).

Seated on boardwalk: Jim Howell, Ada Howell.

(Indentifications courtesy of Colonel Louis Brechemin, Jr.)

In 1887 Andrew Burt was promoted to the rank of Lieutenant Colonel and assigned to the 7th Infantry at Fort Laramie. A favorite quip of his for the next few years: "Captain of the 9th; Major in the 8th; Lieutenant Colonel in the 7th; Heaven help the 6th!" Brevet rank aside, he was twenty years a line Captain before he became a Major, and six years a Major before his Lieutenant Colonelcy. Strict seniority rules were observed and there was no correlation between ability and speed of promotion. Finally, however, he was getting his proper recognition, much to the satisfaction of friends back in the Chicago Press Club who frequently growled, "Why don't they promote Andy faster?"

The Burts moved by rail to Lusk, Wyoming, where they were met by Government ambulance from Fort Laramie. Reynolds vividly recalls his family's arrival at the fort, just as the garrison school was in recess, and "the crowd ran to surround the ambulance and to stare at the new family. Miss Rockwell, the alert teacher, furiously rang the bell and thus relieved us of the mob." Reynolds did not attend this school himself, being sent east with his sister to resume the brief formal education he had in Chicago.

His mother also remembers:

>　　We had already accepted an invitation from Captain Kirtland and his wife to be their guests upon our arrival. He had belonged to the original 18th in the Civil War and had been a bachelor lieutenant in General Gibbon's regiment when we lived in the block house at Fort Sanders in the sixties. Of his family, one of the boys is now [1912] Lieutenant Roy Kirtland of aviator fame.

>　　Every lady in the new post was a stranger to us, but it was not long before they made us at home. They had an inspiring example in the wife of their commanding officer, Colonel Henry Merriam, 7th Infantry. . . .

>　　It seems a strange coincidence that both of our sons started from Fort Laramie at the age of thirteen, though eleven years had elapsed between their birthdays, to leave the army temporarily and live in Cincinnati to attend school. . . . For the first time we were without any of our children. Lonely indeed was the quiet house. . . .[21] [but] there was little time for me to hold my hands and mourn, as we soon left Laramie for our new station, Fort Washakie.

>　　On the way we left the Union Pacific Railroad at Rawlins and took a stage ride of thirty hours; traveling day and night we arrived at our new post before dark one beautiful evening in spring[1889]. We found a small command of 7th Infantry and 9th Cavalry in a little jewel of a post beside a rushing stream.

Colonel Burt's transfer to Fort Washakie as post commander brought him back full circle, after nearly a quarter of a century, to "the Land of the Shoshones." In 1866 the agency for this tribe had been at Fort Bridger (commanded then by young Captain Burt). By a treaty of July 3, 1868, the "Eastern Shoshoni and Bannocks" accepted a reservation of nearly three million acres drained by Wind River, far to the north of Fort Bridger and the new Union Pacific Railroad. In 1872 the southern portion of the area, below the forks

FORT LARAMIE NATIONAL HISTORIC SITE.

Courtesy, National Park Service

"THE BURT HOUSE" OF 1887-1888.
As it appears today adjoining the old Sutler's Store.

of the Popo Agie River, was lopped off by a cash agreement, in order to avoid Indian entanglement with miners and settlers who flocked into that area as the result of the South Pass gold rush. When Colonel Burt officiated at Fort Washakie the reservation still comprised around two million acres; but by subsequent treaties the Shoshone were also relieved of all lands north of Wind River, leaving them today with a triangle of about one-half a million acres. This is the Indian Reservation familiar to tourists who now follow the highway up Wind River and over Togwotee Pass to Jackson Hole.

When the Wind River Reservation was first set aside, the Shoshones were frequently at war with the more powerful Sioux and victimized by unscrupulous whites. Their need for military protection was first met by the establishment of Camp Augur in June, 1867, on the site of present Lander. In March, 1870, this was renamed Camp Brown for Captain Frederick Brown who was killed with Fetterman near Fort Phil Kearny. In January, 1871 Captain Robert Torrey, 13th Infantry, selected a new and more centrally located site for a post on the Little Wind River, while a new agency site was spotted about two miles away, on the South Fork of the Little Wind. In 1878 this was officially renamed Fort Washakie in honor of the Indian Chief. The military post, of stone construction, was laid out in the standard rectangle.[22]

Elizabeth Burt remembers:

> Captain and Mrs. Quinton welcomed us most cordially to their pleasant home, and Captain and Mrs. Olmstead of the 9th Cavalry were most hospitable. Mr. and Mrs. J. K. Moore were a great acquisition to our society.[23]
>
> We were on an Indian reservation where the Shoshone tribe lived on one part and the Arapahoes on another. Both were friendly with us, but avoided each other. Mary Ann was a squaw of the Shoshones and Mollie of the Arapahoes. Each had been taught by wives of officers preceding us to do laundry work, scrub and wash dishes and windows. . . . Sometimes they met by chance at our house. One would sit at an end of our back porch and glower at the other. "Arapahoe squaw no good," would be heard from one, and then would follow a spiteful response, "Shoshone squaw no good."[24]
>
> The Reverend Mr. Roberts was missionary to the Indians, devoting his life to the work. He and his wife lived in a small addition which had been built on the Episcopal chapel. Faithful workers were they in the mission field, where they still live and have brought up their children. Glad were we to learn that their eldest boy had won a Cecil Rhodes scholarship and had gone to England to complete his education. . . .[25]
>
> Another interesting person was the Reverend Sherman Coolidge, an Indian whom the 7th Infantry had captured years ago during an engagement with the Arapahoe. This Indian boy was taken by Captain and Mrs. Coolidge and cared for by them until the Right Reverend Bishop Whipple took him and placed him at school where he was educated for the ministry. When we knew him at Fort Washakie he was an ordained minister of the Episcopal Church. . . . Since then he has married a lady from the East who went to Wyoming as a teacher to the Indians.[26]
>
> Again we met Washakie, grand old man of the Shoshones. Since we saw him years ago, his black hair had become white and hung over his shoulders. . . . Upon one of their festive occasions we were invited by him to be present. It proved to be a Thanksgiving service beginning with what they called a dance. Men and women stood side by side in a circle, moving with slow side step, singing in monotonous

tones what, we were told by Mr. Roberts, was a hymn of thanksgiving to God. Washakie had been confirmed in the Episcopal church and used his influence to convert his tribe, beginning by sending his children to the reservation school. This religious ceremony was followed by a feast that had been cooked in the washboilers and brought hot to the festival. We politely declined the invitation to share the bountiful repast which seemed to consist of all the vegetables raised by them, cooked into a stew. Judging from the eagerness with which they devoured it from tin plates, they at least considered it a treat.

Reynolds Burt, who visited Fort Washakie on summer vacations, remembers that:

Chief Washakie was a fine upstanding man. He often came to call socially on the commanding officer. As they sat on the front porch of our quarters I would watch, fascinated, their hands and gestures as they communicated in Sign Language, the universal language that all tribes of the Plains understood and used. . . .

Services were conducted on Sunday evenings by Rev. Coolidge. The congregation was very small and consisted of officers' families. I do not remember attendance of any enlisted men. No offertory was passed. There was very little free money in circulation. However, the Commanding Officer at each meeting, as the congregation passed out, laid a fifty cent piece at the foot of the improvised altar.[27]

The Commanding Officer promoted baseball. By general and unit contributions an outfit of baseball suits and other equipment was obtained. This was a morale builder. "Washakie" was prominent across the shirt fronts. We played one outside game at the town of Lander on July 4. . . . The civilian team with no practice offered no opposition. The prize was $10.

Calamity followed shortly after this celebration. The sergeant in charge of uniforms deserted taking them with him. Strange as it may seem, with the widest of spaces between ranches and towns, he got away. The general opinion was that the ranchers were disposed to cover for such a man. Baseball was dead for the summer. . . .

The most important form of recreation, however, for military and civilian alike, was big game hunting. Fort Washakie became an assembly point for many expeditions up Wind River and its tributaries, to the Union Pass area, and to Jackson Hole. One such visitor was Owen Wister, a young Philadelphia lawyer, who fell in love with the West and gave up law to write *The Virginian* and other immortal cowboy fiction. Among his recently published letters there is this entry of October 15, 1889, at Fort Washakie:

> Got here at six o'clock Sunday. Spent yesterday in preparations and calling on the people at the Post. All were very pleasant and cordial. I got in terms instantly with the commander thus. He said, "You know, sir, I don't sympathize with you men from the East who come here and shoot our game." "Well, sir," I made answer, "Did you know but how little of it I shot, you would sympathize with me very deeply." He has offered to send an ambulance and a doctor for me if I get hurt. I told him that was a most comfortable idea to start off with. But he'd do it.[28]

Some years later Colonel Burt, who had apparently written Wister to compliment him upon his stories, received this undated note from him, written at 328 Chestnut Street, Philadelphia:

> Dear Colonel Burt: Remember you? Why of course I do—and this long delay in thanking you for your very kind note is because it has just caught up with my shifting addresses. We met in J. K. Moore's store in October, 1889, when the stage came in with your mail and with me. Subsequently we played whist and discoursed, and you and your family were most hospitable to the stranger both before he went up Wind River and after he came down. I am delighted that my stories entertain you. But if I disappoint you about the destiny of Specimen Jones you must forgive me. I am hoping to introduce him to my readers once more before he makes his final bow.[29]

Burt's next assignment, to Rock Springs Barracks, 1890-1892, was not historically memorable, but it was not without incident. The big excitement at Rock Springs had occurred in 1885 when a score of Chinese employees of the Union Pacific Coal Mines were massacred in a race riot. It was because of this shameful affair that United States soldiers were stationed here for a few years, at the request of the Chinese government. The nearest thing to a riot that occurred while the Burts lived in Rock Springs was the fatal explosion of July 17, 1891. Two Finns named Santala and Hilli, while gloriously drunk, began an argument as to which man was the better shot. They chose as their target the door of the Company powder house, containing about a ton of high explosives. The resultant blast left a great crater, made a shambles of the neighborhood, and blew the Finns into shreds. Like the majority of innocent inhabitants, the Burts were shaken up by this episode, but unscathed.[30]

A more pleasant episode here was the marriage of Edith Burt to young Lieutenant Trout, Troop E, 9th Cavalry, who was stationed at Fort Robinson and who soon became involved in quelling the "Johnson County War" between Wyoming cattlemen and homesteaders. It was one year later, while Edith and grand-daughter Elizabeth Dorothy were visiting at Rock Springs, that Colonel Burt received the news that he was promoted to the rank of full colonel and would take over the 25th Infantry at Fort Missoula, Montana.

In many respects the six years at Fort Missoula, 1892-1898, were the best of the golden years. Here at last there was gracious living in a large well-appointed house, near a community which appreciated genteel refinements, and a succession of sparkling and distinguished guests. And from here youngest son Reynolds Burt, who had been a Fort Laramie infant during the Sioux Wars, went to West Point, returning in 1896 with his bride to begin a military career under Andrew's personal command.[31]

A large roughly rectangular area in northwest Montana is cut off from the rest of the state by high mountains. Here in the early 1870's the pioneer communities of Deer Lodge and Missoula felt themselves threatened by the hunting expeditions of Nez Perce Indians from Idaho, and petitioned for a military post. In February, 1876 Colonel Wesley Merritt reported on the situation to the Department of Dakota, recommending such a post at Hell Gate, near Missoula. Later in the year officers of the 7th Infantry surveyed to determine its precise location. In June, 1877 Captain Charles G. Rawn, 7th Infantry, left Fort Shaw on Sun River to occupy the site and begin construction. At an elevation of 3,400 feet above sea level, on a large flat surrounded by mountains, the new post enjoyed a pleasant and healthful climate. To the Southwest fifteen miles away, was snow-clad Lo-Lo, one of the highest peaks of the Bitter Root Range, with the easy gradients of Lewis and Clark's famed Lo-Lo Pass beside it. The fertile valley of the Bitter Root stretched sixty miles southward from the new site.

The most important year at Fort Missoula, militarily, was 1877. A climactic event occurred before construction of the fort was fairly under way. This was the attempted interception of fleeing Nez Perce Indians under Chief Joseph by General Howard and troops from the Department of the Columbia. Troops under Captain Rawn and citizens of Missoula were involved in a futile parley with the rebel chiefs. They joined troops under General Gibbon who arrived

MARK TWAIN AND COLONEL BURT AT FORT MISSOULA,
MONTANA.

at Fort Missoula to launch operations which culminated in the celebrated Battle of the Big Hole.

After a minor campaign against stray hostiles in 1878, it appears
that the duties of the troops stationed at the fort consisted mainly
in policing and escorting the peaceful Flatheads to and from the
buffalo hunting grounds and maintaining federal law in the territory.
Abandonment of the fort was ordered in 1898, when it was evacu-
ated by Colonel Burt and the 25th Infantry; however, upon demand
of the citizens this order was revoked and Fort Missoula lingered on,
unimportantly, until very recent years.[32]

Perhaps the most memorable visitor to Missoula during Burt's
command was the celebrated shock-haired Samuel L. Clemens, alias
Mark Twain, in August, 1895. He had a lecture engagement in town
enroute to the West Coast where he would soon start on a trip around
the world. With his wife and daughter, Clara, he was a dinner guest
of the Burts and returned to the post next morning to watch the
guard mounting ceremony.

Mrs. Burt recalls the occasion:

A most trying occasion for me arose when a message was received from my husband in Missoula, worded, "Mark Twain, his wife and daughter, will dine with us today." Exactly how it was managed I never knew. Six was our dinner hour, and the telegram was received about two o'clock. But it was in the summer, and our garden furnished delicious lettuce and peas. The chicken coop supplied fine broilers. Our good black cook did her best and had a soup and salad. The ice cream and coffee were perfect. The attractive round table was decorated with roses from the garden, amid shining silver. When the guests arrived I knew they did not surmise the state of commotion that had existed that afternoon. After dinner, the band played, the garrison officers and their ladies called, and all was happiness. Mr. Clemens, however, was due at the theatre for his lecture. So pleased were they with their visit that they accepted an invitation to see guard mounting in the morning. . . .

While driving to Fort Missoula my husband said, "Mr. Clemens, I am taking you to a place where you will not be obliged to do the entertaining, but will be entertained." Mr. Clemens threw up his hands and exclaimed, "Great Heavens! Is there such a place of delight on earth?" My husband arranged to have Mr. Clemens surrounded by a number of officers of the fort, and when he started to tell a joke, one of the officers would interrupt, saying, "Beg your pardon, Mr. Clemens, permit me to tell a little incident," and then would give an old army story. After the laugh each time, Mr. Clemens would endeavour to follow with an anecdote of his own, receiving the same interruption; so it went on until in bewilderment, Mr. Clemens exclaimed, "I beg you give me just one chance." After the general laugh he added in that inimitable drawl of his, "Say, boys, I haven't had one put over me as good as that since the old Comstock days."

An amusing incident occurred on our front porch looking over the parade ground at guard mounting. The officers who were not on duty were present also with my husband. When the band in "trooping off" had marched past the guard and was countermarching back to its post, my husband said, "Mark Twain says in one of his books—There are two things I could never understand. One is the solar eclipse and the other is the countermarching of a band." Mr. Clemens replied, "You are right, Colonel, on both counts. I haven't solved the band proposition even now, and as for the other count, I was modest before I was born." . . .[33]

Another visit that is remembered with pleasure was that of Professor Elliot Coues and his wife who arrived unan-

ELIZABETH REYNOLDS BURT, 1902.

nounced. He was rewriting an account of the Lewis and Clark expedition and had come from Washington to go over part of the ground. He brought letters from Secretary of War Lamont, asking Colonel Burt to provide transportation for the party. . . .[34]

Baseball was a passion with Andrew Burt ever since his first post command at Fort Bridger, recognizing its value as a morale builder. An article from the *Daily Missoulian* for April 30, 1907, is significant:

Missoula remembers General "Andy" Burt who as colonel of the 25th was at Fort Missoula so long that he became an old-timer here. General Burt had three fads— his profession, baseball and whist. Andy Burt, as he used to be known in the West so many years ago that it would be a shame to speak of them publicly, is one of the best all-around sportsmen in the country, and although he is on the retired list of the army, he is as much a baseball fan as when baseball was invented.

Andy Burt, one of the best Indian fighters in the army, whose theater of operations was the vast plains of the great West, was the first commissioned officer to step over the line and play baseball with the men. He played shortstop in Company H, 9th Infantry, so many years ago that it has almost been forgotten. It was a bold departure in those days, contrary to the iron rule handed down from the old army before the war of the states.[35]

The 25th Infantry under Colonel Burt was a crack outfit. A sample testimonial is recorded in the report of an inspection of Fort Missoula, September 23-28, 1897, by Colonel George H. Burton, Pacific District:

In all the schools of practical instruction this battalion maintains the same high standing that is held at my two previous inspections. In comparison with other battalions in the district it has no superior. Colonel Burt has practiced the battalion in many movements by Bugle commands with good success. The ceremonies of review and inspection were familiar to the officers and men. The step and dress of the troops at review were commendable. The arms and acoutrements at inspection were perfect. The discipline of the command is praiseworthy.[36]

In the Burt Collection there is an extensive file of letters to the President of the United States in 1896-1897 urging Burt's promotion to brigadier rank. Among the enthusiastic endorsers were Senators Manderson and Thurston of Nebraska, Senator Warren of Wyoming, Ethelbert Talbot (Episcopal Bishop of Wyoming and Idaho), Inspector-General J. C. Breckenridge, United States Army, and General D. S. Stanley, under whom Burt served during the Yellowstone Expedition of 1873: "I have always found him an admirable officer, intelligent, alert and daring." In another endorsement, James W. Drannan, Adjutant General, State of Montana, became eloquent in his praise:

> I knew "Captain" Burt when [I was] a sergeant in the same regiment. The Colonel was universally liked and respected by the enlisted men. If left to a vote of the soldiers who served in the frontier of '66 to '76 Major Burt would be the only man in it. [I] would walk to Washington to help the Colonel as would thousands of old soldiers through the country.

Word of Colonel Burt's achievements in the training and morale departments were not lost on Army brass. With the threat of the Spanish-American War in 1898, the 25th Regiment of Infantry was among the first to be summoned. The Colonel's ability as a leader was extolled in a Chicago newspaper:

> Burt's Men in the Van. Pen Picture of a Typical American Soldier. The 25th Infantry, U. S. A., the regiment ordered to Key West, and which in case of war will be the first to test the mettle of the Spanish troops, is commanded by Colonel Andrew Sheridan Burt. The regiment has been stationed at Fort Missoula, Mont., and both officers and men are veterans. Out there in the Western wilds some barrack room Kipling has composed a regimental ballad:

> We've known him in times of peace,
>   And when in times of trouble
> Have eyes and swords together flashed
>   We felt we knew him double.

> He rides to danger with his men,
>   A fearless form before them,
> And that's the reason why—perhaps,
>   Those very men adore him.

> If bullets sing and rifles ring,
>   May no mischance avert
> Just praise from one—Mars' own true son—
>   Gallant Andy Burt.

Fighting troops always like a hard-fighting leader; one who can get them into more tight places than any other commander and then get them out again successfully they look up to with respect. The 25th both likes and respects its Colonel.

Colonel Burt is a hard fighter and is a descendant of hard fighters. Ancestry and long campaigning have combined to make him the soldier he is. He is described as a man of cool, deliberate judgment, firm decision, quick in action, and noted for bravery among brave men; a strict disciplinarian, yet considerate of his men. . . .

In appearance Colonel Burt is of medium height, lithe, sinewy, bronzed, without a superfluous ounce of tissue, and carrying his years as lightly as might many a man half his age. He has strong regular features, a grizzled moustache, kind eyes that look out piercingly from under heavy brows, the bearing of a soldier, and the polish of a student. His father was an art collector, and some of the best pictures transported west of the Atlantic found lodgement in the home of the soldier, whom today his country beckons to the front.

Colonel Burt's influence over his men is admirable. He has commanded two posts for a year without having a single desertion. . . .

In the early years his young wife frequently crossed the plains in wagons with him and his comrades. . . .

With the leaving of the 25th for the scene of probable combat, it is safe to assert that none of the younger men of the service will bring to the discharge of duty more enthusiasm, discretion, ability and bravery than Gallant Andy Burt.[37]

But the War Department had ideas of its own about the Colonel's usefulness. With the outbreak of war he was relieved of Regimental Command, and made a Brigadier General of Volunteers, being an old Army regular who could be depended upon to weld untrained units into a fighting force. Contemporary newspaper accounts testify to the brisk manner in which he performed these assignments, as well as the warm affection with which he was held by the newspaper fraternity. Typical is a dispatch from Chicamauga Park, Georgia, May 19, 1898:

An Ideal Soldier. General Burt has completely won the officers and men of his brigade by the bluff, soldierly cor-

BRIGADIER GENERAL ANDREW SHERIDAN BURT, 1902.

diality of his manner and the interest he takes in all the affairs of his command. It is a saying in the army that Burt was the whole 25th Infantry, and the men now under his command are beginning to understand the methods which made that regiment a famous and splendid organization. . . .

Mrs. Burt and the General's beautiful granddaughter visited him at his headquarters today and received a jovial welcome. As Mrs. Burt was departing the General said: "Well, I command the brigade, but she commands me. But she's as good a soldier as any of us. Why, she was with me in an Indian fight, and she never even said, "Andrew, come here!"[38]

The colorful veteran was saluted again in the *Chicago Evening Post* for June 14, 1898, while troops were awaiting embarkation at "Camp Cuba Libre" at Jacksonville, Florida:

The Second Illinois, First Wisconsin and First North Carolina are to be congratulated upon their brigade commander, General A. S. Burt. The general has been nearly forty years in the service. He rose from the ranks and is proud of it. No army officer is more considerate of the welfare of his men than this stern old warrior. When anything is wanted for their comfort the general says: "I howl and howl all the way up till I get it." General Burt is no believer in the feather bed soldier. He is as stern as may be in the line of duty, yet has a heart in him four sizes too big for his body. By the way, the general is something more than a dilettante as a playwright and author. He has fathered at least one successful play. His libretto of Robin Hood is a fine production. He is the author of a farce which may be produced some day. It has plenty of scream in it. The general's special hobby is whist. He plays it by telegraph, talks it, writes about it and is ready to fight over it if necessary.[39]

A second report from Camp Cuba Libre appearing on June 20 in the *Mail and Express* also dwells on the merits of the First Brigade:

There have been two reviews of regiments by Major-Gen. Lee, commanding the Seventh Corps. It indicates the advancement in the organization of this Second Division of this corps that today was held the first review of a brigade. It was the review of the First Brigade, Gen. Burt commanding. It was a great compliment to select Gen. Burt's command for the review. The three regiments of the brigade, the 2nd New Jersey, the 1st North Carolina and the 2nd

Illinois were each heartily applauded as they passed Gen. Lee's reviewing station at the Windsor Hotel, in perfect alignment by companies, and with well-maintained distances. General Lee was quite warranted in the congratulations that he showered upon General Burt for the fine condition of efficiency into which he has brought his command.[40]

On December 31, 1898, Andrew Burt was mustered out as Brigadier General of Volunteers, and then rejoined the 25th Infantry as Colonel, with headquarters at Fort Logan, Colorado. He served in the Philippines from August, 1899 to August, 1901. Here he was assigned to command Zambales Province, Luzon. Generals Wheaton and MacArthur complimented him officially for his success in conquering Zambales, cleaning out not only Insurrectos, but all Ladrone bands in the Province, compelling the surrender of General Mascardo, Colonels Arce and Alba, their officers and men.[41]

On April 1, 1902 Andrew Burt was promoted by President Roosevelt to the rank of full Brigadier General in the United States Army.[42] He retired on April 15 of that year, on his own application, after forty years' service. He then made his home in Washington, D. C., becoming quite active in veterans', fraternal and patriotic organizations, operating the Burt-Peckham Information Bureau, making speeches and contributing articles of reminiscences to newspapers and press associations.

General Burt died at midnight, January 11, 1915, aged eighty-three, at his home, and was buried at Arlington.[43] Elizabeth Burt survived him by eleven years.

Many eulogies to this patriotic and devoted soldier appeared in the public press, but the finest tribute of all was written by John McGovern, Chicago newspaperman and old friend of Press Club days:

Private, Corporal, Sergeant, Captain, Colonel, General Andy Burt was as simple as a child and as great as an ancestor. It was my good fortune to see and sit with him once more only a week before his sudden death. When our time to part was at hand, he stood at the elevator on the fourth floor. "John," he said, suddenly, "let me hug you!" And so, like the republicans of Paris, we gave the fraternal embrace. It had never happened to us before. But it was Opportunity. What man ever had greater honor than to clasp Andy Burt within his arms?

I began resenting the fact that Andy Burt was only captain so long back as 1880 or 1881. I cannot unreel the

GENERAL REYNOLDS JOHNSTON BURT.

great spool of moving pictures that carries the scenes of his glory since then. One thing time could not do unto noble Andy Burt. It could not change him in face, form or demeanor. "John," he said, as we sat for the first time in 'Race's palatial restaurant' (Boston Oyster House, upstairs), "John, it is a rotten line!" Andy would love his friend, but he would not praise his bad poetry. And he looked then just as he looked in 1915. His play-spell of recruiting, on Clark Street, in the eighties, could not last always, and there was a big hole in this town when he went on to command at Fort Bidwell, at Fort McPherson [McDowell], at all the hot forts in the Southwest, and finally at Fort Missoula, Mont., where he would welcome the guest and do it with the regimental band! He would make a post holiday! Ah! come! Be a good fellow! Come!

Such was the open heart of Andy Burt. Three-quarters of a century it beat with friendship and love. On that last afternoon he delivered to me the same eulogium of the "Commander"—the wife who had gone gloriously over the world with him. Just as he had written it a quarter-century before, he told me once more, and for the last, loving, loyal time, that Peggy O'Dowd (in *Vanity Fair*) was a beautiful figment of a great man's brain, "but by God, sir, the Commander went through it all." Never did Andy tell of the bullets that flew through him and about him at Mill Springs, Chickamauga, Jonesboro, Atlanta.

In 1885, the sharpest eye in the army—the best sharpshooter. Well, you could see it in Andy's eye.

So Andy is gone, and gone to a sure glory. We saw him march past as private, corporal, sergeant, captain, colonel, or general, always at his country's call—always his noble breast exposed to the bullets of his country's foes— 41 years in active service. May his country remain grateful to his memory; may his descendants rejoice in the distinction he bestowed upon them; may his surviving companions charge themselves anew with the loving guard of his great name.[44]

Notes

CHAPTER 1 — CIVIL WAR ROMANCE

1—"An Army Wife's Forty Years in the Service, 1862-1902," by Elizabeth Reynolds Burt. Typed *Manuscript,* 346 pages, presented to the Library of Congress by Brig. Gen. Reynolds J. Burt, retired, 306 Woodland Terrace, Alexandria, Virginia. Hereinafter referred to as Elizabeth Burt *Ms.*

2—Elizabeth Custer, *Boots and Saddles,* New York, 1885; Margaret Carrington, *Ab-Sa-Ra-Ka, Land of Massacre,* Philadelphia, 1879; Frances Roe, *Army Letters from an Officer's Wife,* New York, 1909; Agnes W. Spring, editor, "An Army Wife Comes West; Letters of Catherine Wever Collins," *Colorado Magazine,* Vol. XXXI, No. 4 (October, 1954).

3—The album is in the extensive collection of General Burt, aforementioned. This, hereinafter referred to as the "Burt Collection," includes Burt family correspondence, news clippings, scrap books, programs, brochures, photo albums, and assorted manuscripts and genealogies.

4—John A. Rayner, *The First Century of Piqua, Ohio,* published at Piqua, 1916; John Johnston, *Recollections of Sixty Years* (reprinted from *Cist's Miscellany,* Cincinnati, Ohio, 1842), Dayton, Ohio, 1915; Miscellaneous data in the Burt Collection, notably a 23-page letter of reminiscences dated January 3, 1895, Julia J. Patterson to her daughter.

5—Genealogical data in Burt Collection.

6—*Ibid.;* Elizabeth Burt *Ms.;* Anon., "Biographical Sketches of Non-Graduates," *Bulletin* of the Fiftieth Anniversary of the Class of 1861, Yale College, pp. 175-176.

7—Theo. F. Rodenbaugh and William L. Haskin, *The Army of the United States,* New York, 1896 ("The Eighteenth Regiment of Infantry," by First Lieut. Charles H. Cabaniss, Jr.), p. 643.

8—Burt Collection.

9—Unidentified news clipping in Burt Collection; Frank Moore, editor, *The Rebellion Record,* New York, 1862, pp. 34, 37, 42-45.

10—Elizabeth Burt *Ms.*

11—John Fitch, *Annals of the Army of the Cumberland,* Philadelphia, 1864, p. 716.

12—Elizabeth Burt *Ms.;* Rodenbaugh and Haskin, *op. cit.,* pp. 643-652; official citations in Burt Collection.

13—John Haskell King, brigadier general of volunteers, 1862, brevetted major general 1865, died 1888.—Frances B. Heitman, *Historical Register and Dictionary of the United States Army, 1789-1903,* Washington, D. C., Vol. I, p. 599.

14—George H. Thomas, West Point, 1836-1840. Achieved fame as the "Rock of Chickamauga" in the famous battle of September 20, 1863, in which Andrew Burt also fought with distinction. Cited in a Congressional Resolution of March 3, 1865, for driving General Hood from Tennessee. Major general in the regular army. "General Thomas was a solid, heavily built man, and bore his massive frame so erect as to exaggerate his height."—George W. Cullum, *Biographical Register of Officers and Graduates of the United States Military Academy, 1802-1870,* New York, 1891, pp. 33-40.

15—William F. Fox, *Regimental Losses in the American Civil War, 1861-1865,* Albany, New York, 1889, pp. 520-521; Frederick H. Dyer, *Correspondence of the War of the Rebellion,* Des Moines, 1908, p. 1715. According to Major Alson B. Ostrander, *An Army Boy of the Sixties,* New York, 1924, p. 267, the 18th Infantry sustained the heaviest "Lost in Action" of all regiments of the Regular Army. At the Battle of Stone's River, where the regiment encountered its hardest fighting, the 2nd Battalion, commanded by Major Frederick Townsend, took 603 officers and men into the fight, of whom forty-eight per cent were killed or wounded.

CHAPTER 2 — JEFFERSON BARRACKS TO FORT KEARNEY, 1866

1—Rodenbaugh and Haskin, *op. cit.,* p. 653.

2—M. Carrington, *op. cit.,* p. 37.

3—Regimental Returns, National Archives.

4—James Van Voast, cadet at Military Academy 1848-1852; major, 18th Infantry, 1863; Fort Laramie, June to December, 1866; Fort Phil Kearny, Dak., to April, 1867; Fort Reno to May, 1868; Fort D. A. Russell to April, 1869; colonel in command at Fort Wallace, Kansas, 1877-1880; retired in 1883 for disability—Cullum, *op. cit.,* Vol. II, pp. 477-478.

5—The site of Jefferson Barracks, just below St. Louis, had been selected in 1826 by General Henry Atkinson as the hub of a system of frontier defense lines extending up the Mississippi and Missouri Rivers. The new post was named in honor of the famous ex-President and signer of the Declaration of Independence, who died on July 4 of that year. During the next few decades as Headquarters, Department of the West, this was the principal training and staging area for troops destined for service on the frontier. During the Civil War the Barracks became the principal recruiting center and hospital facility in the West. In 1866 Elizabeth Burt witnessed the last year of Jefferson Barracks as a command post. In later years it would serve variously as engineer, ordnance and cavalry depots; during World Wars I and II it was a primary induction and demobilization center. In 1892 the original stone buildings around the parade ground, in one of which lived the Burts, were replaced by brick buildings, now occupied by the Missouri National Guard. Still standing, however, are stone buildings in the old Ordnance Depot area which date back to 1843, and which are now operated by St. Louis County as a feature of Jefferson Barracks Historical Park. Meager data is presented in Maj. Henry W. Webb, "The Story of Jefferson Barracks," Manuscript in National Park Service possession; the Missouri Historical Society, St. Louis, is assembling archival data for a definitive study. For a description of the Barracks in the late 1860's, see *Circular No. 4*, War Department, Surgeon-General's Office, "Report on Barracks and Hospitals with Descriptions of Military Posts," December, 1870, pp. 275-284.

6—A transplanted French aristocrat, General B. L. E. Bonneville, was graduated from West Point in 1815 and saw long service on the Indian frontier, with two notable interludes. In 1825 he was detailed to serve as aide to the nation's honored guest, the Marquis de Lafayette. And in 1832-1835 he took leave from the army to engage in a fur trading and exploring expedition to the Far West, an experience made famous by Washington Irving's *Adventures of Captain Bonneville* (New York, 1936). In 1849 during the California gold rush he was briefly in command of new Fort Kearney on the Lower Platte. In March, 1865 he was brevetted Brigadier General for long and faithful service, and placed in command of the St. Louis post. In October, 1866, he resigned from the Army and moved to Fort Smith, Arkansas.—*Dictionary of American Biography*, New York, 1946, Vol. II, p. 438.

7—J. R. Perkins, *Trails, Rails and War: The Life of General G. M. Dodge*, Indianapolis, 1929, pp. 171-198. Dodge, 1831-1916, Congressman, Civil War hero, builder of the Union Pacific, benefactor of James Bridger, first citizen of Omaha, Nebraska and Council Bluffs, Iowa, was one of the giant figures of America's westward expansion.

8—Historical Map of Fort Leavenworth, published in 1956 by the Fort Leavenworth Historical Society; *Fort Leavenworth and the Command and General Staff College*, Public Information Office, 44 pp.; *Historic Kansas*, by Margaret Whittemore, Lawrence, 1954, p. 24; *A Survey of Historic Sites and Structures in Kansas*, Kansas State Historical Society, Topeka, 1957, p. 36.

9—Circular No. 4, *op. cit.*, pp. 284-286.

10—Washington Lafayette Elliott, Military Academy, 1841-1844, Officer in Mounted Rifle Regiment to 1854; brigadier general of Volunteers in Civil War; lieutenant colonel of 1st Cavalry, 1866; retired 1879; died 1888—Heitman, *op. cit.*, I, 402.

11—George Sykes, Military Academy, 1838; major general of volunteers, 1862; colonel 20th Infantry, 1868; brevetted for gallant service at Cerro Gordo, Gainesville, Gettysburg.

—Thomas Hensil Reeve, rose from private with Tennessee volunteers in 1861 to lieutenant colonel, 1865; captain, 39th Infantry, July 1866, retired 1868.—Heitman, *op. cit.*, Vol. I, pp. 942, 822.

12—The official history is that by Elvid Hunt, *History of Fort Leavenworth, 1827-1927,* published at the post, 1926. It is not satisfactory for an analysis of surviving historic buildings.

13—As indicated in Chapter 1, Elizabeth Burt's diaries and letters themselves have vanished; their substance is reflected in the Elizabeth Burt *Ms.* recollections.

14—The course of the Fort Leavenworth-Fort Kearney Military Road, generally following the old Oregon Trail and new stage line, is given by M. Carrington (*op. cit.,* pp. 55-56), who preceded Elizabeth Burt by five months: "There was first a rough ride to the 'Nine Mile Station,' with its uncomfortable stone house. Then came, in turn, the crossing of the Acheson and Pike's Peak Railroad; Kinnekuck, on the Big Grasshopper, beyond Grenada, where the 'kickapoo' Indians were buying and begging; Big Muddy; Ash Point; Big Blue, with Simpson's capital Yankee store of notions; Rock Creek; Big Sandy; Little Blue River, with its perpetual Indian alarms and occasional depredations; Little Blue Station; Spring Creek; Pawnee Ranche; Sand Hill Station; and Valley City, or 'Dog Town,' only nine miles from Fort Kearney."

15—A "brevet" is defined as "a patent conferring a privilege or rank; esp., a commission promoting a military officer to a higher rank without increase in pay." To be brevetted was the equivalent of being higher ranked. Burt was brevetted major in 1864. Hence this passage at this point in Elizabeth Burt *Ms.* is puzzling.

16—Nathaniel Coates Kinney, who would establish Fort C. F. Smith a few weeks hence, became 1st lieutenant in the 18th Infantry in 1861; captain in 1862; transferred to 27th Infantry in September 1866 (as Major Burt would later); twice brevetted for Civil War service. Resigned in 1867.—Heitman, *op. cit.,* I, 602.

17—Henry Beebee Carrington, 1842-1912, lawyer, soldier, author, deserves a better fate than to be remembered as the commander of ill-fated Fort Phil Kearny. He had a brilliant Civil War record as organizer of Ohio and Indiana volunteers and colonel of the fighting 18th U. S. Regiment of Infantry. Although he himself wrote many books on military history, *Ab-Sa-Ra-Ka* (*op. cit.*) was written by his first wife, and published in 1868. Subsequent editions were expanded by Henry Carrington under the sub-title "Indian Affairs of the Plains," leading to much confusion among library classifiers. His first wife was Margaret Irving Sullivant of Columbus, Ohio. His second wife, as of April 3, 1871, was Fannie, widow of Col. G. W. Grummond, and daughter of Robert Courtney.—*Dictionary of American Biography,* New York, 1946, Vol. III, pp. 520-521.

18—Lyle E. Mantor, "Fort Kearny and the Westward Movement," *Nebraska History,* Vol. XXIX, No. 3 (September, 1948), pp. 175-207; Lillian M. Wellman, "The History of Fort Kearny," *Publications,* Nebraska State Historical Society, Vol. XXI (1930), pp. 213-326. The correct original official spelling, of course, is "Kearny," but the misspelled "Kearney" has the sanction of long and established usage. It so appears in the bulk of the official reports and has been adopted by the present nearby city of Kearney. In the present work this helps, also, to avoid the common confusion between this Nebraska fort and contemporary Fort Phil Kearny in Wyoming.

19—Lyle E. Mantor, "Stage Coach and Freighter Days at Fort Kearny," *Nebraska History,* Vol. XXIX, No. 4 (December, 1948), pp. 324-338; Frank A. Root and William Elsey Connelley, *The Overland Stage to California,* Topeka, 1901, pp. 205-206; 233-243.

20—Circular No. 4, *op. cit.,* pp. 332-333; Root and Connelley, *op. cit.,* p. 204.

21—Eugene F. Ware, *The Indian War of 1864,* Topeka, 1911, pp. 560-561.

22—Robert G. Athearn, *William Tecumseh Sherman and the Settlement of the West,* Norman, 1956, pp. 59-64.

23—Bvt. Brig. Gen. O. E. Babcock, Report of October 5, 1866, at Washington, D. C., to Maj. Gen. Rawlins, submitted by the Secretary of War and reprinted in *House Documents* No. 20, 39th Congress, 2nd Session, p. 2.

24—Lt. Gen. W. T. Sherman, Report of August 21, 1866, at Fort McPherson to Gen. J. A. Rawlins, submitted by the Secretary of War and reprinted in *House Documents* No. 23, 39th Congress, 2nd Session, p. 5.

CHAPTER 3 — TO THE CREST OF THE CONTINENT

1—Grace Raymond Hebard and E. A. Brininstool, *The Bozeman Trail,* Cleveland, 1922, Vol. I, p. 266. "Annual Record of Events of the 2nd Battalion, 18th U. S. Infantry, 1866," *Ms.* National Archives, indicates the arrival at Fort Kearney on May 15 of 481 recruits from the General Depot, New York City, under Captains Proctor and Burrowes. These would be a portion of the total of around 1,650 men in the Van Voast column.

2—Elizabeth Burt *Ms.;* M. Carrington, *op. cit.,* pp. 36-44.

3—Aspects of Jim Bridger's well-publicized career appear in later chapters. Of "H. Williams" little is known except that the "H" stands for "Henry." M. Carrington, *op. cit.,* p. 44, says merely that he "had been a guide to several expeditions to the Republican [River] during the winter of 1865-1866." Some writers have confused this individual with Old Bill Williams, a famed mountaineer who was found frozen to death some years earlier. See George E. Hyde, *Red Cloud's Folk: A History of the Oglala Sioux Indians,* Norman, Oklahoma, 1937, p. 144.

4—Vivid pictures of stage coach travel at this period are to be found in Root and Connelley, *op. cit.*, pp. 63-103, 189-232; James F. Rusling, *Across America: or, The Great West and the Pacific Coast,* New York, 1874, pp. 125 *et. seq.;* Frances Roe, *op. cit.*, pp. 207-213.

5—Most overland journalists commented on the ubiquitous prairie dog. See Theo. H. Scheffer, "Historical Encounters and Accounts of the Plains Prairie Dog," *Kansas Historical Quarterly,* Vol. XIII, No. 8 (November, 1945), pp. 527-537.

6—M. Carrington, *op. cit.*, pp. 45-46.

7—Sherman, *op. cit.*, p. 7.

8—LeRoy R. and Ann W. Hafen, editors, *The Diaries of William Henry Jackson,* Glendale, 1959, p. 50.

9—M. Carrington, *op. cit.*, p. 57.

10—Regimental Returns of the 18th U. S. Infantry, National Archives. "Annual Records," *op. cit.*, reflects minor variations of timing and spelling:
"May 19th at 10 o'clock A. M. pursuant to G. O. No. [illegible] Hd. Qrs, 18th Infty commenced the march for the Mountain District, Dept. of the Platte, marched 12 miles and encamped at Twelve mile ranche.
20th. Moved at 5 o'clock, marched 18 miles and encamped 3 P. M. near Plum Creek, N. T.
21st. Moved at 5 o'clock, marched 15 miles and encamped at 1 P. M. near McAnally's ranche, N. T.
22nd. Moved at 5 o'clock A. M. marched 15 miles and encamped at 12 o'clock M. near Dan Smith's ranche, N. T.
23d. Moved at 5 o'clock, marched 17 miles, passing Fort McPherson. & encamped at 12 M. near Morrow's ranche.
25th. Moved at 5½ o'clock A. M. marched 18 miles & encamped at 1 o'clock P. M. near O'Fallon's Bluff, N. T.
26th. Moved at 5 o'clock A. M. Marched 25 miles & encamped at 2½ o'clock P. M. near Alkali Station, N. T.
27th. Battalion remained encamped at Alkali Station.
28th. Moved at 6 o'clock A. M. marched 19 miles encamped at 2 P. M. 3 miles east of old California Crossing.
29th. Moved at 6 o'clock A. M. marched 12 miles encamped 10 A. M.
30th. Moved at 6½ o'clock A. M. marched 16 miles & encamped at 12½ near Fort Sedgwick, C. T.
31st. Remained in camp, furnishing large details to assist in ferrying Platte river . . ."

11—Circular No. 4, *op. cit.*, pp. 334-337; Root and Connelley, *op. cit.*, pp. 498 *et. seq.*; Ware, *op. cit.*, pp. 63-76 *et. seq.* The site of Fort McPherson is less than four miles south of Maxwell, Nebraska, on U. S. 30. Like Fort Kearney, McPherson was on the south or Oregon Trail side of the Platte River. U. S. 30 follows the north or Mormon Trail side of the Platte.

12—Elizabeth Burt *Ms.*; M. Carrington, *op. cit.*, pp. 46-47. According to the latter, witnessed by the Regimental Returns, there was only a brief halt here. It is possible that a portion of the command was detached to remain overnight; certainly the main body did not.

13—Sherman, *op. cit.,* pp. 5-6.

14—". . . received a call from Col. Otis and some gentlemen of the Peace Commission who, with agreeable presents for the red men, were on their way to the Laramie Council."—M. Carrington, *op. cit.,* p. 47. The Peace Commission, headed by E. B. Taylor of the Indian Department, was in session with the Indians at Fort Laramie June 1 to 15; the arrival of Carrington's troops there on June 13 alienated Red Cloud and effectively torpedoed the delicate negotiations.

15—Root and Connelley, *op. cit.,* pp. 219-220, 360, 375-376; *Colorado Magazine,* Vol. VII, pp. 139-146; IX, pp. 70, 178, 218; *Colorado, A Guide to the Highest State,* New York, 1941, pp. 208-210.

16—Fort Morgan is now a county seat. During the gold rush it was a station and a military post on the Overland Trail, known first as Camp Tyler, then as Camp Wardwell. In 1866 it was named in honor of the first commanding officer, Colonel C. A. Morgan. The site is marked by a monument on Riverview Avenue.— *Colorado, A Guide,* p. 202.

17—M. Carrington, *op. cit.,* pp. 51-52.

18—*Ibid.*; William Murphy, "The Forgotten Battalion," *Annals of Wyoming,* Vol. 7, No. 2 (October, 1930). Murphy has it that, "Two of our men got caught in the quicksand and were drowned." This loss is not confirmed in Regimental Returns or "Annual Record," *op. cits.*

19—M. Carrington, *op. cit.,* p. 63.

20—Colonel Carrington's route up the North Platte was the classic Oregon Trail: "June 4 Hd Qrs with 2nd Batt and recruits for Co. A, B, D, E and G 1st Battn en route Fort Laramie. Marched 17 miles and camped on Lodge Pole Creek. June 5th marched to upper crossing of Lodge Creek 18 miles. June 6 marched 28 miles to mud Springs: June 7 march 10 miles. Camped on pumpkin Creek near Court House rock: June 8 march 12 miles camping on North Platte river near Chimney rock; June 9 march 15 miles Camping on North Platte west of Terys ranch. June 10 Waited for priest: June 11 march 18 miles on North Platte west of Fort Mitchell. June 11 marched 21 miles. Camping on Cold Spring: June 13 marched 18 miles camping on Platte river near Laramie. June 14, 15 & 16 occupied in refitting, drawing rations, and turning over recruits of the 1st Batt. June 17 marched en route to Mountain District Dept of the Platte. . . ."—Regimental Returns, National Archives. See also M. Carrington, *op. cit.,* pp. 64-73.

21—M. Carrington, *op. cit.,* p. 54.

22—William Henry Lewis, Military Academy, 1845; major 18th Infantry, 1864; transferred to 36th Infantry, 1866; lieutenant colonel 19th Infantry, 1873; twice brevetted for gallant service in the Southwest during the Civil War; commander at Camp Douglas, Fort Fred Steele, Fort Dodge; died September 28, 1878, from wounds received in action with the Cheyenne Indians near Fort Wallace, Kansas.—Heitman, *op. cit.,* I, 631; Cullum, *op. cit.,* Vol. II, pp. 382-384.

—John McClintock, brevetted captain in 1863 for gallantry at Gettysburg; berevetted major at the end of the war; mustered out of service, 1871.—Heitman, *op. cit.,* I, 657.

—William Elkanah Waters, assistant surgeon, 1861; major surgeon, 1879; lieutenant colonel and departmental surgeon, 1895; brevetted twice for faithful and meritorious service during the war; retired in 1897.—Heitman, *op. cit.,* I, 1008.

23—The trail up the Lodgepole at this time, soon to become the Union Pacific Railroad, was little more than an Indian travois route. It had known limited use as a military short cut between Forts Sedgwick and Halleck. Hitherto the divergent North and South Forks of the Platte had been the main thoroughfares of white travellers.

24—Heitman, *op. cit.,* II, 554, lists Camp Walbach, "on Lodgepole Creek, near Cheyenne Pass." It appears to have been established in 1862 when the Postmaster General ordered the Overland Mail Company to abandon the North Platte and Sweetwater part of the route through Nebraska and Idaho Territories (now Wyoming) and to remove their stations to a southern route from Julesburg to Denver. According to Agnes W. Spring, *Caspar Collins,* New York, 1927, p. 42, Camp Walbach was between Virginia Dale and Big Laramie, on the Denver-Salt Lake City route. Little is known of Camp Walbach and its fate. It is not mentioned, for example, in C. G. Coutant's *History of Wyoming,* Laramie, 1899.

25—The "Wyoming Black Hills" is a term now obsolete. In general it was applied to the present Laramie Mountains west of Cheyenne, and extending north to Laramie Peak. In 1865 General G. M. Dodge had surveyed the railroad route across these mountains, plotting construction via "Sherman Hill" and "Cheyenne Pass."

26—This was the original "overland trail" or "overland stage route" between Leavenworth and Salt Lake City, via Denver, created by the Colorado gold rush of 1859. Its big elbow bend north to west was the site of future Fort Sanders and the city of Laramie (not to be confused with Fort Laramie, at the junction of the Laramie and North Platte Rivers). For a vivid description of this route see Rusling, *op cit.* After construction of the Union Pacific, the new east-west trunkline railroad adopted the name "overland route."

27—To reach the site of Fort Halleck today one drives 80 miles west of Laramie on U. S. 30 to Harris, Wyoming, then 18 miles south by county roads to Elk Mountain. This post was named for Maj. Gen. H. W. Halleck and was constructed in 1862 to protect the overland stage line. It was manned by Co. A, 11th Ohio Cavalry, directed by Colonel W. O. Collins at Fort Laramie. See Agnes W. Spring, *Caspar Collins,* New York, 1927, pp. 42-49.

28—The dangerous North Platte crossing of the Overland Trail would become the site of Fort Fred Steele in 1868. In 1880 there was another disaster here, when a ferry-boat operated by post trader J. W. Hughes capsized with the loss of four lives, including the wife and two children of a luckless emigrant.—*Wyoming, A Guide to Its History, Highways and People,* New York, 1936, p. 238.

29—Before the land that is now Wyoming became a territory in its own right in 1868 it fell within the shifting boundaries of many territories, including Nebraska, Dakota, Idaho and Utah. During 1864-1868 it was mainly within Dakota Territory.

CHAPTER 4 — FORT BRIDGER, AUTUMN, 1866

1—Irene D. Paden, *The Wake of the Prairie Schooner,* New York, 1944, p. 246.

2—Elizabeth Stone, *History of Uintah County,* Glendale, n.d., pp. 41-46; Coutant, *op. cit.,* p. 349.

3—Robert S. Ellison, *Fort Bridger, Wyoming: A Brief History,* Casper, Wyoming, 1931, pp. 12-15; Captain Howard Stansbury, *Exploration and Survey of the Valley of the Great Salt Lake of Utah,* Philadelphia, 1852, p. 74 and opp. plate.

4—Captain Jesse A. Gove, *The Utah Expedition,* 1857-1858, New Hampshire Historical Society, Concord, 1928, p. 97.

5—For details of the "war" see Gove, *ibid.;* H. H. Bancroft, *History of Utah,* San Francisco, 1890, pp. 512-542; Coutant, *op. cit.,* pp. 353-355.

6—J. Cecil Alter, *James Bridger,* Columbus, Ohio, 1951, pp. 427-469; Hebard and Brininstool, *op. cit.,* Vol. II, pp. 232-233. The authors quote John Hunton, patriarch of Fort Laramie. From October, 1867 to April, 1868, Bridger bunked with Hunton in the sutler's store at Fort Laramie. (The date "October, 1868" is obviously a typographical error). See also M. Carrington, *op. cit.,* and Chapters VII and VIII.

7—For a sketch of Major Noyes Baldwin, see *Annals of Wyoming,* Vol. 12, No. 3 (July, 1940), p. 173; Coutant, *op. cit.,* p. 356.

8—Babcock, *op. cit.,* p. 7.

9—Coutant, *op. cit.,* p. 357.

10—Ellison, *op. cit., pp.* 38-43.

11—Rusling, *op. cit., pp.* 142-162.

12—"Report of Brigadier James F. Rusling," October 11, 1866, at Fort Bridger, Utah, transmitted by the Secretary of War and reprinted in *House Documents* No. 45, 39th Congress, 2nd Session, pp. 48-55.

13—Anson Mills, *My Story,* Washington, D. C., 1918, pp. 107-113.

CHAPTER 5 — FORT BRIDGER, CHRISTMAS, 1866
TO SPRING, 1867

1—Hyde, *op. cit.,* pp. 137-141; *Report of the Commissioner of Indian Affairs,* 1866.

2—Mills, *op. cit.*, p. 107. One more discrepancy appears. According to the official roster as well as the account of General G. M. Dodge himself, Anson Mills remained in command at Fort Bridger until August, 1867; but Mills has it that "in the spring of 1867" he was ordered to escort General Dodge, Chief Engineer of the Union Pacific Railroad, on a reconnaissance of a route from Salt Lake City to Oregon, returning after two months to Fort Sanders. From here Mills proceeded to Fort Fetterman where he stayed during the winter of 1867, while the Burts were at Fort C. F. Smith. In 1876 he would be associated with Major Burt again, on the Big Horn and Yellowstone expedition.

3—General Andrew S. Burt, "Washakie, Chief of the Shoshones, and his Christmas Dinner." Release by Beckham Press Service, Washington, D. C., December 27, 1903. Burt Collection.

4—Dale L. Morgan, editor, "Washakie and the Shoshoni; Documents from the Records of the Utah Superintendency of Indian Affairs, 1864-1866," *Annals of Wyoming,* Vol. 29, No. 2 (October, 1957), pp. 195-227.

5—See Rodenbaugh and Haskin, *op. cit.*, "The Eighteenth Regiment of Infantry," p. 653. The 1st Battalion remained the 18th Infantry; the 3rd Battalion became the 36th Infantry.

6—Ellison, *op. cit.*, pp. 47-50.

7—Gen. Grenville M. Dodge, *Biographical Sketch of James Bridger,* New York, 1905.

8—A. K. McClure, *Three Thousand Miles Through the Rocky Mountains,* 1869, p. 169. In 1868-1869 there was new construction. For a detailed description of Fort Bridger at this period see *Circular No. 4,* War Department, Surgeon General's Office, December, 1870, pp. 359-362.

CHAPTER 6 — GETTING INTO RED CLOUD'S WAR

1—John Gibbon, West Point 1847, held the rank of colonel, but was brevetted major general for services at Petersburg during the Civil War. He was variously commander of Forts Kearney, Sanders, Shaw and Laramie. He is best remembered for his battle with the Nez Perces at Big Hole, Montana, 1877. Cullum, *op. cit.*, II, pp. 323-324.

2—The log blockhouse in which Mrs. Burt was sheltered appears in an official inventory of 1870: *Circular No. 4, op. cit.*, pp. 353-354.

3—Perkins, *op. cit.*, pp. 208-215.

4—Christopher C. Augur, West Point, 1843, was brevetted major general in 1865, commanded the Department of the Platte, 1867 to 1871. Cullum, *op. cit.*, II, p. 167.

5—Henry W. Wessels, West Point, 1833, hero of Cerro Gordo in the Mexican War, was brevetted brigadier general for Civil War services. From January, 1866 to December, 1866 he commanded successively at Forts Phil Kearny, Reno, McPherson, Fetterman, D. A. Russell and Laramie, holding some kind of a record for mobility.

Despite his seeming frailty he lived to 1889, age 80. Cullum, *op. cit.,* I, pp. 560-561.

6—Perkins, *op. cit.;* Agnes W. Spring, *The Cheyenne and Black Hills Stage and Express Routes,* Glendale, 1949, pp. 29-35; H. H. Bancroft, *History of Nevada, Colorado and Wyoming,* San Francisco, 1890, pp. 733-738; C. G. Coutant, "History of Wyoming," *Annals of Wyoming,* Vol. 12, Nos. 2 and 4 (April-October, 1940).

7—*Circular No. 4, op. cit.,* p. 340; Coutant, 1899, *op. cit.,* pp. 595-596; *Outline Description of Military Posts in the Military Division of the Missouri,* Chicago, 1876, p. 37; Jane R. Kendall, "History of Fort Francis A. Warren," [formerly Fort D. A. Russell], *Annals of Wyoming,* Vol. 18, No. 1 (January, 1946), pp. 3-66.

8—For Bill Reed's story, see Merrill J. Mattes, "The Sutler's Store at Fort Laramie," *Annals of Wyoming,* Vol. 18, No. 2 (July, 1946), pp. 127-132.

9—The well established trail to Fort Laramie was north from Cheyenne, across the headwaters of Lodgepole and Horse Creeks, then down the Chugwater and the Laramie. The route from Cheyenne to Fetterman was northwestward, joining the new route north from Fort Sanders.

10—Dr. J. M. Christlieb of Omaha, Nebraska: "The standard 'painkiller' of the period for children was paregoric, a camphorated tincture of opium. Laudanum, with higher opium content, was for adult use."

11—Wilson Clough, editor, "Fort Russell and Fort Laramie Peace Conference in 1867," *Sources of Northwest History,* No. 14, reprinted from *The Frontier,* Vol. XI, No. 2 (January, 1931).

12—Merrill G. Burlingame, "John M. Bozeman, Montana Trailmaker," *Mississippi Valley Historical Review,* Vol. XXVII, No. 4 (March, 1941).

13—LeRoy R. Hafen and Francis Marion Young, *Fort Laramie,* Glendale, 1938, pp. 346-352; Alter, *op. cit.,* "Observing the Peace Conference," pp. 427-437.

14—Fort Reno, 1866-1868, named for Major Jesse L. Reno, was one mile removed from Fort Connor, built as a supply base for the Powder River expedition. The Reno site is on Powder River, 28 miles by county road from Kaycee, Wyoming, on U. S. 87.

15—The Fort Phil Kearny site, marked by a restored log stockade corner, is 15 miles north of Buffalo, Wyoming, west of U. S. 87.

16—The most comprehensive account of the Bozeman Trail and related events is Hebard and Brininstool, *op. cit.* See also M. Carrington, *op. cit.,* and official archival records.

17—See *Circular No. 8,* War Department, Surgeon General's Office, 1875, "A Report on the Hygiene of the United States Army, with Descriptions of Military Posts." Washington, D. C., 1875, pp. 346-352. The site of Fort Fetterman, 1867-1882, may be reached today by following U. S. 26 to a point about 2½ miles west of Douglas, Wyoming, then following a dirt road 6 miles to a sagebrush plateau south of the Platte.

18—Frances C. (Grummond) Carrington, *My Army Life and the Fort Phil Kearny Massacre,* Philadelphia, 1911, pp. 65-67. Lieutenant Grummond was killed at the Fetterman affair of December 21, 1866. His widow later became the second wife of Colonel Carrington.

19—The Major Van Voast who was now stationed at Fort Reno, the same who led the column from Fort Leavenworth in 1866, is frequently confused by writers with "Mr. Van Volzpah," a mail carrier who, with his soldier escort, was earlier killed, scalped and mutilated at Brown's Spring nearby.

20—Gen. W. B. Hazen, Report of October 16, 1866, to Major H. G. Litchfield, Department of the Platte, transmitted by the Secretary of War and printed in *House Documents No. 45,* 39th Congress, 2nd Session, p. 3. The Crow Chief, Iron Bull, a fast friend of Major Burt, is cited as the authority for the fanciful "Legend of Crazy Woman's Fork," given by Rev. Edmund B. Tuttle, *The Boy's Book About Indians,* London, 1870, pp. 145-149.

21—Frances Carrington, *op. cit.,* pp. 70-81, quotes the account of S. S. Peters, a survivor, Omaha, Nebraska, July 6, 1908. See also "Annual Record," *op. cit.,* for June 25, 1866, and Murphy, *op. cit.,* pp. 385-386. "Annual Record of Events, 27th U. S. Infantry, 1867," *Ms.,* National Archives, tells of another battle at Crazy Woman: "On August 13, 1867, a force of 250 Indians, enraged by the Wagon Box defeat of August 2, attacked a detachment under Captain H. B. Freeman near Cheyenne Fork of Powder River, severely wounding three enlisted men."

22—Fort C. F. Smith Post Records, National Archives.

23—Colonel John Eugene Smith, 27th Infantry, was brevetted Major General of Volunteers in 1865. He died in 1897.—Heitman, *op. cit.,* Vol. I, p. 900.

24—John Bratt, *Trails of Yesterday,* Chicago, 1921, pp. 100-104.

25—"Annual Record, 1867," *op. cit.*

26—As indicated in Chapter 1, Mrs. Burt's "diaries" have disappeared, but her recollections were written in 1912 with the aid of these diaries.

CHAPTER 7 — FORT C. F. SMITH, 1866-1867

1—J. P. Dunn, *Massacres of the Mountains: A History of the Indian Wars of the West, 1815-1875,* New York, 1958 (facsimile reprint of the 1886 original); Grinnell, George Bird, *The Fighting Cheyennes,* Norman, 1956 (reprinted from the original edition, New York, 1915). Events around Fort C. F. Smith are scarcely noted by Hyde, *op. cit.,* in his history of the Oglala Sioux; they are entirely ignored by recent popular writers such as Stanley Vestal,

Warpath and Council Fire, New York, 1948, and Paul Wellman, *Death on Horseback,* Philadelphia, 1934.

—M. Carrington, *op. cit.,* p. 137; Major Alson B. Ostrander, *An Army Boy of the Sixties,* New York, 1924, pp. 140-163; William Murphy, *op. cit.,* p. 392; Hebard and Brininstool, *op. cit.,* Vol. II, p. 140.

3—Bruce Catton, *This Hallowed Ground,* New York, 1956, pp. 71-72, 97-98, 128.

4—M. Carrington, *op. cit.,* pp. 125, 130-133.

5—James D. Lockwood, *Life and Adventures of a Drummer Boy,* Albany, 1893, pp. 151-154.

6—Hebard and Brininstool, *op. cit.,* pp. 279-281.

7—"October 28th. 2nd Lieut. James H. Bradley, commanding escort from this battalion to Bvt. Major General W. B. Hazen, Assistant Inspector-General, Dept. of the Platte, enroute west, returned, having been absent fifty five days and marched one thousand and four (1004) miles, visiting Gallatin City, Fort Benton, the towns of Helena, Bozeman, etc. Command badly worn down."—"Annual Record, 1866," *op. cit.*

8—M. Carrington, *op. cit.,* pp. 134-137; Hazen, *op. cit.,* pp. 2-6; Nolie Mumey, *James Pierson Beckwourth,* Denver, 1957, pp. 163-174, quoting from the diary of Captain George Templeton; Fort C. F. Smith Post Records.

9—Lockwood, *op. cit.,* pp. 155-164, describes the arrival of the Crows ("a never ending stream pouring over the hills"), Private James W. Thompson's report of Beckwourth's death, Jim Bridger's role as an interpreter, and the immorality of the Crow women.

10—M. Carrington, *op. cit.,* p. 128.

11—"Annual Record, 1866," *op. cit.*

12—Fort C. F. Smith Post Records.

13—M. Carrington, *op. cit.,* p. 199.

14—Carrington's official report, quoted in Hebard and Brininstool, *op. cit.,* pp. 336-337, indicates Fort C. F. Smith forces at this time as follows: "aggregate for duty, 159, and three officers; total present 167." Lockwood, *op. cit.,* refers to "less than two hundred men."

15—Lockwood, *op. cit.,* pp. 166-167.

16—Post Records.

17—Hebard and Brininstool, *op. cit.,* Vol. II, pp. 106-107. Murphy, *op. cit.,* p. 392, referring to "two men who should have monuments," erroneously places the incident at March 1, and has them "bringing some Crow Indians with them, and a lot of mail packed on dogs."

18—Post Records.

19—"Annual Record, 1867," *op. cit.*

20—Burlingame, *op. cit.* Nelson Story is quoted in the Boulder, Montana, *Monitor,* October 25, 1919, cited by Hebard and Brininstool, *op. cit.,* Vol. I, pp. 224-225: "Mountain Chief, one of the renegade Blackfeet, I saw at Fort C. F. Smith the year after [the murder]. I tried to get the commanding officer to put him under arrest, but the officer feared the Indian would be hanged and trouble would ensue, so he would not accede to my request."

21—Granville Stuart, *Forty Years on the Frontier,* Cleveland, Vol. II, pp. 64-66.

22—"Annual Record, 1867," *op. cit.*

23—Post Records.

24—"Annual Record, 1867," *op. cit.*

25—Post Records.

26—Lockwood, *op. cit.,* pp. 176-181.

27—Post Records. Luther P. Bradley, brevetted brigadier general of volunteers during the Civil War, had the rank of lieutenant colonel of the 27th Infantry. He later served with the 9th and 3d Infantry regiments. Heitman, *op. cit.,* Vol. I, p. 234.

28—Post Records.

29—Hyde, *op. cit.,* pp. 144-145, 159.

30—Grinnell, *op. cit.,* pp. 230-244.

31—"Annual Record, 1867," *op. cit.*

32—Robert B. David, *Finn Burnett, Frontiersman,* Glendale, 1937, pp. 152-195. Burnett does not identify General Bradley by name. Lockwood, *op. cit.,* pp. 182-190, claims to have been in the battle, but his account of this episode seems confused and unreliable.

33—Post Records.

34—*Ibid.* Thomas Bredin Burrowes, Captain, 27th Infantry, was brevetted major for heroic action at Jonesboro in 1864. He retired in 1879, died 1885.—Heitman, *op. cit.,* Vol. I, p. 267.

35—Hebard and Brininstool, *op. cit.,* Vol. II, pp. 144-146. English-born Edmund Richard Pitman Shurly, 2nd lieutenant, 18th and 27th Infantry, was brevetted to colonel for gallantry at Fredericksburg and other Civil War battles. He retired December, 1868, apparently from disabilities incurred in the fighting along the Bozeman Trail.— Heitman, *op. cit.,* Vol. I, p. 885.

36—Post Records.

37—Murphy, *op. cit.;* David, *op. cit.*

38—The "Annual Record, 1867," *op. cit.,* makes only fleeting reference to the Indian Commissioner, Matthews, and the need to furnish him escort. It does note the arrival at Phil Kearny on October 23 of Inspector General of the Dept., Bvt. Lieut. Col. Merrill, Paymaster U. S. A., Major Clark, Bvt. Col. Grimes A. Q. M., and other officers of the Department. On the 24th this group left for Fort C. F. Smith. It is remarkable that they apparently escaped involvement in the hostilities that erupted along the Bozeman Trail just a few days later.

39—Post Records.

40—The report of Lieutenant E. R. P. Shurly, Commanding Escort, to George M. Templeton, 1st lieut. and post adjutant, Fort C. F. Smith, M. T., written November 10, 1867, at Fort Philip Kearny, D. T., survives among records of the 27th Regiment, Record Group 94, Office of the Adjutant General, National Archives. The entry for November 4 in "Annual Record, 1867," *op. cit.*, describes the location of the fight as Goose Creek, about 20 miles from Phil Kearny, and indicates the additional loss of two wagons containing sutler's supplies. (Shurly names A. C. Leighton as Post Sutler, Fort C. F. Smith.) The regimental report has Shurly "severely wounded in the foot by a musket ball." Another version of Shurly's fight on Goose Creek is to be found in Tuttle, *op. cit.*, p. 109.

41—Post Records.

42—*Ibid.*

43—Hebard and Brininstool, *op. cit.*, Vol. II, pp. 144-145. This entry explains the seeming discrepancy between the early account of log construction, and the known extent of adobe remains.

CHAPTER 8 — FORT C. F. SMITH, 1868

1—Post Records.

2—*Ibid.* According to Hebard and Brininstool, *op. cit.*, I, p. 235: "In the fall of 1866 at Bozeman, Nelson Story took his oxen and wagon team filled with flour and vegetables to Fort C. F. Smith where he sold the supplies to the government. . . . From that date until the old trail was abandoned in 1868 Story continued to regularly supply this fort with food. . . ." But unlike Richard, Story's name does not appear in the official records.

3—Hyde, *op. cit.*, p. 158.

4—Post Records.

5—Murphy, *op. cit.*, p. 393. "Annual Report, 1867," *op. cit.*, for May: "The garrisons of Philip Kearny and Reno have been severely afflicted with scurvy."

6—Post Records.

7—Edwin J. Stanley, *Rambles in Wonderland,* New York, 1878, p. 28.

8—Burt Collection.

9—Post Records.

10—Hebard and Brininstool, *op. cit.*, II, opp. p. 140.

11—*Ibid., op. cit.*, II, opp. p. 110; Post Records.

12—Post Records as well as the D'Isay sketch are at variance with the Burnett sketch; for example, they show five barracks instead of three. The difference can be explained by General Bradley's reconstruction program in late 1867, after Burnett's departure.

13—In contrast to the "Annual Record" for the preceding two years, the "Annual Return, Record of Events for the Year 1868 of the Twenty-Seventh U. S. Infantry" is fairly skimpy. However, there is this illuminating entry for March 23, 1868: "Bvt. Major General John E. Smith, Colonel, 27th Infantry, with 1st Lieutenant A. H. Bowman, Adjutant, 27th Infantry, left Regimental Headquarters at Fort Philip Kearny, D. T., for Fort C. F. Smith, M. T., to inspect the companies of the regiment stationed there." The general returned to Fort Philip Kearny on April 3.

14—Post Records.

15—*Ibid.*

16—Hebard and Brininstool, *op. cit.,* Vol. II, p. 258.

17—Prior to the appearance of the Burt journal, there was no announced evidence of women at Fort C. F. Smith. Now we know that during the winter of 1867-1868 there were at least five—Mrs. Burt and her sister, the wives of Lieutenant Miller and the unidentified post baker, and Julia Roach, post laundress, whose tombstone is now to be found at the Custer Battlefield National Cemetery. There were also at least six children—Andrew Gano and Edith Burt, the Mormon servant girl Christina, and the three children of the post baker. In the spring of 1868 came the wife of Captain Wishart and children, one of whom soon died. The wives of General Bradley, Captain Burrowes and Lieutenant Shurly all turn up for the first time at Fort D. A. Russell, after the return of these officers from Fort C. F. Smith.

18—Post Records. "Annual Record, 1868," *op. cit.*: "July 28. Companies E, G and H left Fort C. F. Smith, M. T. (abandoned), enroute to the U. P. R. R. . . . August 2, Companies E, G and H arrived at Camp Philip Kearny, D. T. (late Fort Phil. Kearny, D. T., abandoned), en route from Fort C. F. Smith, M. T. (abandoned) to the U. P. R. R. distance marched 95 miles. . . . August 4, Hdqts and Companies E, G and H left Camp Phil Kearny, D. T. en route to the U. P. R. R. and went into camp on the 18th inst. near Fort D. A. Russell, W. T. Distance marched 320 miles.

19—Addison M. Quivey, "Yellowstone Expedition of 1874" *Montana Contributions,* Volume I (1876), pp. 274-275.

20—James H. Bradley, "Sioux Campaign of 1876," *Montana Contributions,* Volume II (1896), p. 183; Journal of Lieutenant E. J. McClernand, 2nd Cavalry, April 1-September 29, 1876, reprinted in *Annual Report of the Secretary of War,* 45th Congress, Volume II, Part II (1877), p. 1365.

21—Additional inscriptions on the transplanted C. F. Smith tombstone: Corporal Alvah H. Staples, Pvt. Charles Hackett, Pvt. Thomas Navin, Pvt. Thomas Fitzpatrick, Citizen Charles Bowman, all "killed by Indians"; Sergt. John Murphy, Wagon Master, Geo. W. McGee, Citizen Daniel Grouse, all "drowned in river"; Pvt. Jeremiah Osier, "died of disease"; Citizen Wm. Bruce Smith, "died of wounds"; Teamster James Strong, "died of injuries"; Pvt. Charles Riley, "died in hospital"; Pvt. Robert Clair, "killed by accident"; Julia Roach, laundress. . . .

CHAPTER 9 — FORTS RUSSELL, SANDERS AND OMAHA, 1868-1874

1—George M. Templeton, corporal in the 149th Pennsylvania Volunteers, August, 1862; captain 32nd U. S. Infantry, 1864; 2nd lieutenant 18th U. S. Infantry, 1866; transferred to 27th Infantry, 1866; captain, October, 1867; died in May, 1870, in Omaha from the effect of wounds received in actions with Sioux Indians.— Heitman, *op. cit.*, Vol. I, p. 950. The owner of Templeton's Journal, referred to in Mumey, *op. cit.*, has reserved it for future publication.

2—Shurly was involved in many Indian fights around Fort C. F. Smith and between that post and Fort Phil Kearny. However, the "wound which cost him his health" was undoubtedly incurred in the desperate Goose Creek fight of November 4, 1867, referred to in Chapter 7.

3—*Circular No. 4, op. cit.*, p. 324, indicates, "Ogallalla, Nebra., 1 co. cav.," among temporary stations in the Department of the Platte, all along the new Union Pacific Railroad. This was the germ of a town which achieved fame as a range cattle shipping point in the 1870's. The present city of Ogallala is at the junction of U. S. 30 and U. S. 26. . . . "Annual Record, 1868," *op. cit.*, indicates that Headquarters and the bulk of the regiment were shipped by rail to North Platte Station, then were dispatched southwestward to scout the Republican and Smoky Hill Rivers country. On December they were in garrison at Omaha Barracks.

4—Elizabeth Burt does not mention any fracas with the Indians while at Ogallala. However, "Annual Record, 1868," *op. cit.* indicates that on October 26, "a party of hostile Indians made their appearance at Ogallala, the station of H Company, but were driven off without loss to the company." The frequency of Indian attacks on these stations and on Union Pacific work crews is indicated in Perkins, *op. cit.* and Tuttle, *op. cit.* as well as official records of the Department of the Platte. "Annual Record" indicates that H Company was at Plum Creek Station in January, 1869. The exact date of Burt's transfer to Omaha Barracks is not given.

5—Colonel John H. King, bvt. major general U. S. A., assumed command of the 9th Regiment in December, 1866. In June, 1869, after more than thirteen years of service on the Pacific Coast, the 9th was ordered to the Department of the Platte, where upon arrival in July the 27th Infantry was consolidated with it. The regiment performed garrison and guard duty on the line of the Union Pacific Railroad until May, 1873.—Rodenbaugh and Haskin, *op. cit.*, p. 528.

6—William Bedford Royall was one of the great cavalry officers of the Civil War and the Indian-fighting Army. His career began as lieutenant in the Missouri infantry during the Mexican War. He was brevetted several times, the highest rank to that of brigadier general for "gallant service against the Indians" at Rosebud Creek, Montana, June 17, 1876 when he fought with Major Burt. He died in 1895.—Heitman, *op cit.*, Vol. I, p. 849.

7—Walter Scribner Schuyler, cadet Military Academy 1866, 2nd lieutenant, 5th Cavalry 1870, captain 1887, was brevetted for action in the Indian Wars of the Southwest and the Big Horn Mountains, (the Mackenzie campaign of November, 1876). He rose to high rank before the outbreak of World War I.—Heitman, *op. cit.*, Vol. I, p. 867.

8—Adolphus Washington Greely, lieutenant 18th Infantry 1863, captain 1865, brevetted major of volunteers 1865, 2nd lieutenant 36th infantry 1867, transfer to 5th cavalry 1869, captain 1886, brigadier general and Chief Signal Officer of the United States Army, 1887. —Heitman, *op. cit.*, Vol. I, p. 473.

9—Jesse Matlock Lee, private 59th Indiana infantry to 1862, 2nd lieutenant 1863, captain 38th infantry 1865, 2nd lieutenant 39th infantry 1866, colonel 10th U. S. volunteers infantry 1898, brigadier general 1902.—Heitman, *op. cit.*, I, p. 624.

10—In May, 1873 companies A, D, E, F, H and I were sent to the Department of Dakota for duty with the Yellowstone Expedition, which formed the escort to the engineers surveying for Northern Pacific Railroad in that year, returning to the Department of the Platte after an absence of over four months.—Rodenbaugh and Haskin, *op. cit.*, pp. 528-529. According to the Regimental Returns, 9th Infantry, Co. H, left Fort Sanders May 21, 1873; arrived at Fort Rice, D. T., June 4, 1873; left Fort Rice on the expedition June 20; returned to Fort Omaha, October 9.

CHAPTER 10 — FORT LARAMIE, JUNE, 1874 TO JUNE, 1876

1—The standard work on the subject to date is Hafen and Young, *op. cit.* See also Merrill J. Mattes, "Fort Laramie, Guardian of the Oregon Trail," *Annals of Wyoming*, Vol. 17, No. 1 (January, 1945), pp. 1-21; and David L. Heib, *Fort Laramie National Monument*, Washington, 1954.

2—Lloyd McCann, "The Grattan Massacre," *Nebraska History*, Vol. 37, No. 1 (March, 1956), pp. 1-26.

3—Spring, *Caspar Collins, op. cit.*; Coutant, *op. cit.*, pp. 406-504.

4—Merrill J. Mattes, *Ms.*, "Surviving Military Structures at Fort Laramie," compiled from Records of the Post Quartermaster, Fort Myer, Virginia; Fort Laramie ground plans, 1849 to 1868, National Archives; W. H. Jackson photographs in files of the U. S. Geological Survey.

5—The fortified corral does not exist in Fort Laramie records or ground plans for 1866 or earlier. It provides background in photographs taken by Alexander Gardner at Fort Laramie in 1867 or 1868. Files of the Bureau of American Ethnology and Missouri Historical Society.

6—Cynthia J. Capron, "The Indian Border War of 1876, from letters of Lieut. Thaddeus H. Capron," *Journal of the Illinois State Historical Society*, Vol. 13, No. 4 (January 1921), p. 477.

7—Fort Laramie Post Records, National Archives.

8—Mattes, *op. cit.;* Fort Laramie Ground Plans, 1868-1876; Fort Laramie Research Photo File.

9—Fort Laramie Post Records; L. G. Flannery, editor, *John Hunton's Diary* (Lingle, Wyoming, 1956), Vol. I, p. 102; Johnny O'Brien, interviewed by Merrill J. Mattes in 1943.

10—John S. Collins, "Stories of the Plains," *Across the Plains in '64*, Omaha, 1904, Part II, p. 49.

11—Charles J. Kappler, *Indian Affairs. Laws and Treaties*, (Washington, 1903), Vol. II, pp. 770-781; *Annual Report* of the Commissioner of Indian Affairs, 1868, pp. 31-251.

12—George E. Hyde, *Red Cloud's Folk: A History of the Oglala Sioux Indians* (Norman, 1937), pp. 162-204; *Annual Report* of the Commissioner of Indian Affairs, 1868-1873.

13—Fort Laramie Post Records.

14—Hyde, *op. cit.*, pp. 210-215; Roger T. Grange, "Fort Robinson, Outpost of the Plains," *Nebraska History*, Vol. 39, No. 3 (September, 1958), pp. 191-240.

15—Regimental Returns, National Archives.

16—It is difficult to identify the exact building occupied at this time by the Burt family. However, the brief description tallies with any one of the three adobe-filled frame quarters that stood south of Old Bedlam, and which are identifiable on successive post ground plans as well as a parade ground photograph by Gardner, c. 1868. Constructed in the 1850's, these quarters were replaced in 1881 by lime-concrete quarters which today stand in ruins.

17—Regimental Returns, 9th Infantry; Fort Laramie Medical History, National Archives.

18—William Ludlow, *Report of a Reconnaissance of the Black Hills of South Dakota*, Washington, 1875; C. C. O'Harra, "The Black Hills Expedition of 1874" and "The Discovery of Gold in the Black Hills," *The Black Hills Engineer* (Nov. 1929).

19—Hyde, *op. cit.*, pp. 220-224.

20—Charles Schuchert and Clara Mae LeVene, *O. C. Marsh, Pioneer in Paleontology*, New Haven, 1940, pp. 139-155; Hyde, *op. cit.*, pp. 224-228. Regimental Returns, 9th Infantry, indicate November 5-

12 as the inclusive dates of the expedition. Bradley, Burt and Mix are among army officers whose solicited opinions later supported Marsh's complaints about agency food.

21—Henry Newton and Walter P. Jenney, *Report on the Geology and Resources of the Black Hills of Dakota,* Washington, 1880, p. 37.

22—John G. Bourke, *On the Border with Crook,* New York, 1891, p. 387.

23—Fort Laramie Medical History; James B. Fry, *Army Sacrifices,* New York, 1879, pp. 118-126. According to Regimental Returns, the inclusive dates of the Co. H escort were February 13-24. Total distance marched, 250 miles.

24—Fort Laramie Post Records.

25—Newton and Jenney, *op. cit.,* pp. 18-35.

26—*Ibid.,* p. 2.

27—Agnes Wright Spring, *The Cheyenne and Black Hills Stage and Express Route,* Glendale, 1949, p. 65, citing Cheyenne newspapers.

28—Newton and Jenney, *op. cit.,* p. 26.

29—*Ibid.,* pp. 243-246.

30—Fort Laramie Medical History; Harry Young (*Hard Knocks,* Portland, 1915, pp. 154-169), a teamster, throws some light on the "Jenny" expedition, with recollections of California Joe, "M. Mc-Gillacuty" and a "Captain Dan Burke" of Company I, 14th U. S. Infantry. The latter, represented as a tough disciplinarian yet popular with his men, is supposed to have commanded a supply train between Jenney's camp and Fort Laramie. Since the 14th Infantry is not alluded to in official records in connection with the Jenney Expedition of 1875, one wonders if Young hasn't confused "Burke" with "Burt," and the latter is actually the hero of the incident Young refers to. (There *is* a "Daniel W. Burke" alluded to by Captain John G. Bourke in events of *1876* at Slim Buttes).

31—Julia B. McGillicuddy, *McGillicuddy, Agent,* Palo Alto, 1941, pp. 24-36.

32—Hyde, *op. cit.,* pp. 240-248; Collins, *op. cit.,* Part I, pp. 76-85.

33—The anonymous author of this article can now be identified as Reuben Briggs Davenport, managing editor of the *New Haven Morning News,* 1890-1895, who covered the Jenney-Newton expedition of 1875 for the *New York World-Herald.* He was also along on the Big Horn and Yellowstone Expedition of 1875, and antagonized Crook and others by unfair criticism of the campaign, which he likened to Napoleon's retreat from Moscow: Oliver Knight, *Following the Indian Wars,* Norman, 1960, pp. 165, 172, 244-282, 319.

34—Fort Laramie Medical History.

35—Spring, *op. cit.,* pp. 135-137.

36—Jesse Brown and A. M. Willard, *The Black Hills Trail,* Rapid City, 1924; Fort Laramie Post Records and Medical History; Regimental Returns, 9th Infantry.

CHAPTER 11 — BIG HORN AND YELLOWSTONE EXPEDITION

1—Similar sentiments, more intense because her soldier husband died in battle, are expressed by Elizabeth Custer, *op. cit.,* pp. 261-269. See also Fairfax Downey, "They Also Served," *Indian Fighting Army,* New York, 1941, pp. 86-100.

2—The principal official sources for the B. H. and Y. Expedition are to be found in various participant Regimental Returns, and files of the Military Department of the Platte, both in the National Archives, and the *Annual Report* of the Secretary of War, 1876. The Fort Laramie Post Records for 1876, which should be in the National Archives, are missing. Fortunately there were two star witnesses in Captain John G. Bourke, *On the Border With Crook* (New York, 1891), pp. 241-381, and John F. Finerty, *War-path and Bivouac* (Chicago, 1890), pp. 45-292.

3—Finerty, *op. cit.,* p. 80; Knight, *op. cit.,* pp. 171, 188, writes about other newspaper correspondents on this campaign; "[Robert E.] Strahorn was not the only correspondent for the *Chicago Tribune* . . . an infantry officer, Captain A. S. Burt, also wrote for the *Tribune* as well as for the *Cincinnati Commercial.*" Knight, quoting from Strahorn's unpublished autobiography (in Strahorn Memorial Library, The College of Idaho, Caldwell), also reveals a conversation between General Crook and Captain Burt on the subject of a soldier's feelings during battle.

4—Capron, *op. cit.,* p. 481.

5—*Ibid.,* p. 485.

6—Bourke, *op. cit.,* p. 297. It was the privilege of an infantry commander to ride horseback on occasion; the enlisted men would "get a ride" only if ill or wounded.

7—Bourke, *ibid.,* pp. 299-300; Mills, *op. cit.,* p. 401.

8—Bourke, *op. cit.,* p. 301; Joe DeBarthe, *Life and Adventures of Frank Grouard* (Norman, Oklahoma), 1958, pp. 114-115.

9—Bourke, *op. cit.,* p. 305.

10—De Barthe, *op. cit.,* p. 115.

11—From official reports of the expedition, National Archives, reproduced in J. W. Vaughn, *With Crook at the Rosebud* (Harrisburg, Pennsylvania, 1956), pp. 224-225.

12—Finerty, *op. cit.,* p. 115.

13—An exhaustive analysis is offered by Vaughn, *op. cit.*

14—Vaughn, *op. cit.*, pp. 48-64, 80, 90-95, 105-116, 154, 170, 178, 182, 195, 224.

15—Burt Collection.

16—Vaughn, *op. cit.*, p. 110. Regimental Returns, 9th Infantry, give only this laconic account of the Rosebud Battle: "June 17 marched down Rosebud about 5 miles when at 8:30 A. M. command engaged a body of hostile Sioux Indians. The fight was of a desultory nature and lasted about four hours, when the Indians were driven off. Casualties in the companies, None."

17—One of the delinquents, inevitably, is represented to be the ubiquitous Calamity Jane. If true, she was involved in this perverse way in more Indian campaigns than any woman on record. A scholarly evaluation is to be found in Roberta Beed Sollid, *Calamity Jane: A Study in Historical Criticism* (Helena, 1958), pp. 24-27. See also Spring, *op. cit.*, p. 112.

18—Capron, *op. cit.*, p. 488.

19—Finerty, *op. cit.*, p. 213.

20—Captain Charles King, *Campaigning with Crook and Stories of Army Life* (New York, 1880), p. 57.

21—Finerty, *op. cit.*, pp. 228 et seq.

22—Bourke, *op. cit.*, p. 356.

23—Classic accounts of the "horsemeat expedition" are given by Bourke, Finerty, Mills and Capron, *op. cits.*

24—Gen. Andrew Burt, U. S. A., "Army Women on the March," article in unidentified, undated newspaper, c. 1904, in Burt Collection.

25—Bourke, *op. cit.*, p. 374; Capron, *op. cit.*, p. 498. Regimental Returns give this summary of the expedition:
"August—Cos C G and H in field with B H and Y Expedition, left camp on Goose creek, W. T. Aug 5 and marched north, crossing and re-crossing the Tongue, Rosebud and Powder Rivers and camping thereon until the 17th when they reached the Yellowstone, went into camp and remained there until the 24th of August. Left camp on the Yellowstone August 24, marched up Powder River 37 miles, from that point crossed the country toward the Little Missouri, arriving at Beaver Creek August 31, 1876. Total distance marched 377 miles.

"September—Cos C, G and H were on detached duty with the B. H. and Y. expedition under the command of Brigadier-General Crook. The companies left camp on Beaver Creek Sept 1 and marched 92 miles to the head of Heart River which was reached September 5, 1876. September 7, 33 miles to North Fork of Grand River; September 8 and 9, 41 miles to Rabbit Creek, Slim Buttes where a Sioux village was captured by the expedition. An attack was made on the troops by Indians about 4 o'clock P. M. September 9 during which Private Robert Fitz Henery Co. H received a flesh wound in the thigh. September 10-11 marched 36 miles to a branch of Owl Creek September 12. 36 miles to Branch of Belle Fourche; September 14 to September 30 the command marched 97½ miles to camp on French Creek, Black Hills, D. T. Half rations were issued to the command September 5 and 6. Quarter rations September 7, and from the 8th to the 15th the command subsisted on horse meat and dried meat captured in the Indian villages."

26—In addition to the standard accounts, Cheyenne and Deadwood newspapers of the time give lurid impressions of the triumphal Deadwood episode.

27—McGillicuddy, *op. cit.,* p. 62.

28—Richard B. Hughes, *Pioneer Years in the Black Hills* (Glendale, 1957), p. 190.

29—Finerty, *op. cit.,* pp. 285-292; Fort Laramie Post Records.

30—Edwin Franklin Townsend, Military Academy, 1850-1854, brevetted lieutenant colonel, 1865, major 27th Infantry, 1868, 9th Infantry 1869, on Powder River expedition November 1876 to June 1877. In addition to command at Fort Laramie, Townsend commanded at Forts Sedgwick, Omaha, Stambaugh, Sully, A. Lincoln and Yates. Retired 1895. Cullum, *op. cit.,* Vol. II, pp. 591-593; Heitman, *op. cit.,* Vol. I, p. 967.

31—Spring, *op. cit.,* pp. 158-159; L. G. Flannery, editor, *John Hunton's Diary* (Lingle, Wyoming, 1958), Vol. 2, pp. 84-91; Collins, *op. cit.,* pp. 36-40.

32—Fort Laramie Medical History.

33—Fort Laramie Post Records.

34—Capron, *op. cit.,* p. 494.

35—Collins, *op. cit.,* Part II, pp. 5-7.

36—Capron, *op. cit.,* p. 487.

37—*Ibid.;* Fort Laramie Post Records; Fort Laramie Research Photo File; Ware, *op. cit.,* p. 57.

38—Collins, *op. cit.,* Part II, p. 39.

39—Capron, *op. cit.,* pp. 476-477.

40—*Ibid.,* p. 490.

41—Fort Laramie Post Records and Medical History.

42—Fort Laramie Post Records; Capron, *op. cit.,* pp. 499, 501.

43—Regimental Returns, 9th Infantry, National Archives.

44—*Record of Engagements with Hostile Indians within the Military Division of the Missouri from 1868 to 1882,* Lieutenant General P. H. Sheridan commanding, Chicago, 1882, p. 72.

45—See Chapter 12, pp. 254-256.

46—Hafen and Young, *op. cit.,* pp. 386-398; Collins, *op. cit.,* p. 6; Hieb, *op. cit.,* p. 31.

CHAPTER 12 — THE GOLDEN YEARS

1—Circular No. 4, *op. cit.*, pp. 329-331; Circular No. 8, *op. cit.*, pp. 363-365. Fort Omaha was originally designated "Sherman Barracks." In 1869 it became "Omaha Barracks." The name "Fort Omaha" did not become official until 1878.

2—For many years Department of the Platte Headquarters occupied the Withnell Building, southwest corner of 15th and Harney in downtown Omaha. The building at Fort Omaha to which Headquarters was transferred in 1878, referred to by Elizabeth Burt, was found to be unsuitable. Headquarters were removed once more to downtown Omaha, this time to the Strange Building, 10th and Farnam.—James W. Savage and John T. Bell, *History of the City of Omaha,* New York, 1894, p. 160.

3—Soon after his election to the United States Senate in 1856 Douglas married Adele Cutts, daughter of J. Madison Cutts of Washington and grand-niece of Dolly Madison, whom she is said to have resembled in charm of manner. She was indisputably the belle of Washington. It was always a mystery that she should have chosen to give herself to this unromantic widower, yet it proved to be in every respect a happy marriage until Douglas' death in 1861 from typhoid fever.—*Dictionary of American Biography,* New York, 1946, Vol. V, p. 401.

—Robert Williams was a graduate of the United States Military Academy in 1850. He served with distinction in the Adjutant-General's Office during the Civil War, being brevetted brigadier general. He was staff colonel and adjutant for the Department of the Platte, 1876-1881.—Heitman, *op. cit.,* Vol. I, p. 1042; Cullum, *op. cit.,* Vol. II, pp. 453-4.

4—"Charles F. Manderson, president of the Omaha Savings Bank, has been a resident of Omaha since 1869. . . . He rose from private to brigadier-general in the Union Army. . . . He was city attorney for three terms, a member of the state constitutional convention of 1871-1874. In 1883 General Manderson was elected to the United States Senate, and in 1889 he was re-elected without opposition." —Alfred Sorenson, *History of Omaha,* Omaha, 1889, pp. 303-304.

5—Regimental Returns, 9th Infantry. It was during this period also that the versatile officer invented an "improved shelter tent" which was heartily endorsed for experimental use by the chain of command up to General Sheridan at Division Headquarters in Chicago.

6—John M. Thurston, "The Murder of Mitchell and Ketchum," clipping from the *Examiner,* Omaha, Nebraska, n. d., in The Burt Collection: See also S. D. Butcher, *Pioneer History of Custer County,* Broken Bow, Nebraska, 1901, pp. 43-62. From 1895 to 1901 Thurston represented Nebraska in the United States Senate. —Arthur C. Wakely, *Omaha: The Gate City,* Chicago, 1917, p. 330. There is a slight discrepancy between Thurston's account and the Regimental Returns, 9th Infantry. According to the latter, Company H left Fort Omaha on April 11 at 8 A. M., and arrived in Hastings at 2:15 P. M. The troops returned to Fort Omaha by rail on April 18.

7—Undated clipping from the *Scoop*, published by the Chicago Press Club, in the Burt Collection.

8—Jay Monaghan, *The Great Rascal: The Life and Adventures of Ned Buntline,* New York, 1952, pp. 1-27, 232-233; King, *op. cit.,* pp. 32-42, 114.

9—News clippings in the Burt Collection.

10—The program for *Robin Hood and Rosalind,* published in Chicago, 1883 reads, "Play by Sheridan Burt. Verses by Elwyn Barron. Music by K. T. Harrison."

11—Circular No. 8, *op. cit.,* p. 502.

12—Reynolds J. Burt, "Sketches of Boyhood Days Out West at Army Posts," *Manuscript* in Phillips Collection, University of Oklahoma.

13—A. S. Burt, "Military History of Colonel Andrew Sheridan Burt, 25th U. S. Infantry," printed brochure with typed addenda, Burt Collection.

14—Undated clippings in Burt Collection.

15—Circular No. 8, *op. cit.,* p. 544.

16—See Roger Grange, *op. cit.,* pp. 191-240. Fort Robinson is now controlled by the United States Department of Agriculture. The Nebraska State Historical Society has a permit to operate a museum in the old post headquarters building.

17—"Dr. Walter Reed, discoverer of the cures for yellow fever, served for three years at Fort Robinson. He arrived August 8, 1884, succeeding Dr. Henry MacElderry. His official rank was Captain and Assistant Surgeon, Medical Department, U. S. A. He was post surgeon."—Federal Writer's Project, W. P. A., *A Military History of Nebraska* (mimeograph), Lincoln, 1939.

18—General Edward Hatch, 1832-1889, died in his fifty-seventh year, at Fort Robinson, Nebraska, from the effects of an accident.— *Dictionary of American Biography,* Vol. VIII, p. 392.

19—Burt Collection.

20—Tuttle, *op. cit.,* pp. 77-99.

21—Ironically, now that there were only two in the family, Andrew's rank entitled him to occupy one of the larger and more pretentious residences at Fort Laramie, second only in size and comfort to that assigned to the commanding officer, Colonel Merriam. This was the new lime-concrete "Surgeon's Quarters" with mansard-style roof, erected in 1885 next to the old Sutler's Store. (Both of these structures are among those now being restored by the National Park Service.) Identification of this Burt residence is positive. In a footnote to his mother's recollections, General R. J. Burt notes: "At this time at Fort Laramie we lived in the 2 storied Field officers quarters at the end of the front officers line next to the Post Trader's store." Colonel Louis Brechemin, in an interview with Superintendent Hieb, Fort Laramie National Monument in 1951, also refers to "the Burt House next to the Post Trader's store."

Brechemin's father was the post surgeon. He explains that Colonel Burt outranked his father for the quarters.

22—Grace Raymond Hebard, *Washakie*, Cleveland, 1930, pp. 251-272; Colonel Homer W. Wheeler, "Reminiscences of Old Fort Washakie," *Quarterly Bulletin* of the Wyoming Historical Department. Vol. I, No. 4, (1924); Hiram G. Nickerson, "Early History of Fremont County," *Ibid.*, Vol. 2, No. 1.

23—J. K. Moore was a "licensed Indian trader" at Fort Washakie.— Hebard, *op. cit.*, p. 225.

24—The strained relations between Shoshone and Arapahoe servants mentioned by Mrs. Burt reflect a deep-seated tribal antagonism. The Arapahoes, decimated by the Sand Creek massacre in Colorado in 1864 and the Tongue River massacre of 1865, were the unruly orphans of the Plains tribes, without an acknowledged home of their own, often given to continued depredations against the whites, usually dependent upon other tribes for sanctuary. In 1877, after the conquest of the hostiles, the Indian Bureau imposed on Chief Washakie's monumental good nature and received his reluctant consent to have the problem Arapahoes placed in the Wind River Reservation temporarily. They have been there ever since, and after eighty years the Shoshones are still inclined to regard them as non-paying and not entirely welcome guests. A discussion of reservation life today is given in *Wyoming: A Guide to the History, Highways and People (American Guide Series)*, New York, 1941, pp. 307-312.

25—See Hebard, *op. cit.*, pp. 245-249.

26—See Rt. Rev. Ethelbert Talbot, *My People of the Plains*, New York, 1906, pp. 12-15.

27—Bishop Talbot held special services at Fort Washakie and other posts once a year, and he includes Colonel Burt among his "valued friends." "The cordial welcome and gracious hospitality extended to me by the officers and their families never failed to make my brief sojourn with them memorable."—*Ibid.*, p. 151.

28—Fanny Kimble Wister, *Owen Wister Out West: His Journals and Letters*, Chicago, 1958. pp. 91-92.

29—Burt Collection. Another letter in the Collection from Owen Wister to "My Dear General Burt" dated at JY Ranch, Teton P. O. Wyoming, October 2, 1911 expresses apologies for delay in correspondence, owing to "pretty poor health." Wister continues: "I have been spending some time here in Jackson's Hole, trying to get strong, with partial success. This country will always be beautiful, but the thing you knew is forever vanished. Another life and another sort of people are here, and it will grow less and less attractive to the lover of the wilderness. The automobile will get here soon, and the smell of gasoline displace the odor of the sagebrush." From this it may be inferred that Colonel Burt, while at Fort Washakie, visited Jackson Hole on at least one hunting expedition. This fabulous scenic area is now within the Grand Teton

National Park. Wister's JY Ranch home will be preserved by the government.

30—Anon., *History of the Union Pacific Coal Mines,* 1868-1940, Omaha, 1940, pp. 63-64, 75-101; Paul Crane and Alfred Larson, "The Chinese Massacre," *Annals of Wyoming,* Vol. 12, Nos. 1 and 2 (1940), pp. 47-55, 153-160.

31—Elizabeth Burt, *Ms.*

32—Thomas E. Blades and John W. Wiks, "Fort Missoula," *Military Affairs,* Vol. XIII, No 1 (Spring, 1949), pp. 29-36.

33—The Burt Collection includes letters to Colonel Burt from S. L. Clemens. Particularly poignant is the entry in a black-bordered letter from London, December 12, 1896: "We are miserable in our oldest daughter's death. She died while Mrs. Clemens and Clara were flying to her across the Atlantic. She would not have died if we had been at home."

34—See Elliot Coues, editor, *History of the Expedition under the Command of Lewis and Clark,* in 4 volumes, New York, 1893.

35—Burt Collection.

36—Burt Collection. There is a similar affidavit from Charles H. Whipple, Major and Paymaster, U. S. A.

37—Burt Collection. Identity of the newspaper and date of issue are not indicated.

38—Undated clipping from the *Cincinnati Enquirer,* Burt Collection.

39—Burt Collection.

40—*Ibid.* Another news report describes the effectiveness of "Burt's trumpet telegraphy" during troop maneuvers.

41—Burt, "Military History," *op. cit.*

42—On the same promotion list, to the rank of major general, was Robert P. Hughes, who had also been with the 18th U. S. Regiment of Infantry when it marched westward from Fort Kearney in 1866. While the Burts proceeded to Fort Bridger, Hughes was detached at Fort Mitchell, at the foot of Scotts Bluff on the Oregon Trail.— Heitman, *op. cit.,* Vol. I, pp. 552-553; Merrill J. Mattes, "A History of Old Fort Mitchell," *Nebraska History,* Vol. XXIV, (April, 1943), pp. 78-79.

43—"General Burt was a member of the Colonial Wars Society of Illinois; Sons of the Revolution, Montana Society; War of 1812 Society; Loyal Legion, Ohio Commandery; Grand Army of the Republic; he was a Knight Templar, a Shriner and an Elk."—Burt, "Military History," *op. cit.* In 1910 he became President of the Veteran Reserve Corps of America.—*Fiftieth Anniversary of the Class of 1861, Yale College,* p. 176.

44—*The Scoop,* Chicago, Illinois, April 17, 1915.

Index

303